Learning, Teaching and Education Research in the 21st Century

Also available from Continuum

Education After Dewey, Paul Fairfield
Educational Research and Inquiry, Dimitra Hartas
Philosophy of Education, Richard Pring
Philosophy of Educational Research, Richard Pring
Researching Education, David Scott and Robin Usher
Rethinking the Education Improvement Agenda, Kevin J. Flint and Nick Peim

Learning, Teaching and Education Research in the 21st Century

An evolutionary analysis of the role of teachers

Joanna Swann

continuum

Continuum International Publishing Group

The Tower Building	80 Maiden Lane
11 York Road	Suite 704
London SE1 7NX	New York NY 10038

www.continuumbooks.com

British Library Cataloguing-in-Publication Data
A catalogue record for this book is available from the British Library.

ISBN: 978-1-4411-6317-2 (paperback)
        978-1-4411-6126-0 (hardcover)

Library of Congress Cataloging-in-Publication Data
A catalog record for this book is available from the Library of Congress.
Swann, Joanna.
Learning, teaching, and education research in the 21st century: an evolutionary analysis of the role of teachers/Joanna Swann.
     p. cm.
Includes bibliographical references and index.
ISBN 978-1-4411-6126-0 (hardback) – ISBN 978-1-4411-6317-2 (pbk.)
1. Learning – Philosophy. 2. Teaching – Philosophy. 3. Popper, Karl R. (Karl Raimund), 1902-1994. I. Title.

LB1060.S93 2011
370.1–dc23
                                                              2011020721

Typeset by Newgen Imaging Systems Pvt Ltd, Chennai, India
Printed and bound in Great Britain

To the memory of Tyrrell Burgess

I may be wrong and you may be right, and by an effort, we may get nearer to the truth.

—Karl Popper, The Open Society and Its Enemies, Volume 2: Hegel and Marx

But as for certain truth, no man has known it,
Nor will he know it; neither of the gods,
Nor yet of all the things of which I speak.
And even if by chance he were to utter
The final truth, he would himself not know it;
For all is but a woven web of guesses.

—Xenophanes, *translated by Karl Popper*, Conjectures and Refutations:
The Growth of Scientific Knowledge

'Do no harm' (and, therefore, 'give the young what they most urgently need, in order to become independent of us, and to be able to choose for themselves') would be a very worthy aim for our educational system, and one whose realization is somewhat remote, even though it sounds modest.

—Karl Popper, The Open Society and Its Enemies, Volume 2: Hegel and Marx

Contents

viii Contents

Part 2 ENCOURAGING LEARNING

Part 3 DEVELOPING TEACHING

8 Research and the Development of Teaching 157

9 Developing a Popperian Science of School Teaching 176

10 Improving Our Practices as Teachers 198

Acknowledgements

First and foremost, I am grateful to Karl Popper, whom I never met and with whom I never communicated, but whose published philosophy has enriched my understanding of learning and, by implication, my conception of what teaching can become. I am also indebted to Tyrrell Burgess for his radical interpretation of the implications of Popper's work for educational practice and for very many informal discussions of these implications over a period of 30 years. I am especially grateful to Tyrrell, John Halliday, Michael Jenkins and my partner, Brian Marley, who between them convinced me of the value of writing a book unashamedly based on my own experience and understanding of teaching. My heartfelt thanks go to John Pratt, with whom I edited two earlier books and from whom I learnt a great deal about the process of structuring academic writing. I am very grateful to David Miller for his valuable critical feedback over a number of years on various papers and publications of mine, and for encouraging and supporting my application for financial assistance from the Karl Popper Charitable Trust. I am indebted to the Trust, not only for the funding that enabled me to obtain six months' study leave for the purpose of writing this book but also for the expression of confidence in the venture that this gesture represented. My thanks also go to Lorraine Harrison and members of the School Management Group of the School of Education and the Education Research Centre at the University of Brighton for making it possible for me to take up the Trust's award.

To the following people I offer my deepest thanks for feedback received on this book, or parts thereof, in draft: David Aspin, Alison Barnes, Herzl Baruch, Jean-Pierre Delage, Chris Downs, Janet English, Lorraine Foreman-Peck, Jon Griffith, Michael Jenkins, Pip Marples, Katrina Miller, Eileen Piggot-Irvine, Bernard Trafford, David Turner, Richard Wallis and, for their particularly detailed feedback, David Miller, John Pratt and Brian Marley. Any errors and limitations in the book are, of course, my sole responsibility.

My thanks also go to Alison Baker, commissioning editor, Rosie Pattinson, editorial assistant, and all other members of the team involved with this book at Continuum.

Finally, I am grateful to Manfred Lube and the University of Klagenfurt/ Karl Popper Library for permission to use quotations from Karl Popper's copyrighted works at the beginning of the book and at the head of each chapter.

Joanna Swann
April 2011
joannaswann@yahoo.co.uk

The Purpose of This Book

We all have our philosophies, whether or not we are aware of this fact, and our philosophies are not worth very much. But the impact of our philosophies upon our actions and our lives is often devastating. This makes it necessary to try to improve our philosophies by criticism. This is the only apology for the continued existence of philosophy which I am able to offer.

—*Karl Popper,* Objective Knowledge: An Evolutionary Approach

Introduction

This book has been designed to challenge some widespread assumptions about learning, teaching and education research – assumptions embedded in the practices of many teachers and in the design of most education institutions worldwide. The assumptions I set out to challenge are those that, as I shall argue, fly in the face of what is now conjecturally known (following Karl Popper's evolutionary analysis of learning) about what does and does not happen when learning takes place. In contesting these assumptions, I also expose and weaken one of the deep roots of authoritarianism in human society. The evolutionary analysis of learning strongly suggests that authoritarian approaches to teaching – those that view the learner's relationship to the teacher as one of dependence (Meighan and Siraj-Blatchford, 2003 [1981], Part 3, in particular, p. 214) and thereby inhibit students from engaging in self-initiated and self-directed exploratory activity – are not as conducive to the promotion of learning as is commonly supposed. In this regard, I use criticism (as construed in the above quotation from Popper, 1979 [1972], p. 33) as a tool to encourage improvement, by strengthening the case against the continued adoption of practices that foster learner dependence.

In addition, this book offers theory for use by those who wish to create or defend the opportunity to practise in accordance with non-authoritarian values. My intention in this regard is to provide philosophical argument to support the defence, pursuit and development of non-authoritarian educational agendas. Relatedly, the book outlines some tested alternatives to common practices. My intention here is to provide food for thought for those individuals and groups already striving to teach in accordance with non-authoritarian values or who wish to begin to do so.

A more ambitious aspiration became apparent while this book was being written: I hope the book will contribute, at least in a small way, to the pursuit of human transcendence. To this end I propose a speculative account of what teachers need to do in order to facilitate the kind of learning that may lead to significant improvements in how we treat each other and ourselves, and in the way we use the world's resources (Chapter 11). Transcendent learning, as I see it, is the kind of learning that enables us, collectively and individually, to progress well beyond what has hitherto been habitual and/or commonplace in our thinking, practices, strategies and institutional systems. It is the means by which, to use Popper's imagery, we 'lift ourselves by our bootstraps out of the morass of our ignorance' and 'throw a rope into the air and then swarm up it – if it gets any purchase, however precarious, on any little twig' (Popper, 1979 [1972], p. 148).

1 Whom this book is for

This book is for anyone who views her- or himself as a teacher. It is for qualified teachers, student teachers, teachers of student teachers, and lay teachers of various kinds, not least parents. Much of the book has been written with no particular student age range in mind, but the thrust of the core argument, including the detailed examples in Part 2 and some of the other examples scattered throughout, is directed towards the teaching of children and, to a slightly lesser degree, adolescents. I have taught in higher education for more than 13 years, but children are the learners with whom I have had the most experience as a professional, and childhood is a period when individuals' long-term development can be significantly enhanced or undermined by their experience of teaching. What I propose regarding the teaching of children and adolescents in schools, if adopted, would have profound implications for teaching in further and higher education.

Although I have spent most of my life in the United Kingdom and have clearly developed my thinking in a Western society, the content of the book is not directed towards any specific country or culture. The principal arguments are not context dependent, and the target readership is global.

I am aware that many readers are likely to be more interested in some elements of the discussion than others. Extensive cross-referencing and some repetition of key points have been included to help the reader who is dipping in here and there instead of reading the chapters sequentially.

2 The nature of the argument

Although my argument is philosophical, it does not focus on words and their meanings, and I do not shy away from the discussion of competing statements of fact – this book is not in the tradition of linguistic philosophy. As a philosopher of education I am, for the most part, mindful of Popper's 'anti-essentialist exhortation':

> Never let yourself be goaded into taking seriously problems about words and their meanings. What must be taken seriously are questions of fact, and assertions about facts: theories and hypotheses; the problems they solve; and the problems they raise.
>
> (Popper, 1992a [1974], section 7, p. 19)

It is important here to recognize a distinction between the facts – that is, what is actually so – and statements of fact (propositions about what is so) and assumptions of fact (whereby the nature of what is so is assumed). The facts are often elusive and, as discussed in later chapters, our knowledge of the facts cannot be made secure. It follows that it is best to view all statements of fact and assumptions of fact as provisional and contestable – hence my reference below to alleged facts.

The core of my argument (in Chapter 2) is a challenge to a commonsense assumption of fact that permeates most education institutions, many teaching practices and much theorizing about learning, teaching and research, namely that '*some learning involves the absorption of informational elements from outside the learner*'. The opposing idea that I present and defend, following Popper, is that '*learning never involves the absorption of informational elements from outside the learner*'. The commonsense idea and my Popperian alternative are mutually contradictory; they cannot both be true.

A rational decision as to whether the Popperian '*learning never involves the absorption of informational elements from outside the learner*' is preferable to the commonsense '*some learning involves the absorption of informational elements from outside the learner*' requires substantial engagement in philosophical thought. Both ideas are metaphysical rather than scientific. They purport to describe what is so in the world and, although they have stimulated the development of scientific theories (in respect of my Popperian theory, see Chapter 9), they are not themselves susceptible to scientific testing; that is, neither can be effectively challenged by reference to hard evidence. They can, however, be critically discussed.

When those who would defend the commonsense idea cite evidence in its support, their favourable interpretation of the evidence is inevitably the outcome of assumptions that are non-scientific but which can be challenged philosophically by argument. In challenging the commonsense idea, I mention research evidence from the fields of psychobiology, neuroscience and consciousness studies, but the premises of my argument are similarly non-scientific. Although the idea that learning never involves the absorption of informational elements from outside the learner may appear to be potentially refutable, a difficulty lies in the nature of what is at issue, namely learning. Learning is a process that often has some potentially observable outcomes, but learning cannot itself be observed. As discussed in Chapter 4, our view of learning becomes distorted if we reduce it to a set of observable outcomes.

The commonsense idea about learning and its competing Popperian alternative – expressed above as statements of alleged fact – are very important, because they have profound implications for what we do as learners and teachers, and for the practice of education research. Simply put, it makes a difference whether you act on one idea rather than the other. If teaching, particularly its conduct and organization in the context of institutions, were to be widely reconceived in light of the idea that *'learning never involves the absorption of informational elements from outside the learner'*, then the outcomes of teaching would be both significantly different and better – not only for individual students but also for the societies in which they live.

3 Facts and values

You may be wondering how my argument will proceed from a discussion of fact – about what does not happen when learning takes place – to an argument in favour of non-authoritarian approaches to teaching, construed here as those in which learner autonomy is fostered and learner dependence is discouraged. The link is an account of what happens when learning takes place, one that shows that the opportunity for self-directed exploratory activity is crucial to the advancement of learning (Chapters 3 and 5). Such activity is not an optional extra or something to be made available to learners only after they have acquired a prerequisite sum of knowledge or skills.

As implied above, I have taken the opportunity to promote non-authoritarian values by drawing on Popper's evolutionary analysis of learning to expose a commonly accepted myth about learning. Drawing on Popper's analysis, I present a new theory of what happens when learning takes place, in light of which I highlight seven sets of key facts about learning (Chapter 5, section 1), most of which are little known and, when known, may subsequently influence what people value. Questions of fact and questions of value arise together in situations but can nonetheless be differentiated (Popper, 2002b [1945], addendum 1, section 13; 1992a [1974], section 40). A question of fact – that is, a question of whether or not something is the case – can be distinguished from whether or not we like or dislike the particular fact (or alleged fact). One may question assumptions of fact about how children can best be helped to learn, and one can question assumptions of value – assumptions about what is to be considered good – about how children ought to be treated. However, although facts and values can be differentiated, what people believe to be the case tends to influence what they value, and, perhaps to a lesser degree, what people value tends to influence what they are prepared to believe. People who believe that children and adolescents have the potential to learn more when their opportunities for autonomous activity are restricted may be disinclined to value approaches to teaching children that have as a primary aim the advancement of learner autonomy. If such people subsequently develop the view that opportunities for self-directed exploratory activity (seen here to involve self-monitoring, self-evaluation and self-regulation) are crucial to learning and that exploratory activity that is both self-initiated and self-directed is vital for the transcendent learning of which humans are capable, they may then be more open to exploring how teaching can best support the development of students – children, adolescents and adults – as autonomous agents. I say 'may' because they may decide instead that it is preferable to constrain learning rather than to allow students greater autonomy.

I am not suggesting that we should attempt to view the content of learning in value-neutral terms, and it would seem inevitable, and only proper, that we are all inclined to favour the learning of some things and discourage the learning of other things. But there is nonetheless an important distinction to be made between, on the one hand, constraining learning by attempting to focus student attention on a lengthy prescribed agenda of subjects, topics or problem areas, regardless of the students' preferences, and, on the other, merely ruling a few fields of learning off limits (for moral reasons or because of resource constraints) and devoting our energies to encouraging students to take responsibility for decisions about the content of their planned programmes of study. I argue that the former, the conventional approach to the curriculum, needlessly limits autonomous activity on the part of the student and by so doing limits student learning, while the latter – the use of student-initiated curricula – does not (Chapters 6 and 7).

4 The nature of teaching

Despite my general concern to avoid focusing on problems about words and their meanings, I have nonetheless found that providing a few definitions in the early stages of a discussion can assist communication. When presenting an evolutionary analysis of learning, there are some terms to which particularly broad meanings are ascribed, and it can be useful to highlight how these terms are used. In addition, as a Popperian learning theorist, I have developed a specific definition of learning that is indicative of an evolutionary analysis. Definitions that relate to the discussion of learning are presented in Chapters 2 and 3; here I give a brief definitional account of teaching.

Teaching, as I construe it, is any activity undertaken on the part of one individual with the aspiration of helping another individual or group of individuals to learn. The teacher does not have to set out to teach anything in particular, and although intentionality is required, I do not subscribe to the view that awareness of the intention to promote learning is intrinsic to the act of teaching. The activities of teaching are many and varied, but teachers, as individuals who wish to help others to learn, may be preoccupied with one or the other of two endeavours: they may be intent on helping another or others to learn something in particular, something conceived by them (the teachers) prior to and/or independent of their engagement with the learner, and something other than the general attributes associated with learning how to learn and the development of full learner autonomy; or they may have a more general intention to promote learning, without privileging any particular set of ideas or capabilities other than those that relate to learning in general.

Of course, 'teaching' may be used with a more restricted meaning, limiting teaching to the first of the two preoccupations mentioned above. It may be defined as the business of initiating students into specific ways of thinking and other activities that the students' supposed superiors have deemed to be worthwhile and important. Such a restricted definition presupposes ways of construing learning that this book is designed to challenge. Teaching is also sometimes construed only in terms of a *conscious* intention to promote learning, but this view would also seem to be unduly restrictive and to disregard what is now known about the significance of unconscious activity in human decision making and action (see, e.g., Nørretranders, 1998 [1991], chapter 9; Gray, 2004, chapter 2; and Wiliam, 2006).

If we accept a broader definition of teaching, it becomes apparent that humans spend a great deal of time teaching each other; that is, we participate in exchanges with the intention of furthering our own learning and that of others. During our interactions, all of us are taught and we all teach others, even if only informally. I do not deny that some other animals engage in teaching activities, but teaching and being taught are important human characteristics. Even when we are on our own, we learn from the use of resources that are designed to bring about learning. Although I think it is incorrect to say that computer software packages and books teach, some of those who create such resources may be construed as teachers, even if they have no personal or direct relationship with their 'students'.

'Can I be said to have taught if the student has not learnt?' My answer to this question is no; if learning has not taken place as a consequence of your actions, it would seem strange to say that you have been teaching. However, I would assert that if learning has taken place you have been teaching, even if it is not the learning that you intended. Indeed, I would suggest that most teaching results in at least some learning that is other than what the teacher intended, and much teaching goes on without the full range of the intended learning taking place. In general, what is problematic about teaching activities in formal education institutions is not that the learner learns nothing; rather, the issue is the extent to which what is learnt is different from, and often significantly less than, what was intended. The pressing problem in the context of formal education is not how to teach but how to teach *better* – a problem that raises questions about learning and what teachers are for, that is, their role and purpose in respect of promoting learning.

5 Research on teaching

I make the case in Chapter 8 for there being two distinct, but not unrelated, types of research that can be used in the development of teaching. One focuses on the formulation of *theoretical* problems and the development and testing of *theoretical* solutions; the other focuses on the formulation of *practical* problems and the development and testing of *practical* solutions.

The first type of research includes not only philosophical research of the kind that has led to this book, but also scientific research and exploratory theoretical studies of various kinds. Some years ago, for example, I published a testable hypothesis regarding the particular approach to classroom learning and teaching that I advocate (Swann, 1999c), and I showed how hypotheses of this kind could be tested as part of a scientific study (Swann, 2003a). This hypothesis and an outline proposal for testing it have been reworked for this book (see Chapter 9). Although aspects of my argument, as acknowledged above, are not susceptible to empirical investigation, the discussion as a whole includes elements that could be empirically tested.

Some readers may wish to argue that the conventional approach to the curriculum – whereby students are rarely permitted to take responsibility for the content of their formal programmes of learning – has been tested and found to work. I therefore stress that what I mean by the testing of a *theory* – for example, a theory about the effectiveness of a conventional practice – is this: it is a critical process that involves, whenever possible, the formulation of a hypothesis that could potentially be refuted and the search for refuting evidence (see, e.g., Popper, 1972b [1963], chapter 1, and 1979 [1972], appendix 1). The testing of a *practice* – for example, the practice of teaching according to a prescribed curriculum – involves a concern not only for the intended and desirable consequences of action but also for the unintended and potentially undesirable consequences (see, e.g., Popper, 1961 [1957], section 21). Testing, as I see it, means evaluating a theory or course of action, often (though not always) in the context of competing alternatives. That a particular way of doing things has been accepted practice for centuries does not mean that it, and any of the assumptions embedded in it, have been rigorously tested.

The second type of research is action research. At its best, action research takes the form of a rigorous attempt on the part of practitioners to improve a practice and/or a situation and, at the same time, to increase their understanding of the practice and/or situation and to present this understanding to a wider audience. Such research can be comparatively inexpensive to undertake. It requires time to think, some freedom to experiment and, almost invariably, the opportunity to collaborate with other practitioners and researchers. In this book, my account of what teachers can do to promote learning arises, to a significant extent, out of a six-year action research project I undertook as a primary school teacher of children aged 7 to 11 years. I also give an account (in Chapter 10) of a systematic, problem-based methodology that I devised for use by teachers and other practitioners who wish to improve their professional practice. This methodology has been adopted for research purposes by myself and others, including researchers involved in the multi-institutional project on Improving Formative Assessment in Vocational Education and Literacy, Language and Numeracy (Swann et al., 2011).

6 Authoritarian approaches to teaching

Roland Meighan identified six different authoritarian approaches to maintaining and achieving social order, each involving a broadly different type of power relationship (1981, chapter 14 and, in a fourth edition, with amendments and additions, as Meighan and Siraj-Blatchford, 2003, chapter 16).

Some of these approaches are 'softer' than others, but all are essentially authoritarian because of the dependence relationships they serve to create and sustain. The six approaches to, or 'forms' of, social order are sequenced below according to 'hardness', with the hardest first:

(i)   The *autocratic* form: order is maintained and/or achieved through fear, physical or psychological, and the image of the teacher is that of 'dictator, commanding officer or ringmaster' (ibid., p. 209).

(ii) The *parental* form: order is maintained and/or achieved through deference, and the teacher's role is akin to that of a controlling parent or, perhaps, a cleric.

(iii) The *charismatic* form: order is maintained and/or achieved through charm or 'personal magnetism, public performance skills or emotional persuasion' and the teacher's image is that of a 'leader with his disciples' or an 'entertainer or pied piper' (ibid.).

(iv) The *organizational* form: order is maintained and/or achieved 'through detailed organization, indicating a clear structure, giving full instructions and deciding ends and means in a systematic way' (ibid.). The image of the teacher here is that of an 'architect, production planner or quantity surveyor' (ibid.).

(v)   The *expertise* form: order is maintained and/or achieved 'through the possession of information demonstrated to be useful or believed to be necessary by the non-expert' (ibid.). The teacher's image here is akin to that of a doctor or scientist.

(vi) The *consultative* form: order is maintained and/or achieved 'through the use of feedback from learners so that they feel that the teacher has taken account of their ideas and responses' (ibid.). The image here is that of a market researcher or diagnostician.

Many people would recognize the autocratic approach, and perhaps even the parental and charismatic, as authoritarian; far fewer would characterize the other three forms as authoritarian, particularly the consultative form. Consultation embodies an authoritarian power relationship when the consultee feels obliged to wait to be consulted and/or the consultant feels at liberty to make decisions that ignore the feedback provided by the consultee. So one of the striking and useful things about Meighan's analysis is that approaches to education which are often assumed to be democratic are revealed in their true colours, that is, authoritarian. Note also that

> In all these [forms] the dependence relationship tends to persist unless the dominant person decides otherwise, though reactions from the submissive persons can occur. However, the degree of dependence appears to vary with each type. With the autocratic it may be 100 per cent, whereas with the other forms it may often be less than this.
>
> (Ibid.)

When we were school students, most if not all of us took the submissive role in all six types of authoritarian approach to teaching, and the softer forms are likely to feature strongly in most people's experience of post-compulsory education. Many of us who are or have been teachers of children will be aware of situations in which most, if not all, of these forms were exemplified in our practice.

> The various forms of authoritarian order . . . can be seen in classrooms in a single manifestation, where a teacher relies almost exclusively on one type to establish and maintain order. They are also seen in combination, where teachers use a variety of forms according to the situation, their moods or the state of their relationship with the class . . .
>
> (Ibid., p. 210)

Authoritarian power relationships and authoritarian systems and structures in education stand in contrast to those that are non-authoritarian, of which Meighan identifies two broad types: democratic and autonomous study. These non-authoritarian approaches to power and social order stress, respectively, *interdependence* and *independence*. It should be noted that there are different forms of democratic order, of which four are identified by Meighan: (a) agreed rules, in which 'order is obtained by appealing to rules agreed at some previous date' (ibid.) and the teacher administers the rules, acting as a judge or referee; (b) representative, in which the class elects representatives, either formally or informally, and these representatives, as spokespersons, can influence decision making; (c) committee, in which 'several representatives are elected or nominated to meet to make decisions' (ibid.); and (d) forum, in which 'all members of a class are involved in open discussion about decisions' (ibid.). I think it important to stress that the activities used to illustrate these democratic forms could all be conducted in a non-democratic and authoritarian way. The setting up of a committee by people in power often functions as a means of deflecting or diluting criticism of the status quo and disempowering those who would suggest alternative strategies and practices. And the seeming openness of a forum discussion may be illusory, for example, if the politics that surround it mean that those present are constrained through fear from expressing their genuine opinions.

Meighan also highlights different interpretations of the idea of autonomous study. (In one interpretation, it is merely a method of teaching and learning and could be used as part of an approach that is broadly authoritarian.) Principles and practices that encompass the idea of autonomous study are presented in my Part 2, and democracy is discussed in section 7 below.

Two points are to be made here. First, when I refer in this book to authoritarian approaches to teaching, what I have in mind are power relationships and systems of creating and sustaining order that may include all six forms of authoritarianism identified by Meighan. Second, as already implied, a non-authoritarian approach to teaching is one in which learner autonomy is fostered and learner dependence is discouraged. Even democratic approaches need to support the development of learner autonomy, as the ability of individuals to make autonomous judgements is a necessity if decision making is to become fully democratic; otherwise, for example, individuals' decisions may be the result of manipulation by others.

In terms of my detailed practical proposals for teaching (in Chapter 7), I mostly propose only what I myself have tried and evaluated. I have not taught (or been taught) in a democratic school, and I have not systematically pursued a democratic approach in my teaching (though I have adopted democratic practices on an ad hoc basis). So for the most part, this book is not focused on making schools and classrooms more democratic; it is, rather, more generally directed against authoritarianism and towards promoting both greater independence on the part of the student and a general capability for developing groups and communities in which interdependence is a key concept. From experience, I can say that student-initiated curricula, as a non-authoritarian approach to decision making in respect of the content of formal programmes of learning, can be pursued in institutions in which the softer forms of authoritarianism otherwise prevail. I suspect that if adopted over a period of time by groups of teachers, the use of such curricula could be a catalyst for developing more and deeper democratic practices at the school level – there are, as Meighan points out (Meighan and Siraj-Blatchford, 2003 [1981], pp. 212–13), possibilities for bridging to democracy from both autonomous study and the softer forms of authoritarianism. In schools and other learning centres in which teachers are systematically attempting to practise in accordance with democratic values, it would seem that a non-authoritarian approach to decision making about the content of formal programmes of learning – such as the one proposed in this book – is essential.

7 Teaching and learning in a democracy

Democracy can be construed in many ways. One way is to see it as a means of protecting an open society (though this is not to imply that all democracies are entirely open or that all open societies are democratic). An open society, as conceived by Popper, is one in which the idea that 'I may be wrong and you may be right, and by an effort, we may get nearer to the truth' (Popper, 2002b [1945], p. 249) is made manifest in the practices of its members and in the organization and structures of its institutions.

In an open society, the conjectural nature of knowledge is recognized, and no person or group has a supreme right to determine what is to be construed as good, true or valid. A relativistic view of truth is not implied. Rather, following Popper (1972 [1963], chapter 10; 1979 [1972], chapters 1, 2, 6, 7 and 8), truth is conceived here as a regulative ideal, as a standard at which to aim (see my Chapter 3, section 7, and Chapter 8, section 4). Although we can pursue truth, we can never know whether we have reached our goal. Popperians reject the idea that the growth of knowledge resides in the accumulation of justified true beliefs. Instead, the aim is to challenge, develop and perhaps overthrow some of our existing, flawed or limited expectations. As discussed in Chapter 4, what is provisionally and pragmatically accepted as true or good is not decided by an appeal to so-called confirming evidence (nor to personal status, popularity, religion, political group or state). The 'authority', insofar as there is one, is that of reasoned argument. But any decision to accept a hypothesis, however good it may seem at present, may later be overturned by the discovery of new facts and the development of new ideas and arguments.

In an open society, criticism and diversity are highly valued; so too is the freedom to access information. Decision making and decision taking are addressed in the spirit of openness; different options are proposed, listened to and considered. Fundamental disagreements will occur, of course, and decisions may have to be taken without consensus. But in a society that is democratic, there will be formal procedures for limiting and curtailing the power of decision makers and decision takers – that is, the society's leaders – without having to resort to violence or coercion. Members of a society may wish to utilize these procedures if their leaders exercise their vested power badly or fail to meet positive expectations. In general, the concepts of an open society and a democracy are two vital resources to which we can refer when attempting to organize our social institutions and conduct the business of our groups, communities and countries in such a way that skirmishing, tyranny and bullying are reduced. A third key resource is our advanced facility for learning.

Three common assumptions about democratic organizations, institutions and governments need to be challenged. First, it is often assumed that once a democracy has been created, the most significant threat to its continuance is from those who express a distaste for it – the 'enemies' of democracy. This assumption is not only mistaken (for discussion see, e.g., Codd, 2005) but also dangerous, in that it encourages complacency and a lack of active and critical engagement within an established democracy. The second invalid assumption is that democracy can be imposed from without. This assumption tempts people to adopt short cuts to democracy that do not take account of the particular circumstances. Democracy requires habits of political and social action that have to be learnt and that can develop only over a period of time. And, of course, the idea of imposing democracy is a contradiction in terms. The third invalid assumption is that democracy is largely a matter of suffrage. This assumption is damaging because it provides the basis for the other two. Although voting is not to be undervalued as a way of getting rid of bad leaders, it is in general useful to regard voting as a tool to facilitate decision making. There can be voting without democracy and democracy without voting – in the forum type of democracy, as mentioned in section 6 above, decisions may be made by all members of the group on the basis of open discussion and without recourse to a vote.

These invalid assumptions limit the development and promotion of democratic processes. In particular, they add weight to the fallacious idea that teaching for democracy is a matter of training people to adopt specific roles. Although any complex society will have a variety of roles to which its members will, by one means or other, be assigned, it is potentially undemocratic to set out to prepare some groups and individuals for some roles rather than others in light of, for example, early demonstrations of achievement. Note also that when I say that democracy requires habits of political and social action that have to be learnt, this is not a matter of students developing theoretical knowledge about democracy, though such knowledge may be useful; rather, what is required is practical experience of real, rather than pretend, democratic decision taking. And, as argued in Chapter 5, students who are taught *about* democracy most often learn the practices of authoritarianism – because the way they are taught in school consistently conveys to them the importance of being biddable and willing to conform, and, despite rhetoric to the contrary, their development as fully autonomous learners is generally inhibited.

8 The provenance of the argument

This book offers a free interpretation of Popper's evolutionary analysis of learning, but, although in places it draws heavily on aspects of Popper's epistemology, none of the chapters is intended as a summary of his ideas. Readers who wish to develop their understanding of Popper's work, including those who wish to critique it, are strongly advised to consult Popper's texts at first hand. Note also that this book is primarily concerned with the learning of individuals, rather than, as in the case of Popper's publications, with the growth of human knowledge in its broader sense.

I am, of course, aware of the work of other Popperian educationists and philosophers who have discussed the link between Popper's epistemology and non-authoritarian values, including Henry Perkinson, who also discusses Popper's evolutionary theory of learning (see, in particular, 1984 and 1971), Ronald Swartz et al. (1980), Joseph Agassi (2008 [1993]), John Wettersten (1999) and Richard Bailey (2000). I have been greatly encouraged by these authors' work but not strongly influenced by it. Next to Popper, the greatest influence on the development of my argument, specifically with regard to student-initiated curricula, has been the work of Popperian educationist Tyrrell Burgess (see, in particular, 1975, 1977, 1979).

While writing this book, I became increasingly aware of having been influenced by radical educationists such as Meighan (see section 6 above), Paul Goodman (1971 [1962]), John Holt (1969 [1964]), Neil Postman and Charles Weingartner (1969), Everett Reimer (1971 [1970]), Ivan Illich (1973 [1970]) and Paulo Freire (1972). The work of Meighan aside, I read parts of these radical authors' books a long time ago, either when I was a student teacher (1968–72) or shortly thereafter as a master's degree student (1974–76). My grasp of their work was minimal at the level of detail and in no sense thorough, but I realize now that I was inspired by their anti-authoritarian sentiments.

Insofar as I am indebted to Popper and Burgess, and to other philosophers, teachers and educationists for ideas, I have striven to give credit where credit is due, but in writing this book I have set out to transcend these influences and create a new argument about teaching.

9 A challenge to Popperians

It should also be noted that I am not an uncritical Popperian. Although Popper clearly acknowledged that learning is a creative process, and a theory of creativity in learning can be drawn out of and developed from his evolutionary analysis, he did not explore the creative aspects of learning in depth; the function of *criticism* in the growth of knowledge was his primary concern. Popperians, too, have largely focused on the significance of criticism in the development of objectified knowledge, and they, by and large, have neglected to explore creativity as a necessary feature of any situation in which learning can be said to have taken place. My interpretation of Popper's philosophy, as well as my account of its implications for the conduct and organization of teaching, goes against the grain in this regard. Compared to most Popperians, I place significantly greater stress on the idea of learning as a creative process and, following from this, on what teachers can do to encourage imaginative activity. (This is not to deny that other Popperians have discussed creativity – see, e.g., Larry Briskman, 2009 [1980] and Ian Jarvie, 2009 [1981].)

10 What this book does not do

Any reader who comes to this book looking for an overview of theories of learning or an engagement with published critiques of Popper's work will be disappointed. This is not that sort of book. Rather, my primary concern has been to present the reader with a set of post-Darwinian ideas that are not widely known and, insofar as they are known, generally not well understood. In this regard, the book serves a descriptive function. With regard to the book's argument, my principal concern is to engage with the reader's assumptions about learning and teaching and to challenge some of the ideas that are embedded in conventional educational practices.

Part 1
Learning

The Challenge of an Evolutionary Analysis of Learning

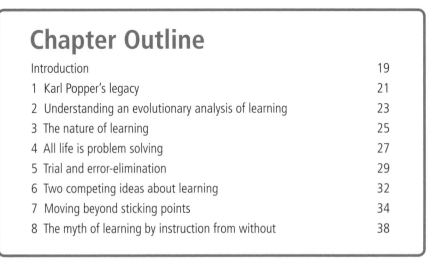

Chapter Outline

We do not discover new facts or new effects by copying them, or by inferring them inductively from observation, or by any other method of instruction by the environment.

—*Karl Popper,* The Myth of the Framework:
In Defence of Science and Rationality

[W]e learn only through trial and error. Our trials . . . are always our hypotheses. They stem from us, not from the external world. All we learn from the external world is that some of our efforts are mistaken.

—*Karl Popper,* All Life is Problem Solving

Introduction

People are inclined to agree that if we are interested in teaching, it makes sense to give some thought to learning. But what is then thought about and discussed is often predicated on the assumption that at least some learning involves the receipt of information or, rather, informational elements from outside the learner. When encouraged to explain how these informational elements are received, many people offer a variant on the centuries-old philosophical explanation that informational elements, viewed as the building blocks of our learning, are absorbed from the environment through the senses and accumulate in our minds as sense data. The idea of informational elements is not, however, widely discussed, and the term 'sense data' is dated and rarely mentioned; rather, the existence of informational elements and the idea that they can be internalized are commonly treated as given. Debates about learning largely focus on what happens next, that is, on how the informational elements come to be processed. Even among educationists who espouse a constructivist view of learning – that is, educationists who view learning as an active process that requires of the learner a personal interpretation of experience and the construction of her (or his) own knowledge – it seems to be widely assumed that processes of interpretation and construction take place only after some primary data have been received.

Having assumed that learning is a process that begins with the internalization of informational elements, educationists are more inclined to discuss learning from a psychological rather than a philosophical perspective. Often of keen interest are those research studies that investigate emotional or cognitive factors pertaining to the development of individuals and groups. Factors of these kinds are considered when thinking about what supports or hinders the learning of particular skills or subjects on the part of children, adolescents and adults.

Without wishing to underplay the value of psychology, I suggest there is a danger in investigating the factors that affect learning on the part of individuals and groups without giving due consideration to philosophical assumptions about learning. Expectations about learn*ers* are invariably linked to assumptions about learn*ing*, that is, to philosophical assumptions about the nature of learning – about what happens in, and factors pertaining to, any situation in which learning can be said to take place. If our expectations about learn*ing* are fundamentally flawed, our attempts to understand learners and the processes that affect their emotional and cognitive development are also likely to be flawed.

The purpose of this chapter is to introduce, from the field of philosophy, an evolutionary analysis of learning. The core ideas of this analysis are highlighted in the seven points below. As indicated in Chapter 1, the discussion is about learning as a subjective process, something that individuals do (mostly, in the case of human learning, in a social context), rather than about the growth of knowledge in its broader sense.

(i) We are conscious of only *some* aspects of *some* of our learning. With regard to the totality of our learning, those aspects of which we are aware are akin to the tip of an iceberg.

(ii) Regardless of how it may seem, learning *never* involves the passive receipt or absorption of informational elements from the environment – neither the social environment nor the physical environment.

(iii) There is *no* transfer of data from the environment to the learner. The learner's response to an external stimulus is always one of interpretation.

(iv) In order for learning to take place, the learner *must* discover (explicitly or, more often, implicitly) a mismatch between an (explicit or, more often, implicit) expectation and experience, actual or anticipated.

(v) Although the discovery of a mismatch between expectation and experience is necessary in order for learning to take place, it is not of itself sufficient to trigger learning. Learning takes place *only* as a result of the individual's creative response to such a discovery.

(vi) In order for learning to take place, the learner *must* problematize a mismatch between expectation and experience and attempt to solve the problem so created. But, even so, problem solving is not necessarily accompanied by learning.

(vii) Learning – *all* learning – is problem solving through which an outcome for the learner is the development of a new disposition (embodying a new preference and/or a new explicit or, more often, implicit expectation).

In the chapter's final section, the evolutionary analysis is extended to challenge the widespread assumption that some learning involves the absorption of informational elements from outside the learner. The character of this assumption seems to me that of a myth, an idea that has existed for some considerable time, but for which there is very little in the way of argument to defend it. If the stated assumption is mistaken – if there is no absorption of informational elements from outside the learner – it undermines the basis for much contemporary theorizing about teaching. It also calls into question many of the practices currently found under the banner of education, including significantly restricting students' opportunities to engage in self-initiated and self-directed exploratory activity.

1 Karl Popper's legacy

As stated in Chapter 1, my argument draws heavily on Karl Popper's evolutionary analysis of learning (in particular Popper, 1979 [1972]; 1992a [1974];

1994a, chapter 1; 1994b; 1999; see also Popper and Eccles, 1977). Although Popper is more widely recognized as a philosopher of science, following the publication of *The Logic of Scientific Discovery* (1972a [1934]), and for his social and political two-volume text on *The Open Society and Its Enemies* (2002a [1945], 2002b [1945]), during the course of his long working life as a philosopher he developed a much broader view of the growth of knowledge and individual learning than these books alone would suggest. His collected writings can be viewed as the exploitation of the idea of natural selection in the analysis of the growth of knowledge, the development of traditions and institutions, and individual learning. As Donald Campbell put it,

> evolution – even in its biological aspects – is a knowledge process, and . . . the natural-selection paradigm for such knowledge increments can be generalized to other epistemic activities, such as learning, thought, and science. Such an epistemology has been neglected in the dominant philosophic traditions. It is primarily through the works of Karl Popper that a natural selection epistemology is available today.
>
> (1974, p. 413)

The conclusion to Popper's selectionist analysis of learning is summarized by the two quotations that head this chapter (from Popper, 1994a, p. 9, and 1999, p. 47). The idea, raised in the first quotation, that 'we do not discover new facts or new effects' by 'instruction by the environment' perhaps needs some clarification. It is another way of saying that, in learning, there is no transfer of informational elements or primary data from one individual to another (the social environment) or from the physical environment to the individual (see (ii) and (iii) in the introductory section above). To say that there is no learning by instruction from without the learner is not to deny that learning takes place *in response to* instruction. Learning can, of course, take place when people are being instructed; in education institutions throughout the world, teachers give instruction and students learn. But these two ideas, of learning *in response to* instruction and learning *by* instruction, are not synonymous. *When learning takes place in response to instruction, it is not the instruction that creates the learning; rather, the learning takes place by means of the activity of the learner.*

According to Popper's account of learning, new expectations, preferences, ideas and theories are never the result of a process in which informational elements have been transferred and in which the learner is to some degree passive; rather, they are created by the learner under environmental and/or internal selection pressure (the latter including, in the case of much human learning, the consequences of thought experiments). In short, *we learn by instruction only insofar as we instruct ourselves – we learn by instruction from within.* At any point in time, those expectations (inborn or the result of learning) which have 'survived' are those that are yet to be eliminated and replaced or modified as the result of the learner's experience of the environment, or the anticipated experience thereof, or the learner's free imagination.

Some 37 years on from the publication of the quoted passage from Campbell (1974, p. 413), evolutionary epistemology remains largely neglected in the study of education (for exceptions see, e.g., Perkinson, 1971 and 1984; Burgess, 1977; Bailey, 2000; and www.takingchildrenseriously.com, the website of the Popper-inspired Taking Children Seriously movement, founded by Sarah Fitz-Claridge and David Deutsch). And, in my experience of education debate at conferences and other fora, Popper's radical theory of learning is sometimes met with incredulity. Some participants wonder how any serious philosopher could have argued that in the development of human capabilities there is no transference of information or informational elements from outside the individual, neither from the physical environment nor from other individuals.

There are, of course, critiques of Popper's work, but the rejection of his ideas is a more complex matter than is often implied when the citation of a critique is followed by the hasty dismissal of his arguments (see Burgess and Swann, 2003, for extended discussion of this topic). The major criticisms of his epistemology have been addressed by Popper himself (see, in particular, Popper, 1974) and by Popperian epistemologists such as David Miller (see, in particular, 1994, chapters 1 and 2, for a defence of Popper's solution to the problem of induction; 2006a, chapters 4 and 5, for a defence of Popper's solutions to the problem of demarcation and the problem of induction). Moreover, critiques of his epistemology usually focus on his philosophy of science rather than his evolutionary analysis of learning. Incorporated into my account are arguments against the generalized points of criticism I have encountered when presenting my own work in the public domain.

2 Understanding an evolutionary analysis of learning

A common objection to the idea that there is no transfer of informational elements from the environment to the learner comes from the assumption that all aspects of learning that involve activity on the part of the learner are invariably conscious. Those aspects of learning about which we remain unaware are then assumed to be the result of passive experiences, including the absorption of informational elements from the social and physical environment. There is, however, considerable evidence – both anecdotal and from empirical studies – to suggest that this assumption is mistaken.

Research in the field of consciousness studies, for example, suggests that we are conscious of a comparatively small proportion of the processes, including processes of learning, in which we engage. We are mostly unaware of how and what we are learning. Note also that when we make a decision, our awareness of the decision comes a fraction of a second *after* we have made it (see, e.g., Nørretranders, 1998 [1991], chapter 9; Gray, 2004, chapter 2, section 2.1; and Wiliam, 2006). It may seem that our conscious minds are regulating all, or most, of our learning activities, but this is an illusion. It therefore follows that the absence of conscious awareness should not be equated with passivity, such as the passivity generally assumed as part of the idea that we absorb informational elements from the environment. Our conscious minds play a role in our learning, but the role is not as great as, and is rather different from, the one often assumed.

With regard to anecdotal evidence, many of us will have experienced going to bed thinking about a particularly intractable problem and waking up the following morning with a solution to it. In general, solutions to explicit problems often spring to mind while we are doing things other than consciously thinking about them.

For some educationists, the term 'unconscious' is associated with Freudian and post-Freudian psychoanalytic theory. I therefore stress that in my account 'unconscious' is not restricted to the psychoanalytic notion of 'dynamically unconscious' (i.e. repressed). I use 'unconscious' adjectivally and never as a noun, as in the idea of 'the' unconscious. The question of whether there is unconscious learning should not be conflated with that of whether some ideas are dynamically unconscious.

In order to understand an evolutionary analysis of learning, it is necessary to assign broad meanings to the terms 'expectation', 'problem', 'knowledge' and 'criticism'. Within evolutionary epistemology, these terms apply to conscious and unconscious phenomena, and they are not confined to ideas that the organism would itself be capable of articulating. I stress in particular that the use of 'expectation' is not restricted to situations in which a person says 'I expect . . .'; it is also used when giving an account of those many situations in which organisms – plants as well as animals – anticipate a situation and are predisposed to respond in one way rather than another. Many animals, for example, exhibit a fearful, poised-for-flight reaction to sudden, loud noises. We can say that their expectation is that a loud noise may signal danger. With regard to our experience of our own background expectations, it is often only in the disappointment of an expectation that the expectation comes to our attention. As Popper observed,

> we become conscious of many of our expectations only when they are disappointed, owing to their being unfulfilled. An example would be the encountering of an unexpected step in one's path: it is the unexpectedness of the step which may make us conscious of the fact that we expected to encounter an even surface.
>
> (1979 [1972], p. 344)

With regard to learning, Popper continued, 'Such disappointments force us to *correct* our system of expectations. The process of learning consists largely in such corrections; that is, in the elimination of certain (disappointed) expectations' (ibid.).

3 The nature of learning

From an evolutionary standpoint, the difference between an organism that learns and one that does not is that only the former develops, in the context of experience, new dispositions – specifically, dispositions that are not purely an outcome of genetic inheritance or haphazard organic change (see Popper, 1979 [1972], pp. 343–4, whose account of learning I have modified slightly). A disposition in this context is a '*disposition to react, or . . . a preparation for a reaction*, which is adapted to (or which anticipates) a state of the environment yet to come about' (ibid., p. 344). An organism's dispositions embody its expectations – its (fallible) knowledge – and its preferences; and while expectations and preferences are both subject to change through learning, it is the disappointment of expectations that, so to speak, drives the learning.

Significantly, changes in expectation are accompanied by changes in what the organism is capable of experiencing and in its potential responses to its environment – that is, what it is capable of doing and what it is inclined to do. An ability to learn is a specific form of adaptability, and the ability to adapt confers, potentially, an evolutionary advantage. Although learning is dependent on maturation, it involves more than the fruition of inborn characteristics. A learning organism develops new expectations, preferences and capabilities that may enable it to function more effectively in the situations in which it finds itself. To clarify what is not learning, an amoeba may respond evasively when it encounters a toxic fluid; that is, its movements are not entirely random. Its response to this kind of problem can become more efficient, in that the period of time it takes to run through its repertoire of genetically programmed behaviours can become shorter; but, aside from this efficiency gain, the repertoire remains unchanged (Petersen, 1988, pp. 34–5). An amoeba is not a learning organism, because it does not expand its repertoire of expectations and responses beyond those that are genetically programmed.

At the physico-chemical level, it can be observed that a learning organism possesses a brain, or at least a nervous system, and that learning involves activity within this neural network. An active neural network is, however, merely a necessary, not a sufficient, condition for learning to take place. Learning is not a process located solely within a neural network; rather, it takes place in the organism as a whole.

The use of 'organism' in my account of learning excludes, by implication, non-biological forms such as those produced in the field of artificial intelligence and robotics. Although I am not committed to the idea of excluding non-biological forms from the category 'things that learn', it seems to me more appropriate to say that human robotic creations – for example, Darwin VIII, a 'mobile brain-based device' (Seth et al., 2004, p. 1185) – *simulate* aspects of learning. While some robots perform in a way that is interestingly analogous to living things, they do not as yet function in the way that living things do. Only living things have problems, which arise in part from their preferences (see below and Chapter 3, section 2); insofar as robotic creations can be said to solve problems, these are initiated and controlled by their human creators – making robots extensions of human enterprise rather than fully autonomous forms. Also, although evolving robotic forms have been created, their development seems to depend on selection applied to *random* changes (see Floreano et al., 2008), which puts them outside the conception of learning proposed above.

With an evolutionary view of learning, there is no implication that what is learnt is necessarily desirable. It is useful here to distinguish between progression and progress (Munz, 2001, and personal communication). Progression involves moving from one state of affairs to a *different* one; progress involves moving from one state of affairs to a *better* one. Learning involves progression, in that the learner proceeds from one state to another, from one expectation to the next; but progress – however it may be construed – may not ensue. People often assume that all learning is 'good' and that the more one learns the better. This is understandable insofar as learning is undertaken in the expectation (conscious or unconscious) that it will be beneficial; improvement is the learner's implicit, if not explicit, aim. But often this aim is not fulfilled. We can, for example, learn things that are false, such as 'spiders have six legs', or detrimental to our personal well-being, such as learning to smoke. As an additional illustration, a child may start school believing in herself as a learner and believing that attending school will be a means of furthering her learning. But as a result of education assessment procedures, the child may learn to see herself as someone who is lacking in ability rather than as someone who is able to learn. Then, although the child still has the potential to learn, her belief in this potential has been diminished. There has been progression – the child's expectations have 'developed' – but not progress, because what has developed is an impediment to future learning.

Some social constructivists are uncomfortable with the idea that learning is an individual activity. I am not, however, denying the importance of the social context of learning. Clearly, what we learn as humans (and how we learn) is bound up with the social dimension of our experience. Uniquely among other animals, we engage with linguistically formulated problems, theories, expectations, hypotheses, assumptions of fact, values and arguments (discussed in Chapter 3). But none of this need lead us to dispute that learning is an activity that takes place at the level of the individual.

4 All life is problem solving

If learning is a process that results in new dispositions, in particular new expectations, what then is the nature of the process involved? According to Popperian selectionism, expectations develop by a critical and creative process of explicit or, more often, implicit problem solving. Here, the use of the term 'problem solving' is somewhat different from its use in education. In education, 'problem solving' is mostly employed when referring to a specific task that has an explicit goal. In evolutionary epistemology, the concept of problem solving is significantly broader; to quote Popper, 'All life is problem solving' (1999, title of book and chapter 9, and see p. 100).

Organisms enter the world laden with expectations. These expectations, contained within each organism's genetic code (its inborn 'instructions'), are fallible: 'Expectations have usually the character of hypotheses, of conjectural or hypothetical knowledge: they are *uncertain*' (Popper, 1990, p. 32). Many expectations are latent until activated by stimuli to which the organism responds – often, in the case of animals, during exploration (Popper, 1992a [1974], p. 52). These inborn expectations – such as, for human babies, 'If I cry I shall be fed' – are about what is so in the world, that is, the world to which the species of which the organism is a member has adapted during the course of evolution. Many expectations are challenged by experience, with the effect that living organisms are continuously engaged in generating solutions to problems: 'Every organism and every species is faced constantly by the threat of extinction . . . this threat takes the form of concrete problems which it has to solve' (ibid., p. 177). In this evolutionary sense, a problem is what exists when there is a mismatch between an organism's expectation and its experience (actual or, in the case of some human learning, anticipated), and, I suggest, when the organism is inclined to do something to address the disequilibrium that the disappointment of its expectation will have occasioned (Swann, 1999a, and section 5 below). This is not to imply that equilibrium can ever be achieved, only that organisms are predisposed to solve problems (Popper, 1994a, p. 4).

Biological organisms have purpose, so to speak, and their fundamental purpose is to survive and propagate their kind. However, the practical – that is, concrete – problems that an organism attempts to solve are not always directly related to its own survival: 'The problem of finding a good nesting place may be a concrete problem for a pair of birds without being a survival problem for these birds, although it may turn into one for their offspring' (Popper, 1992a [1974], p. 177). Similarly, when children are skipping with ropes, the problems they are solving – such as how to jump at the appropriate time and maintain a steady rhythm – are not survival problems. Most problems arise as a consequence of preferences, especially instinctive preferences (ibid., p. 178). But the development and survival of preferences takes place in the context of an organism's principal, if not always most pressing, problem – that of its survival or the survival of its own kind.

Living organisms apply themselves to the solving of problems, but, as mentioned earlier, not all living organisms learn. *Learning can, however, be viewed as a special case of problem solving, one in which a new disposition – a disposition that is neither programmed by genetic inheritance nor the outcome of haphazard organic change – is created.* And, like problem solving, learning is an open-ended process; its consequences cannot be known in advance, though some may be anticipated correctly.

5 Trial and error-elimination

Popper's evolutionary analysis posits that all cases of problem solving and learning embody the same process, a process of trial and error-elimination – also manifest in the evolution of species and the growth of objectified knowledge (ideas expressed in a linguistic, symbolic, artistic or technological form). The process of trial and error-elimination is summarized in the following, oft-cited, simplified schema (Popper, 1979 [1972], p. 243):

$$P_1 \rightarrow TS \rightarrow EE \rightarrow P_2$$

In this schema, P_1 represents an initial problem and *TS* a trial solution applied to the problem. *EE* stands for error-elimination, the means by which some trial solutions are eliminated – either by natural selection or criticism. The elimination of an error gives rise to a new situation and potentially – as shown in the schema – a new problem (P_2).

Following Tyrrell Burgess (1977, p. 129) and in contrast to Popper (see his 1979 [1972], and 1999, chapter 9), I take the view that – in learning and problem solving in general – although mismatches between expectation and actual or anticipated experience are discovered, problems (*P*) have to be created. A mismatch is not of itself a problem. Note, in particular, that in complex human problem situations, any single mismatch may be turned into a number of different problems, all of which will be expectation-laden and, by implication, value-impregnated. For example, in the context of a research project, 'The respondents didn't behave in the way I expected when I administered the questionnaire' can be formulated as a problem of 'how to change the behaviour of the respondents' or 'how to change the way the questionnaire is administered' or 'how to find a more effective way of eliciting the respondents' views' (Swann, 2003b, pp. 20–1) or 'how better to understand what happened'. Also, although life is full of mismatches between expectation and experience, not all of these mismatches are, or need to be, turned into problems. For an organism to have a problem, it must be dissatisfied with, and thus implicitly or explicitly critical of, the state of affairs in which it finds itself – 'hungry', for example – and it must wish, by implication at least, to achieve a state of affairs it deems to be better, such as 'not hungry'. The organism's response to a disappointed expectation is predicated, most often implicitly, on aspirations (such as, 'I want to eat'), expectations about what is possible ('I can get food') and values ('Eating is good').

In a school situation, teachers may be surprised to discover that many of the 9-year-old children in a particular class or group cannot read. But the fact that 'these children cannot read' is not a problem per se. It becomes a problem when one or more of the teachers problematizes the mismatch in the form, for example, 'How can I help these children to become readers?' The creation of this problem requires that value be attached to reading. It also implies the aspiration 'I want these children to become readers' and the (vital) expectation that 'These children can become readers'. The problem of how to help the children become readers does not follow automatically from the observation that they cannot read. A teacher might make the observation and do nothing further about it or might instead create and focus on the problem 'How can I teach this group of children even though some of them cannot read?' I am not suggesting that this last problem is necessarily unworthy, but it is clearly a different problem from the one of how to help the children become readers. (For a discussion of reading from the perspective of the child, see Chapter 3, section 2.)

Although an organism can, in effect, adopt only one trial solution (TS) at a time in response to its specific problem, there are often many possible trial solutions to a problem and a variety of ways in which to respond to a particular type of problem. For example, a fox might assuage its hunger by catching and eating a rabbit or by scavenging for scraps of food among human refuse, and it may generally adopt one type of activity, such as scavenging rather than hunting, as its preferred solution to the problem of how to get food. On any particular occasion, it will do one thing rather than another, but, objectively, there are a number of things it might do, any one or some of which will be more successful than others.

A trial solution, like the problem to which it is applied, is laden with expectations about what is so in the world. These expectations, like those which led to the problem, may be false or merely inadequate – that is, inadequate in the face of the particular problem. The trial itself may be better or worse than any other possible trial. 'Better' and 'worse' in this context are judged according to whether or to what extent the problem is solved and what additional consequences ensue. For example, a fox that eats a chicken may subsequently be hunted and killed by the farmer. A solution is always a trial, in that there is no way of knowing in advance whether it will succeed or whether it is the best possible solution. (It should be noted, however, that many trial solutions succeed despite being embedded with one or more erroneous expectations. A successful trial does not prove the truth of any expectation embodied in it.)

As Popper explained, all trials are 'blind to the solution of the problem' (Popper, 1992a [1974], p. 46); there is no secure knowledge of what the consequences of actions will be (discussed in Miller, 2006a, chapter 5). But a disposition to react in one way rather than another may be conducive to survival, at least in some circumstances. Popper also pointed out that 'the problem often determines the range from which the trials are selected' (1992a [1974], p. 47). The examples he provided were drawn from the work of David Katz (1937, p. 143), who argued that a hungry animal (such as the fox in my illustration) divides the world into edible and inedible things, and that an animal in flight (such as a fox being hunted by hounds) sees escape routes and places to hide. In both examples, any trial is blind in that the animal cannot know whether it will succeed in escaping or in finding food nor what the unintended consequences of its actions might be. But insofar as the animal is acting in response to a problem, then the trial is not quite blind (see Popper, 1994a, pp. 5–6, for further discussion).

The idea of error-elimination (*EE*) pertains to the death of an organism (such as the death of a fox hunted by a farmer whose chickens the fox has eaten), to the elimination or modification of an expectation, preference, theory, hypothesis or behaviour, and to the modification or suppression of a redundant or otherwise unsuccessful organ. In Popper's words,

> new reactions, new forms, new organs, new modes of behaviour, new hypotheses, are tentatively put forward and controlled by error-elimination. . . . Error-elimination may proceed either by the complete elimination of unsuccessful forms (the killing-off of unsuccessful forms by natural selection) or by the (tentative) evolution of controls which modify or suppress unsuccessful organs, or forms of behaviour, or hypotheses.
>
> (1979 [1972], p. 242)

The following quotation from Popper illustrates both the way in which error-elimination can function as a controlling feedback process and the idea that problem solving is continuous and often unconscious:

> If I am standing quietly, without making any movement, then . . . my muscles are constantly at work, contracting and relaxing in an almost random fashion . . . but

controlled, without my being aware of it, by error-elimination (*EE*) so that every little deviation from my posture is almost at once corrected.

(Ibid., p. 245)

Although all processes of trial and error-elimination embody the same 'logic' – as summarized in Popper's simplified schema – the scale and nature of problems and solutions are highly varied. We can differentiate, for example, between discrete problems with solutions that are effected over a period of time, as in the case of a fox finding food, and problems addressed by homeostatic processes, such as those we require in order to remain standing upright, that involve multiple sequences of trial and error, each of which lasts for only a fraction of a second.

Note that the problem (P_2) that emerges from a process of trial and error-elimination is always different from the initial problem (P_1). The process is never cyclical, not even when the initial problem has not been effectively solved. Once an attempt has been made to solve a problem, the trial solution exists in the history of the situation and, whether or not the organism has learnt, a new state of affairs has been brought about. This new state of affairs will pose further challenges for the organism, which may lead to a series of new problems and new trial solutions. This process continues until the organism dies.

6 Two competing ideas about learning

I anticipate that much of the substance of the account of learning and problem solving I have provided will be accepted by most readers as being true of some situations and events, not least because the account is broadly compatible with one of two commonsense notions, namely that we learn from our mistakes. What I suspect many readers will find problematic is the idea that learning is invariably and entirely the result of a process of the kind I have described; what people tend to baulk at is the idea that *all* of our knowledge is either inborn or created by us through a process of trial and error-elimination. The sweeping nature of Popperian selectionism represents a challenge both to orthodoxy in the field of learning theory and to a second commonsense notion – that we learn, at least in part, by absorbing information from our environment.

As made explicit in Chapter 1, section 2, what is at issue here is a choice between two competing theories. One proposes that '*learning never involves the absorption of informational elements from outside the learner'*, the other that *'some learning involves the absorption of informational elements from outside the learner'*. Popperian selectionism, as represented by the first statement, is consistent with experimental evidence such as that found in the work of psychobiologist Arne Friemuth Petersen (1988, 1992, 2000) and also with aspects of the work of neuroscientists such as Gerald Edelman (1992), who has exploited the idea of natural selection in the context of research into brain functioning. However, the work of Edelman (and his associates) and Petersen does not refute *'Some learning involves the absorption of informational elements from outside the learner'* because – as with *'Learning never involves the absorption of informational elements from outside the learner'* – neither the statement nor the theory it represents has the potential to be refuted. Despite the potential for some observable outcomes, learning – the core process to which these statements refer – cannot itself be observed. The competing theories are metaphysical rather than scientific, though they may nonetheless lead to the development of testable – that is, refutable – hypotheses (see Chapter 9). An unfalsifiable theory is not necessarily an underdeveloped or otherwise weak theory. Some theories are intrinsically unfalsifiable, though they can still be critically discussed. Realism is a philosophical position of this kind – one that Popper discussed and defended (see, e.g., Popper, 1979 [1972], chapter 2, sections 4 and 5).

Realism is the idea that entities exist independently of being perceived (commonsense realism) and independently of our theories about them, and this idea may or may not be accompanied by the idea that knowledge of these entities is possible (adapted from Phillips, 1987, p. 205). An antithesis to commonsense realism is an extreme form of solipsism which proposes that the self is all there is and there is nothing outside of the self (the world is my mental construct). Neither commonsense realism nor extreme solipsism is a refutable theory, but it is possible to discuss them as competing accounts of the nature of experience and existence, and there are arguments in favour of adopting one rather than the other. The implications of the two positions are significantly different. Most people favour commonsense realism and act accordingly.

The situation in respect of *'Some learning involves the absorption of informational elements from outside the learner'* (an existential statement) and *'Learning never involves the absorption of informational elements from outside the learner'* (a universal statement) is similar to that of indeterminism, that is, the commonsense belief that 'We are at least sometimes free to act as we choose' (an existential statement), and extreme determinism (a universal theory) which can be represented by the universal statement 'What happens is in every case determined in advance, independently of our choices'. The pairs of theories are similar insofar as each theory in each pair is irrefutable, a reasoned choice can be made between them in light of critical argument, and they have significantly contrasting implications for action. However, whereas in the case of indeterminism and determinism, the position which most people favour intuitively is the one that better survives critical argument – that is, indeterminism (see Popper, 1982 [1956], for a detailed discussion) – in the case of the two competing theories of learning (as represented by the italicized statements), the generally accepted position is, I propose, the one that comes out less well from a critical comparison. The strong case to be made for the competing alternative to *'Some learning involves the absorption of informational elements from outside the learner'* is historically rather recent. Relatively few people know about evolutionary epistemology as it applies to learning and, when it is first presented, people mostly find it difficult to comprehend.

7 Moving beyond sticking points

In my attempts to communicate Popperian selectionism at conferences, in research seminars and in my teaching of undergraduate students of education, I have noted some key sticking points in coming to understand an evolutionary analysis of learning. I certainly do not wish to suggest that anyone who rejects this evolutionary analysis has necessarily not understood it, but clearly, in order to make a reasoned decision as to whether *'Learning never involves the absorption of informational elements from outside the learner'* is preferable to *'Some learning involves the absorption of informational elements from outside the learner'*, it is important that the analysis is understood.

The role of the environment in learning

One sticking point is the need to grasp the role in learning that an evolutionary analysis attributes to the environment. According to an evolutionary analysis, when learning takes place, the process is initiated 'when our knowledge bumps up against our ignorance' (Burgess, 2000, p. 54); that is, as described above, when an expectation – or, more often, a set of expectations – is challenged by some external phenomenon or when we anticipate or create a challenge in our imagination. When a challenge is posed by our environment, what we experience (albeit not necessarily consciously) is a sense that our set of expectations is wrong or not quite right. What happens then, when learning takes place, is that we modify our set of expectations or replace it with a new one. We are entirely responsible for the modification and replacement of expectations.

The environment functions as an eliminatory control, as described above, and also as a resource about whose nature we can only speculate. Although the environment does not transfer data to us, the 'quality' of the environment is important; in particular, some environments provide more scope for learning than others. For example, in order to develop the kind of expectations that comprise sight, the learner has to have access to visual stimuli; sight does not develop in the absence of light.

The role of sense organs in learning

The idea that perception is a creative process is now widely accepted by neuroscientists, psychologists and other researchers in related fields, and is consistent with empirical evidence (see, e.g., Bach-y-Rita et al., 2003, on tactile vision substitution systems). However, aside from evolutionary theory (see, e.g., Wächtershäuser, 1993, on vision), discussions that support the idea of creativity in perception nonetheless often leave unanswered the question of the relationship between external stimuli and sense organs. So it is perhaps not entirely surprising that people in general – including many constructivists – are inclined to think, wrongly, that sense organs receive primary data which are then processed more or less creatively. 'Reception' is assumed to be preliminary to 'making'.

To say that we do not receive primary data through our sense organs is not to deny that these organs provide information; but the way sense organs function is rather different from what is often assumed. Sense organs are, first and foremost, tools for solving biological problems, with different organs addressing different kinds of problems:

> From the point of view of evolutionary theory, our sense organs are the outcome of a series of problems and attempted solutions, just as our microscopes or binoculars are. And this shows that, biologically speaking, the problem comes *before* the observation or sense perception: observations or sense perceptions are important aids to our *attempted solutions* and play the main role in their *elimination*.
>
> (Popper, 1999, p. 7; for a fuller discussion, see chapter 5,
> first published in Popper, 1990; for an earlier discussion,
> see Popper, 1972b [1963], pp. 406–7)

Given an evolutionary analysis, we can see that a sense organ is an evolved structure that provides potentially very complex information in the pursuit of problem solving. But the complexity, as we actually experience it (whether or not it seems that way to us), is in the nature of the organ and its feedback to the brain, the expectations with which it is implicitly laden and the kind of trial-and-error processes in which it enables the individual (and species) to engage. Contrary to what is often assumed, the complexity is not in the nature of the information it absorbs from the environment – as already emphasized, there is no absorption of information or informational elements. The organism *responds* to sensory stimulation, but there is no transfer of data. A sense organ helps the organism to *interpret* external stimuli by a process of trial and error-elimination (see, e.g., Popper, 1999, pp. 63–4). The eye, then, is an organ that has been retained for its ability to solve particular kinds of problems, including the problem of how to evade danger (ibid.). Light enters the eye and impacts on the retina, but there is no absorption of data; rather, the eye helps the organism to interpret visual stimuli, which involves facilitating the making of 'guesses' as to what is or is not present in the visual field.

According to Popper's account, an observation is 'made', rather than being something that happens to us as a result of a passive, expectation-free reception of sense data (Popper, 1979 [1972], appendix 1; 1999, chapter 1). What we perceive (such as what we see or hear) is dependent – though not wholly – on the expectations we bring to the act of perception. I say 'not wholly' because the role of the environment is, as stressed above, crucial. Through our sense organs, we engage with an external reality, a world that exists independently of us; but our only purchase on the nature of that external reality is via our expectations – those that are inborn (including those embodied in our sense organs) and those we develop through learning. And as indicated earlier in the chapter, our attention to our environment is dependent on the kinds of problems with which we are engaged. As individuals and as a species, it may seem to us that we have a fairly complete and accurate impression of ourselves and at least our immediate environment, but what we have is mere conjecture – there is much that we are incapable of sensing (such as radio waves) and much that we have not yet accurately imagined.

What happens when we learn from listening

A common sticking point in understanding an evolutionary analysis of learning is the question of what happens when we learn from listening to a set of instructions, chatting to our friends, and so on. Surely, it is said, we are not engaging in trial and error-elimination. I argue that we are. In order to understand what someone is saying, we must solve a variety of problems; this we do rapidly and mostly at an unconscious level. Whether or not we are aware of it, we are critical and creative listeners. When ideas are conveyed, the listener (as the learner) will have tried out and revised sequences of expectations with regard to both the nature of the situation and what the speaker was trying to convey.

You may be disinclined to acknowledge the imagination required to engage with what someone is saying, not least because such an activity is commonplace and unremarkable. The process itself is not entirely conscious, so you will not be aware of more than a few aspects of it. But regardless of how it seems at the time, any process of listening and making sense of what is being said is hugely creative and is made possible only by a highly evolved, genetically programmed facility for interpersonal communication. This facility predisposes us to learn to interpret what may be called signals, to copy signals and to create them – purely through trial and error-elimination (Popper, 1992a [1974], section 10).

What happens when we learn in response to 'instructive procedures'

An evolutionary analysis of learning helps us to get to grips with the underlying process that occurs whenever learning takes place – regardless of what the learner or teacher did to promote it. And it also accounts for the successes and failures of 'instructive procedures'. One may call what a teacher does instruction, and clearly many people construe a teacher as someone who sets out to impart knowledge. But when students learn in the context of such a process, this does not mean that any informational elements have been transmitted. Rather, what the teacher says and/or does must have challenged the students' assumptions in some way and have provoked them to engage in trial and error-elimination. An individual student may be able to describe some aspects of such a process – 'I used to believe X, but Mrs Smith told me that this was not true, and she played a film clip in which I saw Z ...' – but much of the process will remain unexplained and to some degree inexplicable. By means of instruction, so-called, some students may learn (some of the time and to some extent) something of what the teacher intended them to learn – a very hit-and-miss affair and one that we may judge not only in light of what seems to be effective but also by speculating about the opportunities that may have been lost by not using some other method of teaching (see Parts 2 and 3 of this book).

8 The myth of learning by instruction from without

In this chapter I have introduced the evolutionary analysis that has led to the idea that *'learning never involves the absorption of informational elements from outside the learner'*. In this final section, I pose three challenges to those who would favour the competing view that *'some learning involves the absorption of informational elements from outside the learner'*. In the absence of a satisfactory response to these challenges, I propose that the idea that we absorb informational elements from our environment is a myth – the myth of learning by instruction from without.

First, I invite anyone who wishes to defend the idea that there is learning by instruction from without the learner to make a case for the existence of informational elements, or even to make the case for the existence of sense data. Note also that when basic informational elements are assumed to exist, they are generally also assumed to provide true (or perhaps even certainly true) primary data. Given what we currently know, I suggest that, in Popper's words, 'these data or elements do not exist at all. They are the inventions of hopeful philosophers' (1979 [1972], p. 63). So *the challenge is to identify basic informational elements (whether providing true primary data or not)*.

Second, whereas Popperian selectionism presents a biological description of what happens when learning takes place, the idea that we receive informational elements from the environment is dependent on analogy and metaphor. The learner is often conceived as functioning like a sponge, bucket or radio receiver. But we are not like any of those things. Nor do we have a brain or any other organ that functions in a manner that the use of these analogies implies. The function of the brain is to select and create. It *interprets* physical stimuli, and nothing is taken in or transferred. Analogies between the brain and a computer are also problematic, not least because although memory is an outcome of learning, and memories are used in processes in which there is learning, memory, as it features in biological processes, is dynamic and not of the same character as the memory stored in a computer (see, e.g., Edelman,

1992, chapter 10). Therefore, *I challenge anyone who wishes to defend the idea that there is learning by instruction from without the learner to provide an account of the process by which the informational elements are received – one which goes beyond analogy and metaphor to address the nature of learners as biological phenomena.*

It might be argued that associationism is one such account. Associationism explains the growth of higher-order knowledge by proposing that in such learning an individual selects relevant ideas or elements from repeated acts of observation, makes associations between these ideas and stores the associations in memory. There are numerous critiques of associationism (e.g. Popper, 1979 [1972], chapter 2; James, 1980, chapter 6; and Chapter 4 of this book), and as a philosophical theory it is no longer widely accepted, but what is important in the present discussion is that associationism is 'merely' a theory about how basic informational elements or sense data come to be combined in the 'mind'. What associationism does not provide is any kind of biological account of how these various irreducible elements – the elements that are combined – 'enter the mind' in the first place.

I am aware that Popper's selectionist account of learning has itself been construed as a metaphor because, for example, he proffers the idea of the mind as a searchlight as opposed to a bucket (Popper, 1979 [1972], appendix 1). But although Popper uses analogy and metaphor in his discussions of learning, these are used illustratively and are not a substitute for a biological theory. When Popper uses the searchlight metaphor, he does so within the context of a much broader theory, a 'descriptive epistemology' (Campbell, 1974, p. 413) which explains that the *same* process – as outlined above in section 5 – not merely a similar process, applies to the growth of objectified knowledge, individual learning and the evolution of species.

Third, if you wish to defend the idea that learners receive basic informational elements or sense data from the environment, I would urge you to explain why, in any particular situation, some individuals receive some informational elements and not others. I anticipate that one type of explanation will refer to flaws in the 'receiving mechanisms' of would-be learners. Explanations of this kind, however, usually leave unanswered the question of why people with sensory disabilities or specific limitations of brain function are often highly successful learners; that is, they compensate for what they cannot do by developing what they can do – a propensity we all possess. An explanation is also required to account for the fact that even when there are no assumed flaws in the learner's receiving mechanisms, not everything that could be absorbed is taken in. Selection seems inevitably to be a fundamental part of the explanation. *If you are prepared to accept selection as an aspect of what happens when learning takes place, I would challenge you to defend your decision to reject taking the idea further.*

In short, why should anyone, when presented with this evolutionary analysis of learning, remain faithful to the view that what we know is built upon (or out of) informational elements which are somehow internalized during a process of instruction from without?

What Happens When We Learn

3

Chapter Outline

We can see that life – even at the level of the unicellular organism – brings something completely new into the world, something that did not previously exist: problems and active attempts to solve them; assessments, values; trial and error.

It may be supposed that, under the influence of Darwin's natural selection, it is the most active problem solvers, the seekers and the finders, the discoverers of new worlds and new forms of life, that undergo the greatest development.

—Karl Popper, In Search of a Better World: Lectures and Essays from Thirty Years

The process of learning, of the growth of subjective knowledge, is always fundamentally the same. It is imaginative criticism.

—Karl Popper, Objective Knowledge: An Evolutionary Approach

Introduction

In this chapter, I extend my discussion of Karl Popper's selectionist theory of learning to provide a more detailed account of what generally happens when learning takes place, and more specifically what happens in human learning. This descriptive epistemology is important because, as I argue in Part 2, it has profound implications for the promotion of learning and, therefore, for the theory and practice of teaching. In the last two sections of the chapter, I provide some contextual information that relates Popperian selectionism to one of two broad categories of learning theory that will be familiar to many readers of this book, namely constructivism. Behaviourism, as a category of theory that is antithetical to Popperian selectionism, is discussed in Chapter 4.

Whereas the content of Chapter 2 will stand alone, the content of this chapter will not. Although I revisit some previously introduced ideas, this chapter largely builds on Chapter 2 and presupposes some understanding of it. In particular, I shall take as given the argument in defence of the idea that learning never involves the absorption of informational elements from outside the learner.

1 What happens when learning takes place

Although many disparate processes can be characterized as processes of learning, including Eureka! moments and many imperceptible adjustments of a kind that are not conscious and probably never will be, there is, as argued in Chapter 2, an identifiable process common to any situation in which learning takes place, whether it is the learning of a young child, a university student, a Nobel laureate in physics or someone's pet cat. This process – 'the logic of learning' (Burgess, 1977, p. 127) – is summarized in the following simplified schema of trial and error-elimination (Popper, 1979 [1972], p. 243):

$$P_1 \rightarrow TS \rightarrow EE \rightarrow P_2$$

In this schema, P_1 represents an initial problem. TS is a trial solution applied to the problem. EE stands for error-elimination, the means by which some trial solutions are eliminated. The elimination of an error gives rise to a new situation and, potentially, a new problem (P_2).

Popper's schematic summary of what happens when learning takes place is useful because it helps us to focus on what happens *whenever* learning takes place. The schema highlights the elements characteristic of learning and their relationships. Of course, this schema is a simplification of what happens – there may, for instance, be many possible trials in response to a problem (ibid.; see also my Chapter 2, section 5). But whenever there is learning, the core 'logic' of the situation is essentially the same.

2 Problems

In light of an evolutionary analysis, I define learning as what happens when, and only when, a human or other animal has a problem, attempts to solve it and survives, leading to changes in the learner's dispositions – and, as a corollary, changes in the world – that are not entirely the outcome of maturational or haphazard factors. An individual's initial dispositions embody expectations and preferences that are inborn; they are part of its genetic make-up. Its expectations – which to a large extent comprise expectations of regularity (Popper, 1992a [1974], pp. 48–52) – are, like all expectations, fallible and potentially subject to disappointment in light of experience. In Popper's words,

> every animal is born with expectations or anticipations, which could be framed as hypotheses; a kind of hypothetical knowledge. . . . This inborn knowledge, these inborn expectations, will, if disappointed, create *our first problems*; and the ensuing growth of our knowledge may therefore be described as consisting throughout of corrections and modifications of previous knowledge.
>
> (1979 [1972], pp. 258–9)

Two aspects of the above quotation require further comment. First, in contrast to Popper, I argue that a mismatch between expectation and experience (actual or anticipated) does not per se lead to the creation of a problem. Not all mismatches are acknowledged (not even unconsciously), and those that are acknowledged are not necessarily problematized. Complex learners, such as ourselves, have to be selective – and, as illustrated in Chapter 2, section 5, mismatches can often be problematized in a number of different ways. Second, while all animals enter the world laden with expectations, only some animals – those that learn – correct and modify or replace their previous 'knowledge' in a way that goes beyond their genetic programming. Note that 'knowledge', as used in evolutionary epistemology, is a generic term for all kinds of expectations (conscious or unconscious, inborn or acquired through development and/or learning), assumptions (explicit or implicit) and theoretical constructs (valid or invalid, true or false). In this sense, even an amoeba has knowledge, although, as discussed in Chapter 2, it does not learn.

A learning organism can be said to have a problem when it discovers a mismatch between expectation and experience (actual or anticipated) and has the 'desire' and will to address the disequilibrium occasioned by the mismatch (Swann, 1999a). I use 'desire' to refer to the learner's intention to address the mismatch. As with my use of 'expectation', there is no implication that the learning individual will have expressed, or has even been capable of expressing, a formulation of the kind 'I desire . . .'. An element of what I call desire is necessary in order to problematize a mismatch, and a degree of will is needed in order to act on the desire. Without desire, there is no problem; without a problem, there is no learning.

An organism's desire to resolve a mismatch between expectation and experience (actual or anticipated) arises against the background of its preferences, such as preferences for one kind of environment or environmental feature rather than another. Popper discusses preferences at some length in his intellectual autobiography (1992a [1974], pp. 173–80; see also 1994b, chapter 3) in which he distinguishes between two types of selection pressure: environmental and internal. About the latter he writes, 'Internal selection pressure comes from the organism itself and, I conjecture, ultimately from its *preferences* (or "aims") though these may of course change in response to external changes' (1992a [1974], p. 173). In hypothesizing the success of what may be called 'higher' forms of life, he comments that 'what may perhaps be identified with the higher forms of life is a behaviourally richer preference structure – one of greater scope' (ibid., p. 176). This idea of preferences goes some way to accounting for the broad inclination of a species or individual to do one thing rather than another, and the idea can be used when explaining why an individual would attend to one mismatch between expectation and experience rather than another. Nevertheless, although preferences are part of the general selection process with regard to which mismatches are addressed and which problems are created, a slightly different concept – what I call 'desire' – is needed to account for the motivation to problematize a specific mismatch.

Desires, like preferences, are imbued with values (expectations about what is good), and they also imply hopes (which in turn imply expectations about what is possible). A child who discovers that people read and that she cannot may be motivated by the desire 'I want to read'. Implicit within this desire is the value 'Reading is good' and the hope 'Reading is possible for me'. For the child as a learner, desire, value and hope are just as important as her initial discovery that she cannot read: 'being unable to read' is not a problem per se, but 'being unable to read and wanting to read' is a problematic state which may lead to learning. According to this evolutionary view, a problem – such as that of how to become a reader – is potentially 'a good thing', particularly in the context of human learning. Clearly, the creation of a problem should not be confused with that of making difficulties. And if we are faced with a difficulty, problematizing the mismatch between expectation and experience (actual or anticipated) that is embedded in the difficulty is, potentially, a step towards overcoming the difficulty.

It is not only expectations about what is so in the world that are replaced or modified and potentially developed in learning; hopes, values and desires – which make up the individual's preference structure – are also subject to potential replacement or modification and development. A child whose trial solution to the problem of how to become a reader has been at least partially successful may have developed the expectation – that is, she has learnt – that she can read some texts but not others. The child will have become more dis-criminatory, distinguishing between 'texts I can read' and 'texts I can't read'. The child may develop an expectation that learning to read is a progressive process – 'There are books I can't yet read but will be able to read eventually'. She may also, for example, develop a specific hope in respect of becoming able to read a book that at present is being read to her. In addition, the child is likely to develop preferences with regard to the kinds of texts she likes to read. Such a child may have developed, to use Popper's phrase, 'a behaviour-ally richer preference structure' (ibid.) in comparison to a child who has not yet begun to read.

In contrast, a child who finds learning to read difficult may cease to believe that she can become a reader. I say 'may' advisedly, as it is clearly not always the case that difficulties in learning lead to a loss of hope on the part of the child. However, when there is such a loss of hope – 'Reading is impossible for me' – it is learnt. And with the loss of hope may come a loss of desire – 'I don't want to read'. Such a loss of hope, invariably misjudged, can become a major impediment to learning to read, and can lead to a narrowing of the child's horizon of expectations and a behaviourally poorer preference structure than might otherwise be the case. If a child has not learnt to read, an evaluation of the situation involves a consideration of what the child has done instead.

Nevertheless, I suggest that some problem preferences open up greater opportunities for learning and development, and that maintaining a preference for 'How can I become a reader?' until a satisfactory solution has been created is more conducive to learning than not doing so.

3 Creativity in learning

As highlighted in the first of the two quotations at the head of this chapter, 'life . . . brings something completely new into the world, something that did not previously exist: problems and active attempts to solve them; assessments, values; trial and error' (Popper, 1992b, p. vii). Problem solving, even for the simplest organism, is a creative process, though the degree of creativity exhibited by, for example, an amoeba is minuscule. When problem solving involves learning, a much greater degree of creativity is involved. Learning, like all problem solving, involves creativity in the generation of a problem (P_1 and P_2 in Popper's simplified schema of trial and error-elimination), as discussed above, and in the application of a trial solution (TS) – whether or not the solution is routine; it also involves creativity in the development of a new disposition, specifically a disposition that is not merely an outcome of genetic inheritance or haphazard organic change.

A learning organism may respond creatively when it encounters an unexpected situation by reacting in a way that is not purely the result of prior disposition. That is, when its expectations are not met, the organism responds by creating ad hoc, under environmental pressure, new expectations and perhaps new preferences. These new preferences and/or expectations may be embodied in its trial solution (TS) to a concrete problem. Or if the learning organism's trial solution is less than successful, but not a total failure – that is, if death does not ensue – the organism's preferences and/or expectations may then change (EE), and so too may its subsequent behaviour. As an illustration of the last point, after one or more near misses with vehicles, some domestic cats can learn to cross roads relatively safely.

Error-elimination, though clearly a critical aspect of problem solving, can also result from a creative act. Humans can anticipate situations in the context of thought experiments; they can then imagine how they might react and what the consequences of their actions might be, and in this context they may then create new preferences and/or expectations. Rather than wait for errors to be revealed through happenstance, human learners have the ability to set up test situations, that is, situations specifically designed to facilitate the search for error and/or specific limitation. In this way, they increase their opportunities for discovering and potentially eliminating errors and specific limitations. This is one of the principal means by which we accelerate and expand our learning. Scientific endeavour at its best is the exploitation and development of criticism par excellence. In general, by discovering error and specific limitation, we are put under pressure to create new problems and, with them, new solutions.

Creativity can be viewed as a continuum, at one end of which are responses to routine situations. At the opposite end, from the field of human endeavour, are ideas and inventions that deviate significantly from anything that has gone before and embody one or more of the following characteristics:

(a) the revealing of a hitherto unrecognized mismatch that has far-reaching implications of a practical and/or theoretical nature
(b) the formulation of a new and important problem
(c) the generation of a new and better solution to an existing problem
(d) the development of a new and constructive way of challenging existing expectations.

Our task, if we are committed to advancing our learning, is to search for error and specific limitation in our solutions to practical problems, and in our expectations about ourselves, the physical and social worlds and the world of objectified knowledge (discussed in section 5 below), and what we do in relation to them; we have also to make the effort to develop practices and ideas that are new to us. As Popper put it,

> The process of learning, of the growth of subjective knowledge, is always fundamentally the same. It is *imaginative criticism*. This is how we transcend our local and temporal environment by trying to think of circumstances *beyond* our experience: by criticizing the universality, or the structural necessity, of what may, to us, appear (or what philosophers may describe) as the 'given' or as 'habit'; by trying to find, construct, invent, new situations – that is, *test* situations, *critical* situations; and by trying to locate, detect, and challenge our prejudices and habitual assumptions.
>
> (1979 [1972], p. 148)

Criticism is often conceived in terms of explicit statements of disapproval or rejection, such as 'That's wrong', 'I've made a mistake' and 'This is not a good idea'. But this view is too narrow. Criticism is also embedded in the thought that, for example, 'I could try something else' or the question 'What else might I do?' And it is present in any unstated and even unconscious degree of dissatisfaction that leads an individual to decide to do something rather than nothing, or to do one thing rather than another. For the learner, the more subtle forms of challenge may be more motivationally powerful; for example, asking 'What else might you/we/I do?' may be more productive than saying 'This is not good enough'. In general, the value of criticism should be judged by its effect in a particular circumstance. A criticism, even if valid, may be inappropriate if it ultimately serves to stifle creativity and inhibit subsequent trial and error-elimination (Swann, 1983, and Part 2 of this book, in particular Chapter 7, section 4).

4 The importance of self-directed exploratory activity

According to Popperian selectionism, there is no passive or disinterested aspect to learning. The learning organism exercises preference and, potentially, develops its preferences. It responds to challenges from the environment and, in some cases, seeks new challenges. It modifies or replaces its inborn expectations and its dispositions to react in one way rather than another. The environment acts as a control – it presents challenges and, of course, potential dangers – and it can be said to be stimulating; but it does not transmit informational elements that can somehow be absorbed by the learner. As discussed in Chapter 2, Popperian selectionism posits the view that in learning *all* new expectations arise as the result of trial developments that originate within the organism (see, in particular, Popper, 1994a, chapter 1). (Although the organism is the source of the trials, the trials themselves are sometimes carried out exosomatically; for example, in the case of humans, they can involve the use of pen and paper, computer or conversation.)

The crucial importance for learning of self-directed exploratory action is illustrated by the 'gondola kitten' experiment, conducted and first reported more than four decades ago by experimental psychologists Richard Held and Alan Hein (1963). Their thought-provoking experiment has been cited by authors in a range of fields, including Popper and John Eccles (Popper and Eccles, 1977, pp. 404–5, 434–5; and, e.g., Baxter, 1982, chapter 1). Held and Hein's research has been built upon and refined, and has been influential in the field of evolutionary robotics (Suzuki et al., 2005; Floreano et al., 2008). Their findings are consistent with the general idea that learning is dependent on the opportunity for self-directed exploratory activity – an idea that has been widely investigated in empirical research of various kinds and has, it seems, so far stood up to critical scrutiny. The point of contention in current research is the nature and extent of the activity required for learning (with regard to perceptual learning see, e.g., Mossio and Taraborelli, 2008). As emphasized in Chapter 2, empirical research on learning can refute neither the idea that *'learning never involves the absorption of informational elements from outside the learner'* nor its competing alternative; as a philosophical topic, this is not something that empirical researchers are inclined to discuss. Empirical research can nonetheless facilitate the development of our understanding about various other aspects of learning.

It should be noted that the self-directed activity which took place within the gondola kitten experiment was also self-initiated. The research does not, however, provide experimental evidence in respect of self-initiated activity, only that which is self-directed.

Held and Hein's (1963) research subjects were pairs of littermate kittens which were kept with their mothers and other littermates in darkness for a number of weeks, apart from several hours a day which were spent in an illuminated contraption, later called a kitten carousel. When in the carousel, one kitten was allowed a degree of freedom to explore, while the other was suspended in a gondola (see Figure 3.1). The gondola kitten was able to move its head and limbs to some degree but was otherwise unable to effect any exploratory action. Although the gondola kitten experienced changes in its visual environment, these changes were occasioned by the investigative movements of the other kitten. The kitten carousel was designed so that both kittens were exposed to the same visual stimuli – 'Patterning . . . provided by vertically oriented 1 in. wide stripes of black and white masking tape separated by 1 in. of bare metal' (ibid., p. 874), but only the kitten that was able to explore was responsible for the sequence in which the visual patterning was presented (note: the patterning is not fully illustrated in Figure 3.1). After some weeks, when the kittens were tested to see what they had learnt, the tests indicated that the kittens that engaged in self-directed exploratory activity had developed normal visual competence, but the kittens that had been constrained in a gondola had not.

It would seem that in order to develop the facility for visual discrimination, the kittens needed to be able to engage in self-directed exploration in an environment offering a degree of visual stimulation. The results are also consistent with the idea that when autonomous exploratory activity is

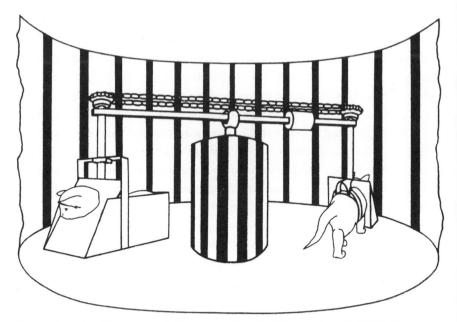

Figure 3.1 Inside a kitten carousel. (Reproduced from Held, R. and Hein, A. (1963), 'Movement-produced stimulation in the development of visually guided behavior'. *Journal of Comparative and Physiological Psychology*, 56 (5), pp. 872–6 (copyright © American Psychological Association. Adapted with permission.)

possible, even a very limited environment, such as that experienced by all the kittens, can be a place for learning.

When the gondola kittens were subsequently allowed to engage in self-directed exploratory activity in an illuminated environment, they developed abilities previously demonstrated only by their littermates. However, in a later experiment (Hein et al., 1970), discussed by Hein (1980), researchers investigated the length of time that gondola kittens subsequently took to develop one of the skills that had been developed by their carousel littermates. It was found that after the experience of being in the gondola, kittens took longer to develop this skill; the results indicated that 'being transported in the gondola, while exposed to patterned light, actually *impeded* later development' (ibid., p. 59; see Floreano et al., 2008, section 61.6, for analogous research and findings from the field of robotics).

The later gondola kitten experiment, like the earlier one, was designed to investigate only the development of visually-guided behaviour on the part of kittens. The results from this later experiment nonetheless prompt me to specu-late that, for a young individual, being placed in an environment that presents a particular type of stimulus, but constrained from the opportunity to receive feedback from self-directed activity in respect of that type of stimulus, impedes subsequent development. I recognize, however, the need to be cautious about drawing conclusions for human learning from experiments with other animals and about relating the findings of research on one limited type of learning to learning of other kinds. But, for ethical reasons, the scope for rigorous empirical research is limited; many individuals, including myself, have concerns about the experimental treatment of animals, and it seems that most people would rightly reject as unethical the kind of highly controlled experiments on children that would be needed in order to test my speculation.

Nevertheless, in general, in light of an evolutionary analysis of learning and seemingly without contradiction from empirical research in other fields, including experimental psychology, 'It may be supposed that . . . the most active problem solvers, the seekers and the finders, the discoverers of new worlds and new forms of life . . . undergo the greatest development' (Popper, 1992b, p. vii). A major difference between ourselves and other species is that we alone are capable of complex and varied thought experiments. We learn not only by exploring our physical environment but also, and rather more significantly, by exploring a world of ideas.

To engage in exploratory activity is to venture into the unknown. As such, it involves a degree of risk – the risk of discovering something unexpected and undesirable, the risk of discovering that one has been mistaken for many years, the risk of trying but not succeeding (failure) and so on (see Burgess, 1977, p. 160). Confident individuals will, in general, be more inclined to engage in exploratory activity – particularly self-initiated and self-directed exploratory activity – and less likely to be passive or diffident in the face of the opportunities and challenges that life presents. I am not advocating foolhardy risk-taking, but it seems clear that significant learning often involves risk. Of course, there are risks in doing nothing as well as risks in acting. And we as humans, with our ability to create and explore a world of ideas and to set up test situations, are in a position to minimize some of the risks (see section 5 below).

5 What is special about human learning

Four interrelated factors are distinctively significant for human learning and have combined to make us the most adept learning organisms on Earth. Of all animals, humans possess the greatest potential for casting off or modifying inborn expectations and developing new expectations, through a process of trial and error-elimination. In the words of David Miller, 'What distinguishes human beings, and even scientists, from other beings is not a superiority in avoiding errors, but a superiority in replacing them' (2006b, p. 157). We are by far the most imaginative beings on our planet, and this propensity for imagination is developed and exploited by means of four distinctive characteristics.

First, we are unique in that we not only experience and engage with physical, personal, social and (as in the case of some other species) cultural phenomena, but also with linguistically formulated problems, theories, expectations, hypotheses, assumptions of fact, values and arguments. These linguistic formulations are what Popper called objective knowledge (see Popper, 1979 [1972]; 1994b, e.g. chapter 1) and what I prefer to call *objectified* knowledge. The forms we create constitute thought-objects; they form part of the content of what we think about, and thinking about them enables us to develop them further. When these thought-objects are externalized in speech or writing, or some other form of expression (including all our symbolic, artistic and technological creations), they become independent of the person or group who created them. We may have forgotten the gossip we shared while queuing for the photocopier, or the article we published a decade ago, but the ideas to which we gave form may nonetheless continue to exist. There is a world of objectified ideas which is no less real than the subjective minds that created it, or the objects and processes that are more often recognized as constituting our external reality or environment. Familiar aspects of the world of ideas become features of our individual experience that are taken for granted – we often use thought-objects without consciously thinking about them.

The above ideas are based on Popper's 3-worlds thesis (see, in particular, Popper, 1979 [1972], chapters 3 and 4), in which he differentiates between the world of physical objects and events (world 1), the world of subjective experience (world 2), and the world of objective knowledge (world 3). For a defence of this thesis, see Mark Notturno (2000, pp. 139–50) and Ilkka Niiniluoto (2006).

Second, our learning differs from that of other animals in that we alone are able to employ both the descriptive and argumentative functions of language. These functions, often ignored or underplayed in discussions of human language capability, have been discussed at length by Popper (1972b [1963], pp. 134–5 and chapter 12; 1979 [1972], pp. 119–22, 235–8; 1994b, chapter 4; Popper and Eccles, 1977, pp. 57–60).

Popper's language thesis was developed from the work of Karl Bühler (see Bühler, 1934, pp. 25–8, cited in Popper, 1972b [1963], p. 293). Bühler identified three principal functions of language – expressive, signalling and descriptive – to which Popper added a further major function, argument. Clearly, many animals express themselves through a form of language. A cry of pain is an example of language in its expressive function. For many animals, expressive language functions as a signal; a cry of pain may signal danger to other animals. But although some non-humans, such as bees, may perhaps use a descriptive language, the degree to which humans have developed this function greatly exceeds that of any other animal. Unique to humans is the use of argumentative language, which arises from and is dependent upon the descriptive function.

Humans are not the only animals capable of thought, but, as is widely recognized, the sophistication and scope of our thinking set us apart from other species. In particular, it seems that we are the only animals with the ability to think about thinking: metacognition. This is made possible by the fact that we have, as mentioned above, abstract thought-objects – expressed in descriptive language – to think about. And thinking about them often involves the use of argument. For example, we use argument in order to reach a decision about whether one idea is better than another. Without argumentative language, we would be constrained to a world of assertions and counter-assertions ('Yes, it is'/'No, it isn't'). With argumentative language, we can convey and develop reasoning ('No, it isn't, *because* . . .'). Argumentative language enables us to challenge expectations of fact and value in a way that goes far beyond the mere exchange of competing descriptive assertions. It involves, among other things, questioning and explicit hypothesizing. It is the principal means by which we can discover and eliminate errors and specific limitations in our expectations without first having to act on them. As such, it is one of our keenest tools for learning.

The ability to describe and argue considerably enhances our facility for creativity (and thus for learning), not only because it enables us to formulate and discuss some of our expectations about what is so in the world, but also because it helps us to imagine circumstances and generate ideas about what might be. And it helps us to imagine ways by which these circumstances might be brought about; when we want something other than what we have, we may be able to develop and select from a wide range of strategies in the hope of improving our situation.

Third, the development of descriptive and argumentative language, and the objectifying of our expectations and other ideas, have enabled us to create theoretical as well as practical (i.e. concrete) problems. The latter, common to all living things, are problems of how to get from one state of affairs to another, such as 'how to obtain food'. Solutions to these problems are states of affairs in which something has been done – for example, food has been obtained. Theoretical problems, by contrast, are problems that exist only in a linguistic form: problems of what is/was/will be the case, what is good, what is aesthetically pleasing (or beautiful), what is logically valid – and why. The test of the solution to a practical problem involves addressing 'What happened?' or 'What is happening?', whereas the test of a solution to a theoretical problem involves addressing 'Is this theory true?' and/or 'Is this argument valid?' (Swann, 2003a).

The significance of the distinction between practical and theoretical problems is explored in Part 3 (see Chapter 8, section 7, for its provenance). As a preliminary illustration, consider the situation in which a team of teachers of young children wishes to improve its teaching of reading: 'How can we improve our teaching of reading?' It would be insufficient for the teachers merely to learn more about the teaching of reading. At some stage, if they are committed to the pursuit of practical improvement, they will have to implement new strategies or practices and evaluate the outcomes. In deciding what to do, the teachers may formulate a range of theoretical problems, including, for example, one or more of the kind, 'What is known about the strengths and limitations of various methods by which reading is taught?' A problem of this kind is solved provisionally by a theoretical discourse. This theoretical discourse may influence the teachers' subsequent actions, but in itself it is not a solution to the practical problem, which can only be solved by action or the decision not to act (or if something else happens that solves the problem).

Note that theoretical problems also include problems *about* practical problems. We can formulate a theoretical problem about how to do something and develop a theoretical solution, but the set of words we use to express our solution to the problem-about-the-problem does not constitute a solution to the practical problem. So teachers may engage in discussion about how to reduce levels of bullying in a school, and they may draw up a policy document containing specific proposals for action, but the content of the policy document is not a solution to the practical problem of how to reduce levels of bullying. The solution to the practical problem is constituted in what is actually done to solve it. In this example, what is done will include the act of developing the policy document, and, perhaps more importantly, what is done after it has been produced.

Although solutions to theoretical problems do not per se solve practical problems, the products of theoretical problem solving – which become part of our objectified knowledge – can enhance our ability to solve practical problems. For example, objectified knowledge often challenges significant assumptions embedded in our plans to act, leading us to revise our plans and (conjecturally) improve what we subsequently do.

Fourth, and as mentioned in section 3 above, whereas other animals are largely constrained to discover errors and limitations by happenstance, we are well equipped – given our facility for descriptive and argumentative language, and our engagement with objectified knowledge – to *search* for them. We are adept at seeking out errors and specific limitations in our expectations by creating test situations (see the earlier quotation from Popper, 1979 [1972], p. 148). When we evaluate the merits of potential solutions or the effectiveness of an adopted solution to a practical problem, we can specify what would count as success and what would constitute failure. We can then test our adopted solution by searching for evidence not only of success but also of failure. We can test our ideas by exposing them to critical scrutiny. Additionally, in the case of some of our universal theories, we can express them in a refutable form and test them rigorously by searching for refuting evidence – to a Popperian, and to those influenced by Popper, this is the distinguishing characteristic of science (see, e.g., Popper, 1972a [1934], chapter 1, section 4; 1972b [1963], chapter 11; 1985c [1974]). By adopting this critical method, we increase our potential for discovering errors and inadequacies and our potential to eliminate or reduce them. Humans, more than any other species, can let our hypotheses 'die in our stead' (Popper, 1979 [1972], p. 244).

In general, the growth of knowledge, whether subjective (i.e. internal to the organism) or objective, can be represented by a slightly modified version of the simplified schema of trial and error-elimination presented in section 1 above and in Chapter 2 (see numerous pages in Popper, 1979 [1972]):

$$P_1 \rightarrow TT \rightarrow EE \rightarrow P_2$$

In this schema, *TS* has been replaced by *TT*, which stands for 'tentative theory' (although in at least one instance, Popper used *TT* to refer to a tentative trial – 1994b, p. 79). As implied earlier in this chapter and in

Chapter 2, a trial solution (*TS*) embodies a set of expectations or, to put it another way, a set of tentative theories (*TT*). Here, 'theory' is used broadly to include implicit assumptions and unstated expectations, such as those embodied in the activities of all organisms. Theories are said to be tentative because we cannot know whether they are true. These tentative theories include expectations of what is so with regard to singular features of reality (e.g. 'This is a child who enjoys stories about animals'), and also general statements about reality, that is, expectations of regularity ('All children enjoy stories about animals' – a false general statement). In human learning, many of these tentative theories are formulated and problematized. For example, when our solutions to practical problems do not work out as anticipated, we may (self-consciously) recognize that our expectations have failed in some way. We may then ask 'Why?' questions – that is, we seek explanations for what we perceive to be the case ('Why is this child not enjoying this book?').

6 Popperian selectionism in the context of constructivism

I have proposed that Popper's epistemology can be appropriately categorized as a form of constructivism (Swann, 1995), a view shared by Denis Phillips (1995 and 2000, chapter 1). There are various forms of constructivism, but the basic tenet of them all is that learning is an active process that requires of the learner a personal interpretation of experience and the construction of her (or his) own knowledge.

Constructivism's long history can be traced back at least as far as the philosopher Giambattista Vico (1668–1744). But, as many readers will be aware, the initial exploration of constructivist ideas in cognitive psychology is generally attributed to two developmental psychologists: Jean Piaget (1896–1980) and, in respect of social constructivism, Lev S. Vygotsky (1896–1934) (but see also the discussion of Otto Selz, 1881–1943, in ter Hark, 2004, 2006 and 2009). Constructivist thinking is also evident in the educational philosophy of John Dewey (1859–1952). Dewey's work (in particular, 1916, 1963 [1938], 1990 [1900/1902]) has been highly influential in the public education sector in the United States and is at the root of many experiential educational initiatives across the globe. The following quotation from Dewey's *Experience and Education* both illustrates the inherent constructivism of his educational philosophy and outlines, in contrast to what he terms 'traditional education', the implications of his philosophy for teaching:

> The trouble with traditional education was not that educators took upon themselves the responsibility for providing an environment. The trouble was that they did not consider the other factor in creating an experience; namely, the powers and purposes of those taught. It was assumed that a certain set of conditions was intrinsically desirable, apart from its ability to evoke a certain quality of response in individuals. This lack of mutual adaptation made the process of teaching and learning accidental. Those to whom the provided conditions were suitable managed to learn. Others got on as best they could. Responsibility for selecting objective conditions carries with it, then, the responsibility for understanding the needs and capacities of the individuals who are learning at a given time. It is not enough that certain materials and methods have proved effective with other individuals at other times. There must be a reason for thinking that they will function in generating an experience that has educative quality with particular individuals at a particular time.
>
> (1963 [1938], pp. 45–6)

During the second half of the 20th century, constructivism as an educational *theory* became increasingly prominent; although the extent of its influence on *practice*, in comparison to behaviourism and to what may be called a more traditional approach, is not clear. Rosalind Driver and Beverley Bell, constructivist educationists and science educators of renown, wrote, 'Learning outcomes depend not only on the learning environment but on what the learner already knows: Students' conceptions, purposes and motivations influence the way they interact with learning materials in various ways' (1986, p. 444) and 'In learning situations we are actively hypothesizing, checking and possibly changing our ideas as we interact with phenomena and with other people' (ibid., p. 448). By 1992, Phillips, contributing to a debate in the United States, felt able to state, 'These days most of us in philosophy of education and in teacher education are constructivists with respect to our *psychology of learning*' (1992a, p. 312). He further claimed constructivism to be the standard view in cognitive psychology, and illustrated the nature of constructivism with a quotation from Donald Norman:

> What goes on in the mind of the learner? A lot: people who are learning are active, probing, constructing. People appear to have a strong desire

to understand . . . [and] will go to great lengths to understand, constructing frameworks, constructing explanations, constructing huge edifices to account for what they have experienced.

(1980, p. 42)

Constructivism is no less influential today, and I do not know personally any academic educationist who is not to some degree a constructivist.

The constructivist teacher believes that what students learn in the classroom is dependent (though not wholly) on their prior expectations, in particular on their previous learning, including learnt misconceptions. The task of the teacher, whether or not there is a prescribed curriculum, is to help students to develop or, as appropriate, replace these expectations – a process which requires the full and active involvement of the students. Constructivism as a learning theory has paved the way for the idea of assessment *for* learning – assessment which facilitates the process of learning and is therefore integral to teaching (see, e.g., Black et al., 2003). Assessment *of* learning can still, however, be viewed as a matter of assessing the extent to which students are able to replicate what has been prescribed. But in the context of a prescribed curriculum, if one believes that learners have to create their own knowledge, the task of the teacher is not the relatively straightforward one of using techniques to shape behaviour regardless of the learners' emotions and mental states and processes (as with the radical behaviourism of B. F. Skinner – see my Chapter 4, sections 7 and 8), but the more complex process of finding ways of helping students to create for themselves what others have decided they should learn.

Constructivism is not generally associated with evolutionary epistemology, and constructivist texts refer largely, if not exclusively, to the learning of humans rather than animal learning in general. Nevertheless, the core idea of constructivism, at least as a psychological theory, is compatible with significant elements of the evolutionary analysis of learning presented in this book, specifically some of those elements that relate to learning that is distinctly human. However, as mentioned in the introduction to Chapter 2, it seems that relatively few educationists, including many of those who would call themselves constructivists, hold the view that in learning *all* new expectations and other ideas are created wholly from within the individual – that is, by the learner. It is often assumed that there is some transference of information to the learner from the social and/or physical environment, and that the processes of interpretation and construction take place after this basic information has been passively received.

7 Radical but not 'radical constructivism'

I would be inclined to describe Popperian selectionism as a radical form of constructivism, were the term 'radical constructivism' not already claimed by members of a group of constructivists – including the influential Ernst von Glasersfeld – who promote an idea that contrasts sharply with Popperian epistemology.

Like Popper and almost everyone else, radical constructivists believe in commonsense realism; that is, they believe there is a world that exists independently of our perceptions, a reality that we all share. And they, like Popper but unlike many constructivists, do not believe in direct experience; in Popper's words, 'there is nothing direct or immediate in our experience' (1979 [1972], p. 36). However, unlike Popper and many other constructivists, radical constructivists argue that we cannot sensibly pursue true descriptions and explanations of our shared reality. For example, Driver and Valerie Oldham wrote, citing von Glasersfeld, 'We cannot "check" our knowledge against an external reality. Our only check is the extent to which our constructions fit with our experience in a coherent and consistent way' (1986, p. 110).

Von Glasersfeld summarized the basic principles of constructivism in the following epistemological terms: '(a) knowledge is not passively received but actively built up by the cognizing subject; (b) the function of cognition is adaptive and serves the organization of the experiential world, not the discovery of ontological reality' (1989, p. 12); and he went on to state that 'to accept the first principle is considered trivial constructivism by those who accept both' (ibid.). I do not propose to hazard a guess as to how influential radical constructivism (as characterized in von Glasersfeld's oft-cited principles) is now, but the ideas that we cannot check our knowledge against an external reality and that we cannot sensibly pursue the truth about the nature of that reality were prevalent – as part of the postmodern position – in education debates during the last two decades of the 20th century and into the 21st century. These ideas are antithetical to Popper's evolutionary epistemology (see Chapter 8 for further discussion) and have a bearing on the present discussion of what happens when we learn.

Popper's view of truth in relation to learning is expressed in the following quotation:

> All acquired knowledge, all learning, consists of the modification (possibly the rejection) of some form of knowledge, or disposition, which was there previously; and in the last instance, of inborn dispositions. . . . All growth of knowledge consists in the improvement of existing knowledge which is changed in the hope of approaching nearer to the truth.
>
> (1979 [1972], p. 71)

Crucial to an understanding of this position is the distinction to be made between the pursuit of certainty and the pursuit of truth. The objection of radical constructivists and others to the idea that we cannot reasonably pursue the truth about our shared reality lies in their failure to distinguish between the quest for certainty and the quest for truth.

The idea that we can describe, explain or otherwise represent the world has been criticized on the grounds that there is no certainty that our accounts reflect what is actually there. The general argument suggests that there is no way of checking, say, theory T_1 as an account of reality except by reference to T_2; but, of course, T_2 is no more certain or secure than T_1, and so on, to the point where we may have a number of theories that interrelate and support each other but which nevertheless fail to provide us with certain or even secure knowledge of the nature of reality. As von Glasersfeld put it, 'there is no logically feasible way of checking the "objective truth" of knowledge if the object of that knowledge is accessible only through yet another act of knowing' (1985, p. 92).

The idea that we cannot achieve certainty is correct – the pursuit of certainty is futile – but abandoning the quest for certainty does not inevitably mean abandoning the quest for truth. Instead of seeking to establish certain or secure grounds for knowledge, we can best consider the process by which knowledge develops. If we are prepared to regard truth as a regulative ideal, a standard at which we can aim (see, e.g., Popper, 1979 [1972], pp. 29–30, 264–5), and if we accept that our knowledge will always remain conjectural and therefore provisional, we can see that the process by which knowledge develops is one of trial and error-elimination. At a pragmatic level, for example, we want many of our expectations about reality to be true – expectations such as 'I can drive through this narrow gap between two vehicles without causing any damage' and 'This is an effective method for helping children to learn to read'. Our expectations about reality are our *fallible* knowledge and, contrary to what radical constructivists and postmodern thinkers have argued, they are *checked* by reality whenever we find that 'our knowledge bumps up against our ignorance' (Burgess, 2000, p. 54, and see my Chapter 2). Given the distinctive features of our learning outlined in section 5 above, we can use our imagination to hypothesize the nature of reality – to pursue but never conclusively attain the truth. As mentioned previously, at least some of our hypotheses, those that form part of what we call science, can be tested by the search for refuting evidence. In general, and when *truth* is our standard, hypotheses that have not withstood criticism are abandoned, at least until there is a reason to re-evaluate the criticism.

Addressing Some Problematic Ideas about Learning

It is not the repeated impact on our senses which leads to a new discovery, but something entirely different: our repeated and varied attempts to solve a problem which, unsolved, continues to irritate us. It is essential here that these 'repeated' attempts differ from each other, and that we repeat the same attempt only when it appears to us to be successful, and only in order to try it out again; that is, in order to test, if possible under varying conditions, the hypothesis that it leads invariably to a successful solution of our irritating problem.

—*Karl Popper,* Realism and the Aim of Science

All reflexes are unconditioned; the supposedly 'conditioned' reflexes are the results of modifications which partially or wholly eliminate the false starts, that is to say the errors in the trial-and-error process.

—*Karl Popper,* Objective Knowledge: An Evolutionary Approach

Introduction

In Chapter 2, I drew on Karl Popper's evolutionary epistemology to challenge the commonly held but mistaken expectation that at least some learning involves the absorption of informational elements from outside the learner – what I call the myth of learning by instruction from without. In this chapter, I draw on Popper's epistemology to outline and challenge various influential ideas about learning that often accompany and/or embody this myth.

I begin with the theory of induction. Unlike Popper's lesser-known evolutionary analysis of learning, his critique of the theory of induction has been extensively debated in the philosophy of science, where it has been influential despite being very widely rejected. Although it seems that, in general, researchers in the physical sciences no longer use the theory of induction, at least not in its purest form, to guide their methodology, I have noted occasions in which scientists have given non-inductive accounts of their work in television documentaries, only for the programme's voiceover to present an inductive overview. Among those who are not scientists or philosophers, the case against induction would seem to be not so much rejected as overlooked. The idea of induction endures to this day as a myth about the nature of scientific method, and the outcomes of science are still construed in some quarters as an 'accumulation of highly confirmed, or highly probable, or well-supported hypotheses' (in a critique – Miller, 1982, pp. 19–20).

The following assumptions about learning relate to the theory of induction:

(i) There can be learning without a problem and without trial and error-elimination.
(ii) Learning sometimes involves abstracting ideas, expectation-free, from experience.
(iii) Expectations are reinforced by confirming evidence.
(iv) Learning is, in general, enhanced by repetition.
(v) Learning sometimes involves expectation-free association.

The first two assumptions have been criticized in Chapter 2. In the present chapter, I critically discuss the remaining assumptions and add to my earlier critique of the second assumption. With regard to the fourth assumption, I offer an evolutionary analysis of repetition in the context of practical learning. The chapter concludes with a critique of behaviourism as an associationist theory of learning antithetical to Popper's selectionist analysis.

1 The theory of induction

Historically, the pursuit of knowledge has been construed in different ways at different times. Despite this variety, to a large extent the history of science (at least prior to the mid-20th century) can be viewed as the search for certainties or secure knowledge, and the history of philosophy can be characterized as the search for the sources and justification of such knowledge. These are the kinds of ideas that postmodern thinkers set out to challenge; however, their approach, as mentioned in Chapter 3, section 7, is in conflict with, and can be criticized by, Popperian evolutionary epistemology (for a discussion from education, see Atkinson and Swann, 2003).

Central to the pursuit of certainty, of particular significance in modern times (at least in Western societies) has been the idea of inductive method, formulated early in the 17th century by the English philosopher Francis Bacon (in his *Novum Organum*) as a way of achieving secure knowledge of the natural world. Bacon's theory, radical at the time, prioritized the role of experience in the pursuit of knowledge of the physical world. His theory of induction was hugely successful, in that it offered a new way of comprehending the natural world, and it led to an explosion of discovery and invention.

In a critical account of induction, Tyrrell Burgess represented its 'logic' in the simplified schema shown below (1977, p. 131), which can be contrasted with Popper's simplified schema of trial and error-elimination (presented in my Chapter 2, section 5, and Chapter 3, sections 1 and 5):

$$O_n \rightarrow H \rightarrow V \rightarrow L$$

Induction, as a theory of the growth of scientific knowledge, is the idea that universal theories arise from a series of singular observation statements (O_n). Singular observation statements can take the form 'This is a . . .', such as 'This is a 5-year-old child who enjoys stories about animals'. A scientist who exploits the theory of induction in her (or his) methods records a series of observations – in which each observation is assumed to be, or treated as though it is, expectation-free – in the hope that eventually a hypothesis (H) in the form of a universal theory will emerge, such as 'All 5-year-old children enjoy stories about animals'. Once such a hypothesis has been derived from a series of observations, the discovery of further confirming evidence is thought to verify it (V). If the confirming evidence is sufficiently strong, the theory may be accorded the status of a law (L).

According to the theory of induction, only knowledge in the sciences reaches the L stage. But the earlier part of the schema highlights a set of broader expectations about the growth of knowledge, namely that in at least some processes in which such growth takes place, there is no problem and therefore no trial and error-elimination; ideas can be abstracted from a range of evidential material; and both repetition and confirming evidence play a crucial role.

2 Belief in regularities

As many readers will be aware, the 18th century philosopher David Hume demonstrated that the theory of induction is logically flawed because there is no logical reason to assume 'that instances, of which we have had no experience, must resemble those, of which we have had experience' (Hume, 2010 [1739–40], Book 1, Part III, section VI, p. 57; see also 1999 [1748]). For an inference to be logically valid, the conclusion must not go beyond the evidence presented in the premises. Therefore inductive inference – reasoning from repeated instances of experience to other instances (conclusions) of which there is no experience – constitutes a logically invalid argument. No number of true singular observation statements of the kind 'This is a 5-year-old child who enjoys stories about animals' can entail the universal theory 'All 5-year-old children enjoy stories about animals' – there may still be one or more, as yet unobserved, who do not.

A problem that followed Hume's discovery that the theory of induction is completely in error is 'Why . . . do all reasonable people expect, and *believe*, that instances of which they have no experience will conform to those of which they have experience?' (Popper, 1979 [1972], p. 4). Hume's criticism of induction was devastating, but he was unable to solve the problem it raised, except to say that while repetition is powerless in terms of logical argument, people are nonetheless conditioned by dint of repetition to believe that similar instances will occur in the future. For example, according to the theory of induction, repeated daily observations of the sun rising have led us to believe that the sun will rise again tomorrow; the belief that 'The sun rises every day' is derived from repeated observations of daily sunrise and justified by further repeated observations of the same kind.

Popper (1972a [1934], chapter 1; 1979 [1972], chapter 1; 1985b [1956]; and 2008 [1930–33]) followed Hume by accepting that the theory of induction is logically invalid, but, unlike Hume, he denied that induction ever takes place, psychologically or otherwise. Popper drew attention to an asymmetry between verification and falsification: while no number of true singular observation statements can verify or prove the truth of a universal theory, one true singular observation statement can refute it. Therefore, although no number of true statements of the kind 'This is a 5-year-old child who enjoys stories about animals' will prove the truth of the universal theory 'All 5-year-old children enjoy stories about animals', the statement 'This is a 5-year-old child who does not enjoy stories about animals', if true, will refute it. A universal theory is always provisional and unverifiable, but some such theories can be refuted. It must be stressed, however, that the status of refuting evidence is itself conjectural and provisional – we may be wrong in thinking we were wrong.

Popper's imaginative response to Hume's critique led to a new theory of how knowledge grows and a new theory of what happens when an individual learns. A singular observation statement is significant insofar as it relates to a universal theory which it may contradict, and an individual's observation is relevant and possible only in the context of an expectation that the individual holds about herself or about some aspect of the physical or social environment or the world of objectified knowledge. With regard to the problem raised by Hume's critique, the idea of *belief in regularity* can be replaced by the idea of an inborn *need for regularity* (Popper, 1992a [1974], pp. 48–52). As Popper wrote in one of his earlier selectionist accounts of learning,

> Without waiting, passively, for repetitions to impress or impose regularities upon us, we actively try to impose regularities upon the world. We try to discover similarities in it, and to interpret it in terms of laws invented by us. Without waiting for premises we jump to conclusions. These may have to be discarded later, should observation show that they are wrong.
>
> (1972b [1963], p. 46)

Regularities are needed, expected and sought, but often not found. Indeed, both learning and the growth of objectified knowledge are prompted not by the acquisition of true or almost certainly true information, but (as discussed in Chapter 2) by the discovery of error (or, in some cases, specific limitation) in existing expectations. A learning organism comes to terms with a disappointed expectation of regularity by creating a new expectation of regularity. For example, 'I shall be fed whenever I'm hungry' may become 'I shall be fed at satisfactorily regular intervals'. The individual assumes that the future will be like the past or the present until experience challenges this expectation or until a challenge is anticipated.

Clearly, the expectations of regularity we create, like those which are inborn, are not necessarily true. I further suggest that, interestingly, it appears that we sometimes create false expectations not just because of ineptitude, but because we are desperate for regularity and for regularities of particular kinds. Having a false expectation of regularity can feel better, and it may be more useful, than having no expectation. Expectations of regularity are not only potentially useful because, insofar as their consequences are true, they enable us to make accurate predictions and thus exercise a greater degree of control over ourselves and our physical and social environment; there is also a sense in which they can be comforting because they make us feel secure. An expectation of regularity can be comforting, even when reasoning leads us to believe it may be false. On the negative side, however, the discovery that a comforting expectation of regularity is false may breed insecurity and may even lead to neurosis.

With regard to our expectations – including explicit theories, both universal (e.g. 'All 5-year-old children enjoy stories about animals') and non-universal (e.g. 'Many 5-year-old children enjoy stories about animals') – we do, of course, have to assume that many are true. But though we act on assumptions of truth and can pursue truth as a standard, we can never know for sure that truth has been achieved. Note that a large number of confirming instances does not necessarily make the truth of a universal theory more probable, even if the theory has not been refuted. If there is one 5-year-old child who does not enjoy stories about animals, it makes no difference whether you have previously found 10 or 10,000 who do; the universal theory 'All 5-year-old children enjoy stories about animals' is false. The existence of a large number of confirming instances can be offset by one refuting instance. The discovery of evidence which seems to support a universal theory may be comforting to us, but it does not logically strengthen the theory. Such evidence may lull us into a mistaken sense of security.

Given that all knowledge is conjectural, *all* attempts to justify particular claims to knowledge are futile. No claim to knowledge is effectively warranted by seemingly compelling evidence or good reasons. With regard to the role of reason in the growth of knowledge, Popper developed a new form of rationalist epistemology, critical rationalism, whereby reason serves not to justify claims to knowledge; rather, its role is in the criticism and, more broadly, the evaluation of such claims (for further discussion, see Chapter 8, and Chapter 9, section 2). Critical rationalism has broken the link between rationality and justification such that, with regard to science,

> What is rational about scientific activity is not that it provides us with reasons for its conclusions, which it does not, but that it takes seriously the use of reason – deductive logic, that is – in the criticism and appraisal of those conclusions.
>
> (Miller, 1994, p. ix)

Despite the importance of Popper's work, comparatively few people have a sound understanding of much of what he proposed and argued. His epistemology is often considered a mere postscript to Hume. For example, he is often mistakenly thought to have proposed falsification as an alternative means by which secure knowledge may be achieved – secure knowledge of what is not so. But a decision as to whether or not a theory has been falsified is always a matter of judgement, and all judgements are potentially flawed. The underlying theme of all Popper's work is that of how to advance our knowledge, not that of how to achieve foundational knowledge of what is or is not so – such knowledge is, quite simply, beyond our reach. (For more detailed accounts of induction's bankruptcy, see, in addition to Popper's own texts, Miller, 1994, chapters 1 and 2, and 2006a, chapter 5.)

3 The role of so-called confirming evidence

Although most people, when presented with Hume's critique, are prepared to accept that the theory of induction embodies a logically invalid argument, it seems that far fewer are prepared to accept the idea that inductive processes do not occur and that any impression that they do is illusory. One reason seems to be that, notwithstanding Popper's critique, many of us do have a sense that at least some of our theories, or expectations, become more strongly held as a consequence of what might be construed as reinforcement by dint of repeated exposure to confirming evidence. This raises the question of what happens when an individual's attachment to an expectation becomes stronger, but the expectation itself is not changed.

I posit that what seems like the reinforcement of an expectation in light of confirming evidence is in fact a situation in which the individual's *attitude* towards the expectation has changed – as per a process of trial and error-elimination. As argued in Chapter 3, section 2, it is not only our expectations that change in learning but also, at least on some occasions, our preferences and what may be called our attitudes. It is possible, therefore, to distinguish between the process of trial and error-elimination as it applies to the content of an expectation and the process of trial and error-elimination as it applies to the individual's attitude towards the expectation. When an individual becomes increasingly convinced of an expectation in light of evidence that appears to support it, this can be explained in terms of the individual's need for regularity. The individual is seeking to increase her sense of security. Her implicit problem is 'How can I achieve a greater sense of security?' Her (methodological) trial solution is to look for evidence that confirms one or more existing expectations of regularity.

Confirming evidence 'supports' the learner's need for security. Which is not to say that the content of the expectation is made more secure by the 'discovery' of confirming evidence: it is not. We can often find evidence to suggest that our solutions have been (or are) successful, but this does not mean that (a) the solutions were (or are) the best available, (b) they have no undesirable, unintended consequences or (c) the expectations embodied in them are true (note: all false expectations have some true consequences). Through learning we create expectations, some of which may be true. But we cannot learn that they are true, though we may become increasingly convinced of their truth. Rather, they stand provisionally until shown to be false. We learn that some of our expectations are false; though, as mentioned above, even when expectations appear to have been falsified, the evidence on which this judgement is made may be misconstrued or misleading. All expectations are conjectural.

Once upon a time, in the not so distant past, people thought the sun moved round the Earth. When they sought confirming evidence, they found it every day. But the expectation 'The sun moves round the Earth' was not confirmed by what they saw; rather, what was reinforced was the conviction that the expectation was true. This reinforcement occurred because of a need for regularity. The regularity of the sun going round the Earth was needed, sought and found. The evidence, as people interpreted it, enabled them to feel more secure; but it did not help them to pursue the truth about celestial mechanics. As we now know, their expectation about the solar orbit was false. But many people were reluctant to abandon the idea that 'The sun moves round the Earth' and were resistant to considering evidence that undermined it. Positing that the Earth was at the centre of the universe made them feel secure.

An individual may welcome the discovery of error or inadequacy as a catalyst for improving what she knows and what she knows how to do.

Alternatively, when such evidence is found, the learner may resent it because it undermines her sense of security. Of course, some occasions for discovering error or inadequacy are better than others. It is, for instance, better to make such discoveries in pilot studies, models, role play or other relatively safe contexts. But as would-be learners, the more mistakes and specific limitations we can find, the better. Not finding that we are mistaken, or not recognizing our limitations, may make us feel good (at times this is important), and a degree of dogmatism can be valuable during the developmental stage of an idea (Popper, 1992a [1974], pp. 41–2). But in the end, the successful pursuit of learning necessitates being mistaken and/or having expectations or abilities that are subject to specific limitations, and discovering that this is the case. What appears to us as confirming evidence may encourage us to develop an idea, but it may also lead to complacency and, ultimately, torpor. Strange as it may seem, we do not and cannot learn from situations in which our expectations remain unchallenged; we learn only from situations in which they are shown to be false or at least inadequate for our present needs.

4 Error, inadequacy and specific limitation

Popper stressed the importance of the discovery of error rather than the discovery of inadequacy or specific limitation. His concern with theoretical rather than practical problems led him to emphasize the two-valued system of logic in which a statement is classified as either 'true' or 'false'. In day-to-day learning, however, a useful distinction can be made between error (where an expectation is false) and inadequacy (where an expectation or set of expectations does not provide us with the kind of information we need for the problem we wish to address) (Swann, 1999a). If there is some clarity about the way in which our expectations are inadequate, we may say that we have identified a specific limitation.

As an illustration, a teacher would be expressing the discovery of an error if she said, 'I thought the students understood my explanation, but when I questioned them afterwards I realized that I was wrong'. In contrast, the discovery of an inadequacy would involve a mismatch between what the teacher knows and what might be known, as in, 'I want to convey this idea to the students, but I don't know how'. Both scenarios involve a mismatch between expectation and experience, but in the second (a case of 'wanting to know but not knowing') a practical mistake may be anticipated and avoided by the recognition of an inadequacy, in this case a specific limitation.

The implications of this distinction can be illustrated by the following account of learning from reading, which also contrasts with the idea of reading as an inductive process; that is, it is entirely different from the idea that ideas can be abstracted, expectation-free, from reading material.

There are three main ways in which reading a book can help someone to learn; two are direct, the other is indirect. These ways of learning are not mutually exclusive; all three functions of a book may come into play at any reading. Intrinsic to all three ways of learning are processes of trial and error-elimination that are embedded and at least partly unconscious, such as those discussed in Chapter 2, section 7 – reading is never a means of learning by instruction from without.

First, a book may challenge the assumptions or existing theories of the reader (the would-be learner). On reading the book, the reader may discover a mismatch between the expectations she brings to her reading and the ideas in the book. The book may (a) contradict the reader's current expectations or (b) contain ideas that expand upon them. In the case of (a), there is potential for discovering error, and in (b) an unforeseen limitation is potentially revealed. An individual may therefore be encouraged to think, 'Are my ideas correct? Are my ideas adequate?' If the answer to either question is 'no', reading the book may result in learning by provoking the reader to formulate one or more new problems.

Second, the reader may bring to a book a question (or set of questions) to which she seeks an answer (or answers). The reader has previously experienced a mismatch between what she knows and what she wants to know; she has identified an inadequacy in her current knowledge. On the basis of a desire to resolve the mismatch, a problem may be formulated, such as 'How can I find an answer to the question "what is wood made of?"' In this situation, reading a book may provide – through a process of trial and error-elimination – part of a solution to a pre-existing problem.

Third, the reader may find in a book ideas which match those she already holds to be true or valid. In this circumstance, insofar as there is no mismatch, no learning will take place with regard to the substance of the ideas in the book. However, the content of the book may be treated as confirming evidence and, implicitly, as a solution to the problem of how to feel more secure. Such 'evidence' may, therefore, make the reader feel good and can boost confidence. This feel-good factor may provide an individual with encouragement to continue working on ideas. It may also, of course, lead to complacency.

What the reader 'observes' in the book will be dependent, though not wholly, on prior expectations. And reading will not necessarily result in 'good' learning; it may confirm prior erroneous expectations or lead to new errors. I suggest that when reading for learning (in contrast to reading for pleasure), it is, whenever possible, better to formulate one's principal expectations in advance; testing expectations or hypotheses is more conducive to bold and critical thinking than is answering questions. The practice of formulating and reflecting on one's ideas prior to reading is something that teachers can promote when seeking to support the development of thinking, instead of encouraging students to see reading as the first step. In contrast to the implications of Popper's evolutionary epistemology, it is still common for students to be encouraged to observe a situation and report what they see, or to read a book or listen to a teacher in order to get some ideas.

5 Observation

While the theory of induction does not exclude the idea that an observation can be the result of an active intention, the observation itself is conceived as, or assumed to be, expectation-free. But as discussed in Chapter 2, there is a strong case to be made for the idea that all observations are expectation-laden, and all are *made* rather than passively experienced: what we observe is dependent not only on what there is to be observed, but also on the expectations we bring to the act of observation (see, e.g., Popper, 1979 [1972], chapter 7 and appendix 1). An observation requires both an observer and a thing observed, and for the observer to observe this thing there must necessarily be some prior expectation or idea. For instance, if a child is asked to observe a tree, the question arises, either implicitly or explicitly, 'What is to be observed about the tree?' In this situation, identifying which features are to be observed becomes a problem. It may be tackled by asking the question or by the child identifying something to observe based on expectations created in prior learning. It is, of course, possible to guide observation by suggesting features to be observed, but, even so, the child's understanding of what is suggested and her awareness of the tree will be dependent on existing ideas. Whatever is seen (heard, read or cognitively assembled) in any situation is not only dependent on what is actually there but also on the prior expectations (implicit assumptions or explicit theories) of the observer: there is always something prior to an observation. All observation is expectation-laden. This is no less true for observations of the physical world than it is for those of the social world.

That some event, state of affairs or object is observed to be 'similar to what we've already observed' is itself dependent on expectations developed in the search for regularities. As Roger James put it,

> seeing things as similar depends upon interpretation, anticipation, and expectation. We cannot therefore explain anticipation and expectation as being consequences of repetition. For even the first repetition-for-us would only be interpreted as such if it is seen as similar, and seeing something as similar depends upon expectation.
>
> (1980, p. 88)

Once we accept that there is no direct transfer of 'what can be known' into 'what we know', it becomes clear that our observations may be mistaken. For example, we may be wrong about whether 'this is a 5-year-old child who does not enjoy stories about animals'. We may, individually and collectively, misconstrue the evidence. Our observations are also limited. We cannot observe everything, and we may miss something important to us. Consider, for example, Oetzi, the mummified remains of a 5,300-year-old man, found in the Tyrolean Alps in 1991. This stone-age corpse has been extensively studied, yet it took researchers almost a decade to discover that the man had, shortly before his death, suffered an arrow wound. Initial speculation, prior to this discovery, was that he had been caught in a storm and died of exposure. It was only when a researcher studied a new set of x-rays that the arrowhead was observed. Although the arrowhead is discernible on the original x-rays, the earlier researchers, who did not anticipate such a find, simply did not notice it. In the normal course of events, often we do not observe things that we do not expect to find – in the way that the first Oetzi researchers did not expect to find an arrowhead. Our expectations may be challenged when we are looking for challenge and when, merely by happenstance, we experience (without anticipation) the metaphorical 'bump' that occurs when our expectations are disappointed (see Chapter 2, section 7).

6 The role of repetition in learning

So far I have drawn on Popper's epistemology to challenge the idea that repeated observation of a particular phenomenon facilitates the abstraction of a universal hypothesis about the phenomenon. Repetition does, however, have a role to play in learning, in the way mentioned in the first of the two quotations that head this chapter (Popper, 1985a [1951–56], p. 40): repetition provides an opportunity for trial and error-elimination in response to a problem.

In a discussion of how children learn, Richard Bailey (2000, chapter 5) presents a Popperian analysis of the role of repetition (see also, Petersen, 1988, section 7). As Bailey points out 'It would be absurd to deny any role for repetition; as any sports player or musician knows, practice is an essential prerequisite of high quality performance' (2000, p. 92). He goes on to argue that what repetition can do, specifically in the context of learning a skill, is increase efficiency. It can do this in two ways, in both of which, I argue, we can see that the idea of a problem and that of trial and error-elimination are retained rather than eliminated.

First, when pursuing a goal – such as 'becoming able to ride a bicycle round a park' (my example) – our repeated attempts to attain this goal can become more efficient, in the sense that our sequence of activities or movements becomes simpler because we learn to eliminate what is superfluous to the task. In learning to ride a bicycle, practice is the means by which we learn to eliminate the unnecessary fumbling which, among other things, impedes our ability to balance. Each attempt to ride the bicycle constitutes a trial solution to the practical problem of 'How can I ride this bicycle?' Throughout each attempt, we must undertake a sustained process of trial and error-elimination in which a developing sequence of micro-problems is created and addressed so that, 'Gradually, through practice, the skill becomes honed and more "to the point"' (ibid.). Even if progress is extremely slow, each attempt to ride the bicycle, each placement of foot on pedal, is different (any sense of exact repetition is illusory). If the bicycle is the appropriate size, if we have sufficient strength in our muscles and if we are confident, we may progress quickly; if not, progress may be slow and we may fail to achieve our goal. Either way, there is no exact repetition, merely a general repetition of climbing on the bicycle and attempting simultaneously to gain and maintain balance while pedalling.

Second, repetition can assist the learning of a skill by enabling elements of the activity sequence to become habitual and relatively unproblematic. The general repetition of an activity or movement sequence provides us with the opportunity to learn to master the more routine aspects, to the point that we can relegate their execution to a lower level of consciousness, allowing us to concentrate on those aspects of the process that are more complicated or important (ibid., p. 93). In the case of learning to ride a bicycle, when we have mastered basic balancing and pedalling, we may decide to take the bicycle out on the road. In learning to cycle proficiently in this context, we must learn to deal with a broader range of manoeuvres and considerations, such as positioning in traffic lanes, responding to traffic signs, avoiding collisions with motor vehicles, and so on. In transferring our basic skills to this more complex situation, it would seem essential that some, perhaps much, of what we need to do must become habitual and not remain at the forefront of consciousness.

Although the process by which the mundane becomes unconscious may be innate rather than learnt (see Popper in Popper and Eccles, 1977, p. 131), I nonetheless disagree with an aspect of the following statement from Popper (ibid., p. 134): 'Repetition, or practising, is no way of acquiring new adaptations: it is a way of turning new adaptations into old ones, into unproblematic background knowledge; into unconscious dispositions.' Repetition, or practising, is, I agree, a way of turning new adaptations into unproblematic background knowledge, and I also fully accept that repetition, or practising, does not lead to new adaptations through any kind of inductive process. But to say that it is not a way of acquiring new adaptations seems to be somewhat misleading insofar as for learning organisms, as the first part of my cycling example illustrates, general repetition of the kind that takes place when we practise often involves the creation of new problems and new solutions, that is, new adaptations developed by 'repeated and varied attempts to solve a problem' (Popper, 1985a [1951–56], p. 40).

All this quite clearly runs counter to the idea that learning in the context of repetition is an example of learning without a problem and without trial and error-elimination. Note that the above analysis of the role of repetition in learning applies to the rote learning of multiplication tables, a process by which ideas encapsulated in simple formulae are made memorable by pattern and repetition. Using this technique, many of us have become able to remember that, for example, 'seven nines are sixty-three'. When reciting a multiplication table, our focus of attention may have been on the rhythmic repetition of the formulae, but the underlying process was nevertheless one of problem solving through a sustained process of trial and error-elimination. During this process, a series of subtle changes occurred, including efficiency gains of the kind described above. As emphasized earlier in the book, the fact that we were unaware of any trial-and-error process does not mean that there was none.

7 Associationist theories of learning

Associationism is a broad term for a category of philosophical theories of learning, some of which are compatible with, and in some cases have traditionally accompanied, the theory of induction. As stated in Chapter 2, section 8, associationism proposes that, in learning, an individual selects relevant ideas or elements from repeated acts of observation; the mind recognizes that ideas (or elements) are associated and stores the associations in memory. As Popper described associationism in a critique,

> Ideas or elements are associated if they occur together; and, most important, *association is strengthened by repetition*. . . . In this way we establish *expectations* (if the idea *a* is strongly associated with the idea *b* then the occurrence of *a* arouses a high expectation of *b*).
>
> (1979 [1972], p. 63)

Conditioning theories of learning – that is, stimulus-response and response-stimulus theories – are modern psychological equivalents of associationism, in that they presume that learning develops by associating one phenomenon with another and that the repetition of such pairings reinforces the association. More complex knowledge is thought to be built up from a series of simple associations. Associationism as a philosophical theory promotes the idea that learning involves the absorption of informational elements from the environment. In accounts of conditioning, this issue is usually left unaddressed, although some kind of learning by instruction from without would seem to be implied.

There are a number of different conditioning theories, but operant conditioning, the theory of the behaviourist B. F. Skinner, has been one of the most influential in the context of education debate and practice. The theory of operant conditioning posits that a learning individual's behaviour is modified by its consequences. The learning individual makes an association between its behaviour and a stimulus and is inclined to repeat behaviour (its responses) which it associates with rewarding stimuli, and it is disinclined to repeat behaviour which it does not associate with rewarding stimuli (see, e.g., Skinner, 1974, chapter 4). As Mark Tennant puts it,

> Skinner argues that organisms simply emit responses which are gradually shaped by their consequences. When a response (bit of behaviour) has a rewarding (reinforcing) consequence, it is more likely to occur again; when it has a non-rewarding consequence, it is less likely to occur again. In this way we acquire a repertoire of behaviour which is literally 'shaped' by the environment.
>
> (2006 [1988], p. 94)

Note that behaviour which reduces the occurrence of a non-rewarding consequence is also reinforced (negative reinforcement):

> A negative reinforcer strengthens any behavior that reduces or terminates it: when we take off a shoe that is pinching, the reduction in pressure is negatively reinforcing, and we are more likely to do so again when a shoe pinches.
>
> (Skinner, 1974, p. 46)

Negative reinforcement should not be confused with punishment, which Skinner did not favour: 'punishment is designed to remove behavior from a repertoire, whereas negative reinforcement generates behavior' (ibid., p. 62).

Skinner's version of behaviourism can be viewed as a form of selectionism, whereby through trial and error the learner's behaviour is modified – controlled – by its consequences. But Skinner's selectionism is very different from Popper's, not least because for Skinner the learner's trials are viewed as if they are entirely blind, in the sense of not being expectation-laden, problem-centred or exploratory (James, 1980, pp. 88–9); whereas for Popper, trials are expectation-laden, and although 'blind to the solution of the problem' (Popper, 1992a [1974], p. 46) – that is, blind in the sense that their consequences are not known in advance – they are not quite blind insofar as the learner's action is directed towards the solving of a problem (Popper, 1994a, pp. 5–6; and my Chapter 2, section 5).

Skinner's basic thesis about learning and the way he developed it have important implications for those who work with children. In his words, 'The application of operant conditioning to education is simple and direct. Teaching is the arrangement of contingencies of reinforcement under which students learn' (1968, p. 64). Following Skinner, if one wishes to encourage a behaviour, one rewards it. What one tries one's utmost to avoid is intermittently rewarding behaviour one wishes to extinguish, because intermittent reward may strengthen the response. A teacher who adopts Skinnerian behaviourism will plan for and monitor the student's learning in great detail, with the intention of developing a programme of tasks that will enable the student to progress from learning basic ideas or skills (evidenced by the student's responses or behaviour) to learning those that are more complex. At each stage, correct responses on the part of the student are reinforced. The teacher aims to minimize the occurrence of incorrect responses, and if such responses occur, they are usually given minimal attention (to avoid reinforcing them). The idea of 'learning from error' (to use a phrase from Berkson and Wettersten, 1984) is anathema to the Skinnerian teacher.

8 In opposition to behaviourism

The origin of the term 'behaviourism' is usually attributed to John B. Watson, who published an article entitled 'Psychology as the behaviorist views it' (Watson, 1913). He and subsequent behaviourist psychologists argued that psychology should be redefined as the study of observable behaviour and that attempts to examine inaccessible and unobservable mental events should be abandoned (Tennant, 2006 [1988], p. 93).

Although Skinner's idea of operant conditioning – whereby 'consequences' are used to 'modify' behaviour – is often viewed as the representative idea of behaviourism, rather more important is the idea, which Watson introduced and Skinner developed and did much to promote, that the learner's introspected internal states or processes are either to be regarded as unimportant or as mere by-products of her 'genetic and environmental histories' (Skinner, 1974, p. 17). Skinner argued,

> we can look at those features of behavior which have led people to speak of an act of will, of a sense of purpose, of experience as distinct from reality, of innate or acquired ideas, of memories, meanings, and the personal knowledge of the scientist, and of hundreds of other mentalistic things or events. Some can be 'translated into behavior,' others discarded as unnecessary or meaningless.
>
> (Ibid.)

It follows that assessment of learning and, ultimately, of social progress, should focus only on what can be observed and measured. In general, social endeavour need not be complicated by thinking about intentions, preferences and emotions. Some people find this idea reassuringly simple, and it has been hugely appealing to would-be social engineers, including politicians (see Chapter 10 for relevant discussion). But for those who experience the effects of behaviourism as a daily reality, behaviourism in practice can be a distressing experience. In England, for example, many of the social structures by which our lives are framed are designed to shape our behaviour, disregarding our emotional states, ignoring many of our personal and social needs and values, and marginalizing our capacity for imagination. Intentions, preferences and emotions exist and they matter; the pursuit of social progress is doomed to fail until or unless social policy takes these factors fully into consideration.

As theories of learning, behaviourism and Popperian selectionism can be contrasted in two key respects.

First, according to Popperian selectionism, as I have outlined it in this chapter and in Chapters 2 and 3, learning can take place without any immediate and observable change in behaviour; what occurs may merely constitute a change in potential, characterized as a change in disposition. There will be physiological changes associated with any change in disposition, but most often a change in disposition cannot be clearly matched with a physiological change. This is not to deny that some kinds of learning are associated with activity in specific parts of the brain; but changes in disposition are often not readily observable, and they may develop 'unseen' over a period of time.

Within education systems, formal processes of education are usually evaluated according to what students can be observed to be able to do. However, if we view learning as a change in disposition (involving a change of preference and/or expectation), which may or may not be accompanied by observable changes in behaviour, then we may be more cautious about the unarticulated, unobserved and unintended consequences of formal education. It may be more straightforward, for example, to evaluate a literacy programme in terms of what the children become able to read; but rather more important in the longer term might be the effect of the programme on the children's attitudes towards reading. A behaviourist might argue, however, that there are ways of observing and measuring changes in children's attitudes towards reading, for example, by reference to behaviours that might be elicited in the context of test situations. But in practice, attempts to evaluate attitudinal shifts in this way are usually eschewed in favour of attempts to measure more concrete changes in skills and knowledge, not least because attitudinal shifts are often elusive and more difficult to evaluate.

Second, conditioning theories – as a feature of behaviourism – invariably embody some of those aspects of the theory of induction that I have highlighted and challenged above. In particular, they mistakenly assume that direct experience is possible, that is, that there is expectation-free observation and association without prior expectation. But contrary to what is proposed by the idea of operant conditioning, for an individual to make a connection between her behaviour and its consequence, she must first have an expectation that such a connection is possible. And in order to view an occurrence as a repetition of a previous occurrence, that too requires a prior expectation. Also, there can be no exact repetition of rewarding consequences because, to use Popper's words, 'All the repetitions which we experience are *approximate repetitions*' (Popper, 1972a [first English edition 1959], p. 420) – the individual has to *make* a connection, which invariably will be expectation-laden.

(See also the second quotation at the head of this chapter, from Popper, 1979 [1972], p. 67.)

Popperian selectionism and Skinnerian theory also differ in that the latter is compatible with determinism, and the former is not. For Popperians, the individual is more than the sum of her genetic and environmental histories; problem solving in general and learning in particular involve elements of free will – life is a genuinely creative process whereby what the individual does, though it is influenced by her histories, is not determined by them. Skinner, by contrast, questions the possibility of free choice (see, e.g., Skinner, 1974, p. 20), and he describes determinism as 'a useful assumption' (Skinner, 1968, p. 171). His behaviourist philosophy neither assumes nor requires the idea of free will.

I emphasize that it is the theoretical framework for operant conditioning and stimulus-response theories that is in conflict with Popperian selectionism. I am not suggesting that observational data have been misreported or even that behavioural therapies and other behavioural practices are invariably useless. The key issue is one of interpretation. As James put it, 'The wealth of observation that has accumulated from learning experiments is not invalidated by the suspicion that conditioning and association are untenable hypotheses, but the observations will need reinterpretation in the light of a better theory' (1980, p. 91). Popperian selectionism is just such a theory. In Part 2, I explore its implications for encouraging learning.

Part 2
Encouraging Learning

What Promotes and What Inhibits Learning

5

Chapter Outline

Institutions for the selection of the outstanding can hardly be devised. Institutional selection may work quite well for such purposes as Plato had in mind, namely for arresting change. But it will never work well if we demand more than that, for it will always tend to eliminate initiative and originality, and, more generally, qualities which are unusual and unexpected. . . .

It has been said, only too truly, that Plato was the inventor of both our secondary schools and our universities. I do not know a better argument for an optimistic view of mankind, no better proof of their indestructible love for truth and decency, of their originality and stubbornness and health, than the fact that this devastating system of education has not utterly ruined them.

—Karl Popper, The Open Society and Its Enemies,
Volume 1: The Spell of Plato

Introduction

In the three chapters that comprise Part 2 of this book, I speculate on the implications for practice of the evolutionary analysis of learning presented in Part 1 (my expanded interpretation of Karl Popper's selectionist theory of learning). In this chapter, the focus is on what, broadly speaking, promotes learning, and what inhibits it. I begin by proposing a set of facts about learning and consider the commonsense implications of both the nature of learning, as it is defined in this book, and these facts. (Common sense is notoriously fallible, but it is nonetheless a good starting point – see Popper, 1979 [1972], chapter 2, section 2.) Core ideas are revisited from different angles, namely one's own learning, learning how to learn, characteristics of an environment conducive to human learning, promoting the learning of others, educational settings not conducive to learning, and significant impediments to learning in school. In places, list format has been used for ease of reference. Of necessity, there is a degree of conceptual repetition between some of the chapter's sections.

Of course, the question of what promotes and what inhibits learning is, to a significant extent, empirical, a matter of try it and see. A hypothesis for empirical testing that has been formulated with reference to the ideas presented in Part 2 and a method for testing it as part of a science of school teaching are outlined and discussed in Chapter 9. A methodology for testing and developing the ideas in professional practice is offered in Chapter 10.

1 Key facts about learning

If we construe learning as a change in disposition – characterized as a change in preference and/or expectation – that is not purely the outcome of genetic inheritance or haphazard organic factors, then in light of my evolutionary analysis of learning, the seven sets of statements about learning below can be regarded as statements of fact.

(i)   *Activity:* All aspects of every process of learning involve activity on the part of the learner. There is no passive aspect to learning. Learning never involves the passive receipt or absorption of informational elements from outside the learner.

(ii)   *Creativity:* All learning involves a degree of creativity on the part of the learner. Creativity is required in the (conscious or, more often, unconscious) formation of a problem and in the development of a new (for the learner) preference and/or expectation. Creativity may also be brought to bear on the way that expectations are tested or in some other way subjected to potential challenge.

(iii)   *Discovery of a mismatch:* In order for learning to take place, the learner must discover (explicitly or, more often, implicitly) a mismatch between expectation and experience, actual or anticipated. All learning requires the experience of a challenge (in essence, a criticism) either from the environment or from an internal stimulus (such as a thought experiment), a challenge which leads to the discovery (explicit or implicit) of error or specific limitation.

(iv) *Problem solving:* All learning is an outcome of problem solving, a process of trial and error-elimination.

(v) *Desire:* In order to have a problem, the learner must have the desire (explicit or, more often, implicit) to address a mismatch between expectation and experience, actual or anticipated. Without desire there is no problem, and without a problem there is no learning.

(vi) *Assessment:* Learning alters the learner's potential, and although changes in behaviour may be indicative of learning, much learning takes place without any observable change in behaviour.

(vii) *Human learning:* Our learning is greatly enhanced by our facility for developing descriptive and argumentative language and, relatedly, the ability to create and engage with objectified knowledge – a world comprised of linguistically formulated problems, theories, expectations, hypotheses, assumptions of fact, values and arguments.

All the above statements are, of course, conjectural and open to critical discussion. But I would urge any reader who would reject all or any of them to formulate a reasoned challenge that takes cognizance of Part 1 of this book. For the remainder of Part 2, the facts about learning highlighted by the above statements will be treated as givens.

2 Method in promoting one's own learning

Before thinking about how to promote the learning of others, it is useful to consider how to promote our own learning. In order to promote our own learning, we need to engage in exploratory activities of various kinds. Exploratory activity is not risk-free, and we need to be prepared to experience the discomfort that often comes when expectations, particularly those that are deep-seated, are challenged; the discomfort that comes from making practical mistakes, such as falling off a bicycle; and the hurt we feel when we try our best to achieve something but do not succeed. A degree of confidence is essential if we are to accelerate our learning (see Burgess, 1977, p. 160). Confident people believe in their potential to succeed, and they are more likely to persist in the face of difficulties. Someone who is confident as a learner may feel that something good may obtain from situations which are not found to be entirely successful. To discover error (e.g. in the context of an argument) and to be able to say 'I was wrong' can be a kind of success whereby we become liberated from ignorance. And although it is better to be able to do something well, if we do something badly but have some inkling of what we did wrong and how it might be put right next time, we are on the road to liberation from incapacity. People who are not afraid to take risks, and to expose themselves to the possibility of discovering errors and specific limitations within their current expectations and capabilities, are in a much better position to learn than those who are reticent or passive.

This is not an argument in favour of foolhardy risk-taking. While exploring, we need to be mindful of potential risks and strive to avoid creating circumstances that will lead to our learning being constrained in the future, for example, as the result of death, severe injury or significant social penalties. (I should add the ethical point that we should be mindful of the broader consequences of our actions.) So, for example, although one cannot learn to ride a bicycle without the risk of falling off, one might decide to minimize the effects of a fall by wearing appropriate head and elbow protectors. In general, with regard to the most significant practical problems, we can reduce the risk of making mistakes by subjecting proposals for action to critical evaluation and by treating current practices (and policies) as trials to be tested.

Quite simply, if we wish to promote our own learning, we are best advised to set out to create problems (not to be confused with making difficulties – see Chapter 3, section 2) and solutions and to be willing to subject the processes we adopt, and their outcomes, to critical scrutiny. We should also shun methods that assume one or more of the following fallacious ideas:

  (i) We can receive ideas ready-made from the environment (from observation, teacher instruction, books, etc.).
 (ii) We can learn inductively, that is, by the abstraction of general ideas from a series of expectation-free observations.
(iii) We can copy what we see or hear without engaging in trial and error-elimination.
 (iv) We can engage in repetition without trial and error-elimination.
  (v) We can learn from situations in which our expectations remain unchallenged.

In light of Popperian selectionism, these assumptions would seem not to be conducive to learning, though this is not to imply that learning does not take place when processes that assume them are adopted. Humans are habitual learners and learn despite ill-conceived strategies and misconceptions. The issue at stake here is how can we accelerate and expand our learning. In other words, 'How can we learn more?'

If we wish to accelerate our learning, whatever the problem area or subject field, we must strive to find ways to encourage ourselves and others to search for errors and specific limitations in our expectations and related actions. We can search for errors and specific limitations by conducting thought experiments; by engaging in practical try-it-and-see activities; by putting what we think and do in a public form or context, and by inviting other people to provide critical feedback and, when possible, engage in dialogue with us. Of course, as mentioned in Chapter 4, some occasions for discovering error or specific limitation are better than others. It is, for example, better to make such discoveries in pilot studies, models, role play or other relatively safe contexts. But as would-be learners, the more errors and specific limitations we can find the better. (The identification of error is, as stressed in Chapter 4, section 2, a conjectural issue. All of us – children, teachers, education theorists and policy makers – can be mistaken about what is wrong.)

The method described above is essentially one of self-regulation, and as such it has a counterpart in the conception of learning how to learn developed by the influential educational psychologist Ann Brown: 'Mature thinkers are those who provide conflict trials for themselves, practice thought experiments, question their own basic assumptions, provide counterexamples to their own rules, etc.' (1987, p. 108). Such self-regulatory procedures may not always be adopted self-consciously; indeed, those who learn most are likely, habitually and unconsciously, to adopt a critical approach. But the most proficient learners will be able and prepared to think consciously about their learning when a habitual strategy has failed, when the risks are great and when the situation is both complex and unfamiliar (Swann et al., 2003). Moreover, researchers (as learners) in the physical or social sciences can strive to formulate some of their expectations as refutable hypotheses and subject them to severe critical empirical testing (see Chapter 9).

In describing the critical method above, I largely concur with Kurt Klappholz and Joseph Agassi who, in an article about methodological prescriptions in economics, asserted that

> there is only one generally applicable methodological rule, and that is the exhortation to be critical and always ready to subject one's hypotheses to critical scrutiny.

Any attempt to reinforce this general maxim by a set of additional rules is likely to be futile and possibly harmful.

(1959, p. 60)

Where I disagree with Klappholz and Agassi is in their use of the word 'always'. In the early stage of developing an idea – a new preference and/or expectation – the individual may need to be dogmatic and wary of premature criticism. Preferences and expectations have to be created before they can be criticized (Popper, 1992a [1974], pp. 41, 48). Too much criticism too soon can stifle creativity; criticism, therefore, is not always appropriate. Also, much depends on the nature of the criticism (see my earlier discussion at the end of Chapter 3, section 3, and see Chapter 7, section 3).

Exploratory activity, which is generally associated with the most significant learning, is imbued with criticality, in the sense that it is motivated by a dissatisfaction with the present state of affairs and may imply such thoughts as 'I could try something else' and 'What else might I do?' Damaging criticism is that which leads the individual to cease to explore and develop ideas that might turn out to be productive. Of course, some ideas which initially look valuable turn out not to be, but developing and then eliminating such ideas from our enquiries is often invaluable for learning.

There is no a priori formula for fostering creativity and imagination in one's own learning, no prescription for how to turn a mismatch into a problem, how to produce a trial solution or indeed how to be critical. What works for one individual may not work for others; and what works in one situation may not work in another. Popper's characterization of creative thinking is nonetheless useful. Although he does not expand on the idea of imagination, he stresses the importance of having a deep interest in a problem, persistence (in developing a solution) and an unfettered criticality:

what is essential to 'creative' or 'inventive' thinking is a combination of intense interest in some problem (and thus a readiness to try again and again) with highly critical thinking; with a readiness to attack even those presuppositions which for less critical thought determine the limits of the range from which trials (conjectures) are selected; with an imaginative freedom that allows us to see so far unsuspected sources of error: possible prejudices in need of critical examination.

(1992a [1974], p. 48)

A belief in the importance and power of imagination in general, and in one's own creative potential in particular, would seem to be conducive to learning. The practice of imaginative criticism requires both an inclination to challenge the given or habitual (Popper, 1979 [1972], p. 148) *and* the intention to create something new and potentially better. Individuals are inclined to seek out and entertain criticism of their ideas and the capabilities in which they are embodied if they think they can respond positively to it. It can be expected that people learn more when they have confidence in their ability to deal creatively with the discovery of error and specific limitation. If we are intent on promoting our learning, we need to find ways to handle challenges to our expectations and current capabilities without losing self-confidence and without damaging our creative potential.

3 Learning how to learn

A concept of learning how to learn can be developed from the method described above for promoting one's own learning. Given this method, an individual who has learnt how to learn is someone who, when intending to learn, will consciously or unconsciously:

(a) seek to identify mismatches between her (or his) current expectations and experience (actual or anticipated) – that is, she will deliberately expose her expectations to the potential discovery of error or specific limitation

(b) problematize some of the mismatches that are discovered – that is, she will treat them as problems about which something is to be done

(c) create (trial) solutions

(d) test solutions by subjecting them to critical scrutiny; that is, seek to identify mismatches between her current expectations (as embedded in actual or envisaged trial solutions) and experience (essentially the same as (a)).

All learning, including unconscious learning, involves (b), (c) and the discovery of a mismatch. But only individuals who have learnt how to learn engage in (a) and (d).

The principal difference between someone who has learnt how to learn and someone who has merely learnt in a particular problem area is that the former individual searches for errors and specific limitations in what she knows, feels and does, whereas the latter waits for errors and specific limitations to be discovered by happenstance or through the initiative of another person. This is not to say that there are no other differences between someone who has learnt how to learn and someone who has not; but the inclination to subject one's expectations to critical scrutiny is crucial. Subjecting one's expectations to critical scrutiny may involve self-evaluation alone, self-evaluation in the light of feedback from peers or others, and/or reference to evidence and other potential challenges of various kinds. It involves the use of argumentative language, though this may be internalized (i.e. unspoken) and is often unselfconscious.

The individual who has not learnt how to learn may be inclined to adopt methods that are not conducive to learning (though their use may nonetheless be accompanied by learning). In light of a Popperian analysis, *un*conducive methods include the following:

(a) proceeding as though ideas can be received ready-made from the environment (from observation, teacher instruction, books, etc.)
(b) collecting information in the hope that new ideas will emerge
(c) seeking confirmation of existing beliefs on the assumption that the accumulated weight of evidence of similar cases strengthens ideas
(d) repeating activities on the assumption that repetition alone will result in improvement.

Someone who has learnt how to learn may sometimes adopt these methods, but when she does so, the method of learning how to learn is not being used.

The learning of someone who has learnt how to learn will, like that of any other learner, involve a desire (implicit or explicit) to change her current knowledge or capabilities for the better; an expectation that positive change is possible for her; and sufficient will and energy to act upon her desire. The will to act requires that the individual be sufficiently confident to risk the discovery of error or specific limitation (see section 2 above). In a particular circumstance, the individual may, for good reason, lack confidence – if she is not, in fact, in a safe place for making such discoveries. But some individuals habitually construe learning as potentially threatening, perhaps because they have learnt to associate the discovery of error or specific limitation with some kind of sanction. They may desire to learn but may, through fear or anxiety, be hesitant to act on the desire. Such anxiety or fear constitutes a significant constraint on both learning and the exploitation of learning how to learn. In general, when a student lacks confidence, the teacher's primary task is to encourage confidence rather than offer criticism. A confident student will respond to criticism of her ideas better and be more inclined to subject her expectations to critical scrutiny than a student lacking in confidence.

A basic level of learning how to learn involves at least some learning about learning, but this learning about learning may never be publicly expressed by the learner. And even if an individual could at one time articulate what she had learnt about learning, the ability may have been lost or diminished because it was no longer needed once the activities of learning how to learn had become habitual. Although the development of learning strategies involves thinking, an individual who has learnt how to learn may often not need to think consciously about how she learns. But when habitual learning strategies fail, engaging in problem formulation – responding to a mismatch by creating one or more *explicit* problems – is likely to be productive, at least in some problem and subject areas (which is not to suggest that this strategy will be appropriate in all circumstances).

Progress in being able to learn how to learn involves applying learning how to learn in a wider range of contexts; being consistently more disposed to practise learning how to learn in fraught and psychologically charged situations; and greater depth with regard to various aspects of being able to learn how to learn – this will require greater depth of learning about learning, and greater depth of self-reflection (Swann et al., 2003). An individual who has developed a stronger ability in respect of learning how to learn may, for example, be more inclined to be bold in her hypothesizing – she will recognize (perhaps only intuitively) that ill-conceived ideas can subsequently be eliminated or improved through critical discussion. With regard to fraught and psychologically charged situations, an individual with strong capabilities in respect of learning how to learn will be more resilient in the context of events which would otherwise serve to undermine her confidence as a learner.

I have not attributed value to the nature of what is learnt when the ability to learn how to learn is exploited. Rather, I propose that an individual who knows how to learn does things that are more likely to result in learning (worthwhile or not). The introduction of judgements about what is worthwhile, valid or true with regard to the content of what is learnt would raise questions such as 'Who is to make these judgements?' and 'When values and factual knowledge change, does this mean that a judgement that someone has learnt how to learn may need to be revised?' In general, although learning is embarked upon with the aim (often unconscious) of bringing about improvement, this aspiration may not be fulfilled (see Chapter 2, section 3). Given a decision to attribute value to learning, one may argue that a process leading to a rapid change in expectations is preferable to one that reduces the speed of change. 'Bad' learning is that which reduces the speed at which the individual discovers errors and specific limitations and inhibits the individual's ability to respond creatively to such discoveries. 'Good' learning enables the individual to increase the speed at which errors and specific limitations are discovered and new ideas, practices and products are created.

This concept of learning how to learn can be applied to group learning (Swann et al., 2003). A group that has learnt how to learn is able to engage in collective self-directed activity (including self-evaluation) that is intended to promote, and is effective in promoting, learning with regard to those expectations (and their associated preferences) of its members that form part of the group's intellectual, artistic and technological capital and which influence the members' contributions to shared endeavours. Working collaboratively, members of such a group will deliberately expose to critical scrutiny, as a means of improving them, the expectations, desires and preferences which significantly affect the group endeavour. In general, they will be supportive of imaginative activity on the part of individuals within the group on the grounds that such activity may lead to the creation of cultural (and other) resources for the benefit of the group.

Although learning how to learn is associated with the exercise of autonomy as a learner, it is important to distinguish between the two ideas. Learning how to learn involves self-directed activity, but the self-direction may occur in response to the initiative of another person, such as a teacher. A student who has learnt how to learn may exercise a degree of autonomy in respect of her programmes of learning but may lack the confidence and other attributes associated with full autonomy. A learner who is *fully* autonomous is someone with the ability and inclination to make independent and critically informed decisions regarding the timing, location, method, purpose *and* content of planned learning. 'Has learnt how to learn', as conceived here, is a necessary but not sufficient condition for achieving full learner autonomy. In general, when I talk about teaching for autonomy, supporting students in learning how to learn is subsumed within this.

4 An environment conducive to human learning

The opportunity to function in an environment conducive to learning also has a significant bearing on the extent of our learning. In light of the nature of learning and key facts about learning, as stated in section 1, it would seem likely that, for individuals, learning is promoted in environments which have the characteristics outlined in (i) to (vi) below. The characteristic highlighted in (vii) is not directly linked to evolutionary epistemology but is important as it relates to how the other characteristics are interpreted in specific situations.

Autonomous activity

(i) The learner has opportunities to engage in *self-directed* exploratory activity. 'Activity' here includes physical activities (specifically, practical trial and error-elimination) and cognitive activities (conscious or unconscious thought experiments). The extent to which the exploration required to support learning involves physical activity and the type of physical activity required will depend on the nature of the learning and the personal characteristics of the individual concerned.

(ii) The learner has opportunities to engage in *self-monitoring, self-evaluation and self-regulation*; that is, to reflect on and take continuing responsibility for her actions and their outcomes. Indeed, it can be argued that, for humans, self-monitoring, self-evaluation and self-regulation are crucial features of self-direction.

(iii) The learner has opportunities to exercise preference to the extent of engaging in exploratory activities that are not only self-directed but also *self-initiated*. 'Preference' as used here is not a synonym for 'choice'; preference is a matter of what the individual really wants to do, and choice is about selecting from a proffered set of options. The distinction is illustrated by the difference between being asked 'What would you like to eat?' and 'Which of these menu items do you fancy?' Of course, choice may coincide with preference when the individual's preference is also one of the presented options, but often this is not the case.

Stimulation, regularity and challenge

(iv) The environment presents opportunities and challenges to which the learner is capable of responding. An environment that is conducive to learning is one in which there are *stimuli* to which the individual can respond (e.g. as mentioned in Chapter 2, section 7, sight does not develop in the absence of light). It would seem also that some *regularities* and non-random features must be present and that *challenges* presented must not be so overwhelming that the individual cannot function effectively. For the human learner, stimulation, regularity and challenge are to be found not only in what might be called the natural environment but also in the world of objectified knowledge (as characterized in (vii) of section 1 above).

A safe place

(v) The environment is supportive of *the search for error and specific limitation* in that (a) the discovery of error and specific limitation is not penalized and (b) unnecessary risks are, as far as possible, avoided (specifically, the risks of occurrences that would ultimately curtail learning). There is no risk-free environment (even an environment that seems free of physical risks may be psychologically damaging), and doing nothing or very little will often mean reducing the potential for learning and may have other negative consequences. But some environments (as discussed later in this chapter and in Chapter 7) are clearly – with regard to self-esteem, self-confidence and physical well-being – safer places in which to learn than others.

Human language capabilities

(vi) The environment encourages the learner to develop her facility for *descriptive and argumentative language*. That is, it supports the learner in becoming able to create accounts of the environment (physical and social, concrete and conceptual) and her experience of it, and in developing strategies and making and acting on decisions in light of a critical discussion of the known possibilities. By implication, the learner is supported not only when engaging with objectified knowledge but also when creating such knowledge.

Personalized support

(vii) The environment is *responsive to the individual* who, while sharing many traits with other humans, has a distinct character and individualized learning needs. In practice, this means that the individual must have direct contact with at least one other human (preferably more) and this contact, if learning is to be maximized, needs to be appropriately responsive to the individual's personal qualities. For example, some individuals are more self-challenging than others and require less encouragement to engage in exploratory activities. Also, what one individual experiences as welcome encouragement, another may experience as an unwanted intrusion. Sometimes, however, unwanted intrusions are conducive to learning.

My intention above has been to highlight only those characteristics of a learning-conducive environment that pertain to most learners and to a broad range of contexts; further discussion is provided in later sections of this chapter and in Chapters 6 and 7, in which the implications of these ideas are explored. I recognize that some of the listed characteristics may not be directly relevant to self-contained activities – such as, for example, learning safety regulations – but they are relevant to the type of broad context in which the learning of specific information (or a specific skill) is most readily accomplished.

Point (vii) above acknowledges that there are important differences between individuals, and it means that how the other points are best interpreted depends on the individual learner. The set of characteristics as a whole, and in particular those in (iv) to (vii), implies that an environment that has no supportive social dimension is not learning-conducive. My claim is not that effective learning cannot take place without reference to supportive others but that people learn more when they function in an environment in which they can benefit from educational relationships (with peers and non-peers). This is true not only for children but also for adults, although the intensity and frequency of support required would seem, in general, to be less for adults than for children. So, again, although my account of Popperian selectionism in Part 1 of this book focuses on learning as an individual biological process, the account is not at odds with the idea that social factors have an important bearing on how human learning is advanced and promoted (as well as how it is curtailed).

5 Promoting the learning of others

In Chapter 1, I defined teaching as any activity undertaken on the part of one individual with the aspiration of helping another individual or group of individuals to learn. The teacher does not have to set out to teach anything in particular, and although intentionality is required, an awareness of the intention to promote learning is not intrinsic to the act of teaching. The activities of teaching are many and varied, but teachers, as individuals who wish to help others to learn, may be preoccupied with one or the other of two endeavours: they may be intent on *helping another or others to learn something in particular*, something conceived by them (the teachers) prior to and/or independent of their engagement with the learner, and something other than the general attributes associated with learning how to learn and the development of full learner autonomy; or they may have *a more general intention to promote learning*, without privileging any particular set of ideas or capabilities other than those that relate to learning in general.

Teaching, as construed here, is something that humans spend a great deal of time doing: we participate in exchanges not only with the intention of furthering our own learning but also that of others. Significant aspects of what we learn are a consequence of being taught. If we were not taught by our parents, other family members, our peers and, on a more formal basis, teachers in schools, colleges and universities, humans and human society would be very different. This is not to marginalize the importance of incidental learning and learning by (trial and error) attempts at imitation, but these activities alone are insufficient to enable a child to become functionally proficient in human society. Even an autodidact will have benefited from some teaching, particularly as a young child, and will have utilized materials produced by people motivated by the desire to promote learning in others. Of course, as stressed earlier in the book, what we learn is not necessarily what our teachers intend; often we do not learn what teachers wish us to learn, and invariably we learn things other than or in addition to this.

Teaching is at the heart of the idea of personalized support set out in (vii) of section 4 above; it is central to the idea of an educational relationship – that is, a relationship that supports learning. A school teacher, for example, can reflect on and strive to develop educational relationships between herself and groups of students (including whole classes and groups within classes) and individual students. Students, too, can develop educational relationships with each other, as individuals and groups (small and large). (Relationship skills for teachers are noted in Chapter 7, section 9.)

With regard to the general intention to promote the learning of another, the teacher-as-educator's general role, given a Popperian account of learning, is to encourage would-be learners to engage in autonomous, open-ended trial and error-elimination. The teacher will strive to offer learners a safe place in which to learn, one in which they can be permitted and helped to seek to identify mismatches between their current expectations and experience (actual and anticipated); problematize some of the mismatches that are discovered; create trial solutions; and test these solutions by subjecting them to critical scrutiny. In so doing, the teacher will strive to foster a belief in the value of imagination and creativity, a critical attitude towards ideas, and the confidence to take appropriate risks and learn from them. The teacher, to varying degrees (depending on the circumstances), will help would-be learners to develop their facility for descriptive and argumentative language, and their knowledge of, and ability to engage with, suitable resources – other people, ideas in the public domain, cultural artefacts and natural phenomena. And throughout these endeavours, the teacher will bear in mind that learning is an open-ended process that is, to a large extent, subject to unconscious and uncontrollable factors. The intention to provide a safe place in which to learn has implications for, among other things, the use of summative assessment (see the next section) and behaviour management practices. With regard to the latter, while rules, privileges and sanctions may be necessary to discourage and prevent behaviours which are undesirable because, for example, they inhibit the learning of other students, the purpose of any sanction should be to maintain the efficacy of the learning environment rather than to punish the student.

The teacher's role as described above is both facilitatory and critical, and is undertaken as part of an open-ended commitment to the promotion of human learning and in the service of the would-be learners. But supposing the teacher wants would-be learners to learn something in particular. What then must she do?

Most of what I have said above also applies to the teacher with a prescribed learning agenda. The difference is that the teacher will not, in the context of that agenda (and in some cases not ever), be inclined to encourage would-be learners to engage in *self-initiated* trial and error-elimination. The would-be learners' learning aspirations must – unless they are identical to those of the teacher – be suspended or distorted in favour of pursuing the teacher's intended outcomes. I do not wish to suggest that this is never an appropriate line to take: in many circumstances, there is a case to be made for communicating safety rules, teaching literacy and numeracy (see Chapter 7, section 7), encouraging the development of social skills, and so on. But if the teacher's agenda consistently overrides that of the would-be learners, they may fail to develop their capability for self-initiated learning; the capability may remain rudimentary or be applied only to learning in a limited range of problem areas. Moreover, when individuals' time is taken up with the learning agenda set by another person, this may distract them from focusing on, challenging and developing the expectations that have the greatest influence on the way they interact with the world.

Assuming a Popperian account of learning, the teacher with a prescribed learning agenda – such as a prescribed curriculum – must also come to terms with the fact that there is no direct transfer of ideas from her to the would-be learners. Therefore, the would-be learners still need the opportunity to engage in trial and error-elimination, and they must have the desire and will to do so. The teacher who knows what she wants others to learn sees her primary task as that of how to manipulate their will and interest – usually according to some notion of what is 'for their own good' or 'for the good of society'.

Teaching, like learning, is generally regarded as a good thing and, as indicated above, it is intrinsic to the human condition. But, like learning (see Chapter 2, section 3), the consequences of teaching are not always beneficial. Our teaching can, despite our good intentions, encourage learning that is detrimental to the learner's well-being and long-term learning. And we can, quite simply, waste others' time when they could be engaging in activities more conducive to learning. The learning that teachers should strive for in the short term is that which leads to greater learning in the longer term. We should, as far as possible, avoid creating situations in which students discover mismatches between their dispositions and experience only to adjust their dispositions in ways that discourage future learning. For example, a child may go to school thinking she can make mistakes without being penalized, only to discover that being seen to make a mistake results in some form of rebuke or sanction; she may thus learn to expect the discovery of error to be accompanied by an unpleasant experience. She may also judge that further unpleasant experiences can be avoided by not making (or by not being seen to make) mistakes. She may decide (probably unselfconsciously) that one of the best ways to avoid penalties is to do as little as possible, because the more one does, the greater the risk of errors or specific limitations being revealed. Clearly this may become a serious inhibition to learning.

Teaching is further complicated by the fact that individuals, including teachers, have multiple preferences and aims. Also, every individual is susceptible to engaging in actions and thought processes which embody conflicting values. Professional teachers, for example, collectively and individually have multiple reasons for their participation in an education system, and the institutions of such a system serve a number of different purposes. There are many reasons for the existence of teaching as a profession and for schools, colleges and universities as institutions. People want paid employment; some need the stimulus of students for their own research work; schools take care of children while their parents are at work. These and many other reasons, as they apply to professional teachers and their institutions, are not necessarily in conflict with student learning. But some of the functions of an education system may conflict with the provision of a learning service, in which case at least some of what teachers are individually and collectively expected to do within the system is likely to be at odds with the promotion of learning (see below and Chapter 6). Practices and structures develop which actually, if not intentionally, inhibit learning.

6 Educational settings unconducive to learning

In this section, I list some of the most significant environmental inhibitions to human learning found in educational settings, both formal and informal. In limiting the list to nine items, I am taking for granted that the student's physiological needs and many of her emotional needs are being met outside the educational setting. An educational setting may need to be more supportive and less challenging for a student whose basic physiological and emotional needs are not being met elsewhere. (Students who are so tired that they fall asleep in the classroom should not be woken in order to 'get on with their learning'.) For the purpose of this discussion, I am assuming that the educational setting is neither highly chaotic nor physically dangerous; although some classrooms and schools exhibit these characteristics, they are not the norm (at least not in primary schools and in secondary schools outside inner cities). For the most part, the listed characteristics pertain to formal schooling at the primary and secondary levels, but institutions of higher education are not immune to displaying some of them. My claim is not that the listed characteristics are present at all times in every part of every education system, or that they necessarily prevent learning; rather that many individuals experience these factors during the course of their education and that the presence of these factors serves to limit their learning. Students learn despite these inhibitions (see the second part of the quotation at the head of this chapter from Popper, 2002a [1945], p. 144), but without these inhibitions they could learn significantly more:

(i)   The student is *prevented from engaging in exploratory activity*, specifically activity which is self-initiated and self-directed, because she is coerced or manipulated into doing other things. For example, the individual is required, for much of the time, to listen to 'unwanted answers to unasked questions' and 'to study for the sake of passing examinations' (Popper, 1992a [1974], p. 40).

(ii) The student is, more generally, *discouraged from engaging in exploratory activity* – that is, discouraged from engaging in the most open-ended forms of trial and error-elimination – because the discovery of errors and specific limitations is often penalized by casual put-downs, punishment or other sanctions, or results in the individual being ignored or discriminated against in some other way. The learner does less to reduce the risk of negative responses.

(iii) Although self-monitoring, self-evaluation and self-regulation may be valued, *other-monitoring and external evaluation and regulation are the norm*. Student responsibility is conceived largely in terms of complying with teacher instructions and meeting prescribed standards. The environment offers limited support for the development of self-regulated responsibility and self-conceived standards.

(iv) The student is *discouraged from exercising autonomy* with regard to many of the decisions made about the what, when, how and why of her planned learning. These decisions, particularly those concerning what is to be learnt, are made independently of the student by those who devise education policy, that is, education policy makers and/or teachers. Consequently, the student is inhibited from developing the personal attributes associated with effective decision making of this kind – the attributes associated with the most effective patterns of lifelong learning.

(v) The student is encouraged to view her worth according to a *limited range of academic and vocational achievements*. Self-esteem and confidence then become factors of the student's success or failure in respect of a narrow range of prescribed standards. Students who do not readily achieve often learn to see themselves as failures and lose hope in their ability and potential as learners. Some of those who succeed may be anxious that their worth can be undermined at any time by the discovery that they do not deserve the recognition they have been given, and they are subsequently reluctant to extend their learning efforts into new fields of enquiry.

(vi) Assessment processes, formal and informal, are to a significant extent directed towards *evaluating the student* rather than towards the promotion of learning. Lack of early success in a field of endeavour is hastily attributed to lack of innate potential; the student is then categorized according to some notion of innate ability or potential in that field. Often, students are further attributed with generalized qualities: 'bright' or 'very able', 'average' or 'less able'. Students deemed less able are often given an impoverished curriculum, one which, for example, focuses on learning basic skills rather than a curriculum that provides more creative opportunities and allows for the development of deeper levels of understanding.

(vii) The student is encouraged to develop *values and beliefs that are unconducive to learning* (see, for example, the beliefs numbered (i) to (v) in section 2 above). As an illustration in respect of values, there are students who learn, in the context of classroom discussion, to value only what the teacher says and to disregard the contributions of their peers. Such students may see their own contributions largely in terms of whether they can provide the responses the teacher expects. Consequently, they may learn not to value their own potential to engage in more wide-ranging thought processes.

(viii) The student is given only *limited support for the development of argumentative language* and is, in particular, discouraged from engaging in critical discussion with regard to the social structures in which she is placed and the socially constructed information with which she is presented. The student is encouraged to be critical only in respect of her own achievements.

(ix) The environment is *generally impoverished with regard to stimuli and resources*. Resource availability is constrained not only by economic factors but also, and often more importantly, because access to resources is controlled by teachers, functioning as gatekeepers, who have a limited conception of what might be relevant to the student's learning. Students are denied access to objectified knowledge, including critical discussion, outside of what is specified in the prescribed curriculum. They are constrained to concentrate on problems and projects only within the periods of time determined by the teacher and/or school. They are not encouraged to regard each other as resources for mutual learning.

7 Significant impediments to learning in school

The evolutionary analysis of learning presented in Part 1 and the basic implications of the analysis set out in this chapter suggest that, if we wish to promote learning, we should be wary of corralling children and older students in environments that

(a) inhibit activity, particularly autonomous activity that is exploratory, self-initiated and self-directed

(b) discourage criticality and creativity

(c) suppress desire and curtail the exercise of preference

(d) generally limit opportunities for trial and error-elimination.

Education institutions, particularly those for older children and adolescents, are, however, very often environments of this constraining kind.

Curtailing self-initiated trial and error-elimination

Self-initiated trial and error-elimination is, from the early years, increasingly curtailed and is usually little encouraged again until – for those students who stay with the system – the doctoral level (and even then it is often restricted). Opportunities for teacher-initiated trial and error-elimination are also often limited, although some recent initiatives with regard to formative assessment promote such activity. Teachers are being encouraged, for example, to develop classroom dialogue and promote peer- and self-assessment of students' work. These initiatives notwithstanding, it is still true to say that in most schools and classrooms there is surprisingly little student activity, and even less activity that is likely to be conducive to the kind of learning that leads to further learning in the longer term, both within school and without. And the formative assessment movement, though valuable in the pursuit of pedagogical improvement, does not address what I see as the tyranny of the prescribed curriculum (discussed in greater detail in Chapter 6). Students are rarely encouraged to adopt a trial-and-error approach to the assumptions that underlie their engagement with anything other than what their teachers want them to learn; seldom are they encouraged to initiate and develop their own formal programmes of learning.

The limited opportunities for trial-and-error activity that I have noted are supported by the ideas that student learning can be controlled by the teacher and that the outcomes of teaching and learning are largely predictable. Both of these ideas are consistent with what I call the myth of learning by instruction from without (Chapter 2, section 8). Of course, one does not have to be a Popperian in order to doubt their truth, but Popper's selectionist theory offers ammunition, so to speak, in this regard. If learning by instruction from without is a myth, and if it is better to view learning as invariably a critical and creative process of trial and error-elimination, then the advancement of learning through education and teaching is not a matter of presenting people with basic information and helping them to interpret and utilize it. Rather, it is a matter of encouraging people to create ideas and test them. To return to one of the earlier quotations from Popper (1979 [1972], p. 148 – see my Chapter 3, section 3), 'imaginative criticism' is the means by which we 'transcend our local and temporal environment'. I suggest that formal systems of education generally do very little to bring about the transcendence that Popper describes.

Of course, students learn something when they are taught – they could scarcely do otherwise – but what they learn is often not what their teachers intend. More importantly, we need to entertain the idea that students' learning may be significantly less than it might be. We should not be complacent about the success of our education institutions; we have the potential to 'do education' much better.

Those who teach, administer or make policy on the assumption that there can be learning by instruction from without tend to practise and formulate policy as if what is learnt in school is what is taught. What is assessed is what is explicitly taught; the broader and longer-term consequences of being taught in a school are not considered. No matter then, for example, that students who are *taught about democracy* most often *learn the practices of authoritarianism* – because the way they are taught in school consistently conveys to them the importance of being biddable and constrains them from developing as fully autonomous learners.

Traditionally, educationists have vastly underestimated the human potential for imaginative criticism – because they have not recognized the extent to which it lies at the heart of what we, including the youngest children, do in order to succeed at even the most basic tasks. When educationists act on the assumption that there is some transference of information from environment to learner, they tend to focus their efforts on what they think they can control – on their own input as policy makers or teachers. The natural inclination of children to engage in exploratory activity – trial and error-elimination – is then curtailed. What cannot be controlled tends to be viewed with suspicion rather than treated as the primary resource. It follows that teachers initiate most of the planned learning activities, and students are expected to rely on teachers for fundamental decisions about what to do and when to do it. Mostly, students are not encouraged to question or criticize the material with which they are presented. The task of the student is to learn the syllabus, not question it. For much of the time, students are expected to replicate the arguments of others rather than develop arguments of their own. Creativity is a concept largely confined to 'the arts', and outside of those fields of activity (and to some degree even within them) it is not usually encouraged.

Formal education worldwide is largely controlled and organized by people who wish, perhaps for all the right reasons, to instruct, people who are preoccupied with a desire that children, adolescents and older students learn specific things – things that they, the controllers and organizers, deem it important to teach. Thus a major obstacle to the exploitation of Popperian selectionism in educational practice is that those who wield the most power within formal systems are largely disinclined to favour the open-ended pursuit of learning and are not predisposed to encourage either imagination or free-ranging criticality.

Penalizing the discovery of error and specific limitation

Anyone who believes that discoveries of error and specific limitation are crucial to learning will be perturbed by the extent to which formal education discourages such discoveries. As mentioned earlier, not only are opportunities to engage in trial and error-elimination limited in formal education institutions, many schools are also unsafe places in which to discover errors and inadequacies, because revealing them often occasions a penalty of some kind. In schools worldwide, teachers are expected to produce students who give 'the right answers' and perform tasks according to narrowly conceived standards. In such circumstances, teachers will often be inclined to penalize failure to understand, failure to give the prescribed answer, failure to agree, and failure to conform to narrowly conceived norms. In general, 'getting it wrong' is likely to result in a loss of esteem, a lowering of teacher expectations and less 'high quality' attention.

Some readers may wish to argue that school students need to learn the ways of the world outside of school, and learning that there are penalties for failure is part of this. But schools and their teachers have a more important, overarching role to play: that of promoting student learning in general. When any of us expects the discovery of error and specific limitation to incur a penalty, we are likely to try to avoid such discoveries: we do less, we learn less. In the worst of circumstances, doing less becomes habitual. Perhaps the most damaging consequence of penalizing the discovery of error and specific limitation is not that learning opportunities are lost in specific contexts (as in 'I'll maintain a low profile in this place' or ' . . . with this person'), but that some individuals learn to associate the discovery of error or specific limitation with some form of sanction, and they operate on that assumption (a learnt expectation) in situations in which it does not apply (in which penalties will not be forthcoming).

The tendency to penalize the discovery of error and specific limitation seems to be contingent on the way that schools are instrumental in the process of social selection that influences post-school opportunities, wealth and status. For many students – indeed, for most school students in England – the selection process is introduced into their education at an early age. The status of students, teachers and schools alike is determined by the extent to which the students 'do well' in school. Doing well equates with grasping the prescribed curriculum or, more accurately, with passing prescribed tests and examinations. In such a system, it is all too easy for a mismatch between the student and the curriculum to be construed as failure on the part of the student. The failure of students may be blamed to varying degrees on the students themselves, their parents, teachers and the education institutions. This failure is often implicitly construed to be a failure of transmission.

A society able to operate without the selection of individuals is an unlikely prospect, but, in general, selection systems do not encourage everyone to compete – many people give up – and they discourage individuals from revealing their ignorance and incapacity as a prelude to development. When the function of education institutions and their employees is the selection of individuals, criticism – in a variety of subtle but inhibiting forms – is applied to the student rather than encouraged on the part of the student. At the societal level, imagination is fostered with regard to developing ways of selecting individuals for subsequent life opportunities – in the development of summative tests and examinations – not in the trial-and-error activities of students (see Popper, 2002a [1945], chapter 7, section 5, including the first part of the quotation at the head of this chapter, from p. 143).

I am not making a case for the outright rejection of public examinations and externally accredited qualifications, and particularly not in the case of adults and adolescents aged 14 years or older. Standards of competence are always an issue in the awarding of qualifications, and when students make errors (which may include errors of omission) and demonstrate certain specific limitations, they may not receive the desired qualification. However, if a qualification is to be more than a rubber stamp for the knowledge and capabilities which students brought to their course of study at the outset, they must necessarily discover errors and specific limitations in their thinking and other activities during the period of study. Moreover, the best courses, by encouraging a positive attitude to the discovery of error and specific limitation, are vehicles for a considerable amount of learning of a less prescriptive nature.

Given the human predilection to create false dualisms, I suspect that some readers may at this point be under the impression that what I am proposing as an alternative to the present state of affairs is some kind of laissez-faire system of schooling in which students are encouraged to do what they like without reference to thoughts about standards and without critical evaluation and accountability. As will become clear in the remaining chapters, such an impression is mistaken. What I propose is neither an endorsement nor a mere modification of conventional approaches to teaching in education institutions. Nor is it an abandonment of structure, standards and accountability.

6 Against the Intensive Use of Prescribed Curricula with Children and Adolescents

There are no subject matters; no branches of learning – or, rather, of inquiry: there are only problems, and the urge to solve them.

—Karl Popper, Realism and the Aim of Science

If I thought of a future, I dreamt of one day founding a school in which young people could learn without boredom, and would be stimulated to pose problems and discuss them; a school in which no unwanted answers to unasked questions would have to be listened to; in which one did not study for the sake of passing examinations.

—Karl Popper, Unended Quest: An Intellectual Autobiography

Introduction

Given what is known about learning, as set out in Part 1, and given the broad implications for promoting and inhibiting learning, as discussed in Chapter 5, in this chapter I make the case for reducing the use of prescribed curricula in formal education and for largely replacing their use – particularly for students who are children or adolescents – with student-initiated curricula, that is, curricula conceived and formulated by students as a means of advancing their own learning. The thrust of my argument is this: the use of prescribed curricula originates in mistaken assumptions about learning, and the intensive use of prescribed curricula with young learners restricts the development of learner autonomy – crucial for lifelong learning. Moreover, the intensive use of prescribed curricula embodies and promulgates negative values associated with coercion and social and personal manipulation.

My discussion assumes two ideas with regard to values. First, an educational practice may have unintended consequences that conflict with the espoused values of the teachers and policy makers who are responsible for the practice. Second, the way in which students are treated during the course of their education embodies values, and these are as much a part of values education as the values that teachers explicitly set out to teach. The values that a student learns from the process of being taught may not be those that the teacher explicitly sets out to teach.

I acknowledge that currently, and for some time to come, most teachers in formal education institutions will be required to work with prescribed curricula, at least to some degree and for part of the time. But if teachers and educationists in general begin to think differently – that is, to challenge more vigorously the theory, policy and practice of prescribed curricula – there is the potential for different and better practices to develop. Note also that it is the *intensive* use of prescribed curricula with children and adolescents that I am challenging in this chapter; I am not suggesting that teachers should never have a prescribed agenda or that prescribed curricula are always inappropriate in the context of post-school courses leading to professional qualifications. The question of what should be taught to all children is discussed in Chapter 7, sections 7 and 8. (For relevant discussion of how to organize studies leading to professional qualifications, see Meighan and Siraj-Blatchford, 2003 [1981], pp. 236–43; Burgess, 1999; Pratt and Cocking, 1999.)

1 The ubiquity of prescribed curricula

It is said that travel broadens the mind. Features of one's home environment hitherto taken for granted are challenged by what one experiences elsewhere.

One begins to think differently and, very often, to behave differently. But as far as expanding one's view of education is concerned, travel – whether actual, by visiting education institutions abroad, or virtual, by studying first-hand accounts, film, the internet, and so on – is unlikely to provoke a re-evaluation of core assumptions about the responsibilities of the student in a formal educational setting. The national curriculum and its related structures for children and adolescents in England, as discussed in section 3 below, represent (at the time of writing) an extreme approach to curriculum prescription, and the situation in other countries will inevitably be somewhat different (and this is true even of countries within the United Kingdom – Scotland's national curriculum, for example, is not statutory); but in schools and classrooms worldwide, decisions about curriculum content are usually made not by the students themselves, but by teachers, the school board, the local education authority or the central government. Students are sometimes given a menu of curriculum options from which to choose, but if they would prefer to learn something completely different, this predilection will seldom be catered to or even acknowledged. Student-initiated curricula are rare within formal education.

'Quite right, too', some readers may respond. Others may think that the development of student-initiated curricula is appropriate for older students but not for the very young. Others still may regard the idea as fine in principle but impractical for normal classes in ordinary schools. This chapter and Chapter 7 are designed to challenge the assumptions of readers who fall into any of these three categories.

The relationship between the development of student-initiated curricula and the development of learner autonomy can be empirically investigated (see Chapter 9). But funding priorities tend to dictate what gets researched. Those individuals currently responsible for decisions about research funding are not, generally speaking, interested in testing hypotheses about the relative merits of using prescribed curricula and student-initiated curricula. As acknowledged in Chapter 1, some readers may wish to argue that the conventional approach to the curriculum has been tested and found to work. But what I mean by testing in this context is the formulation of a hypothesis that could potentially be refuted and the search for refuting evidence (see, e.g., Popper, 1972a [1934], chapter 1). It means investigating the unintended and potentially undesirable consequences of action (Popper, 1961 [1957], section 21). It means judging a theory or course of action in the context of competing alternatives and giving each of these a fair hearing. That a particular way of doing things has been accepted practice for centuries does not mean that it, or any of the assumptions embedded in it, has been rigorously tested. Of course, not all practices require testing (nor could they all be tested), but the traditional approach to education has been widely criticized, and it is therefore an appropriate candidate for testing.

The practice of planning a curriculum without the involvement of the students for whom it is designed originates from a time before constructivist theories of learning had begun to be influential. The basic tenet of constructivism – that learning is an active process requiring of the learner a personal interpretation of experience and the construction of her (or his) own knowledge – stands in contrast to the historically more dominant idea that learning is to a significant extent a passive process, involving the transmission of information from the social and/or physical environment to the learner, mediated in the context of education by a teacher.

If one believes that learning involves the passive receipt of information, curriculum development and pedagogy can be treated as separate concerns. The task of the curriculum developer (who may also be the teacher) is to decide what is to be taught – the concepts, facts, values and attitudes deemed to be appropriate and worthwhile – and the task of the classroom teacher is to present the material to students in such a way that they can imbibe it. Yet students tend to be more active than the teacher anticipates; they will try to make sense, for example, of unarticulated features of the situation in which they find themselves (including what sociologists have called the 'hidden curriculum'). Whatever the teaching approach, students will invariably learn things additional to, if not different from, those the teacher intended.

Constructivist approaches to teaching, with or without a prescribed curriculum, are explicitly designed to encourage greater activity – thinking, in particular – on the part of the students. But even if one accepts that the core tenet of constructivism constitutes a valid account of learning, it does not follow that the use of prescribed curricula has been undermined. Constructivism in its basic form problematizes the transmission of curriculum content, recognizes the importance of teachers interacting with students, and supports the idea that students learn more when they are actively engaged in the learning process. However, it seems that most constructivist educators do not exclude the possibility of learning from transmission; they generally assume that some learning is the result of some processes in which the learner is passive. Also, as discussed in Part 1, Popperian constructivism differs from most other forms of constructivism in that it challenges the idea that learning can take place *by* instruction from without the learner, which is not to deny that learning takes place *in response to* instruction. Learning in response to instruction is explained by trial and error-elimination – and, indeed, all of the activities in which teachers and students engage can be explained in this way.

The idea of education-as-transmission endures in part as a view of how some learning takes place and in part as a metaphor for a process of enculturation. It is consistent with what many teachers and policy makers intuitively feel to be true or regard as common sense, and its resource implications appear, at face value, to be preferable to the implications of the idea that learning is always a process of trial and error-elimination without any direct transmission of information from the environment. Educating in accordance with the transmission metaphor *seems* both reasonable and cost effective, and the use of prescribed curricula *seems* to be the most effective and efficient means of transmission.

2 Tyrrell Burgess's legacy for the curriculum

Early in 1976, I was a full-time primary school teacher working to complete my MA dissertation, entitled 'Karl Popper: some implications for the curriculum' (Swann, 1976). 'Some' in this title was used advisedly, and perhaps 'a few' would have been more correct. For although I understood the radical nature of Popper's evolutionary epistemology and rightly suspected that it had radical implications for teaching and the curriculum, I could not claim to have made any significant progress in conceiving what the range of these implications might be.

I then came across an article, 'Choice is not enough – go for responsibility', published in *Where, the Education Magazine for Parents*. The author, Tyrrell Burgess, made no mention of Popper, but as I read the article I became aware that he was a Popperian: 'knowledge is a matter of posing problems, of solving them and of testing the solutions' (Burgess, 1975, p. 6) – a view which Burgess contrasted with the traditional idea of knowledge as 'an infinite accumulation of facts, arranged in subjects' (ibid., p 5). I discovered also what I had hitherto been unable to conceive for myself, namely, that for school curricula to be consistent with Popper's epistemology they must be developed by the children and adolescents themselves, albeit with the support of teachers and parents, not least because for most of us the urgent need is to solve our own problems, and this is as true of children as of adults. What we need to know depends on what we want to do. It is method that gives mastery, not information.

(Ibid., p. 6)

Noting that 'On the traditional view of knowledge, a "curriculum" of a set of subjects is inevitable; on the problem-based view it is absurd' (ibid.), Burgess proceeded to outline how to develop a problem-based education. In just 1,000 words, he provided a well-argued procedure for the teaching of adolescents in secondary schools. Much of what he wrote is also broadly applicable to teaching in primary schools and, as I discovered slightly later, the core ideas were already being practically exploited in higher education at the School for Independent Study – founded in 1974, with Burgess as the first Head of School – at what was then North East London Polytechnic (NELP) (now the University of East London). The following quotations give a flavour of Burgess's insight:

The first step would be to help a group of pupils to formulate their problems. This is a serious business, and would need to take some time. It would not be enough to have a discussion one morning and think that has settled the matter. People are so unused to formulating problems that they need time to consider and reconsider. Most people do not discuss problems at all, but jump straight to a solution and spend their time worrying about that. What is more, there is a need to be clear about the problems of individuals, so as to see which of these the whole group, or most members of it, have in common. We must avoid imposing problems on people for all the world as if they were a curriculum.

(Ibid.)

The next task is the proposal of solutions – and these solutions will be the programme of study and activity which each individual proposes to follow, both on his own and in groups. . . . the role of the group teacher will be crucial. He or she will be a provider – of reference, background and library material; of personal tuition and instruction; of the resources of the rest of the school, both human and material. . . . No specialist will teach unless somebody or some group has asked him to do so. Gone for ever is the captive audience, making the best of a bad job under the pre-ordained curriculum.

(Ibid.)

The final step in all this is the testing of solutions. Pupils, parents and teachers need to know how far the planned programmes have actually met the problems they were designed to solve. . . . They [the pupils] need to be self-conscious, not only about their problems and programmes but also about the status of their own achievements. The question of assessment becomes less the jumping through of externally designed hoops than an essential element in personal responsibility for one's school life and work.

(Ibid.)

Burgess also outlined two means by which accountability could be achieved:

First, the whole educational organisation of the school can be reported to the governors or managers, and can be approved by them. . . . It would secure the public interest in the plans of individual schools.

The second check is the inspectorate . . . If the inspectors were to inspect – the work of the pupils in formulating problems, the progress of the proposed solutions, the tests employed to measure failure – they would not only be earning their money but would be making a serious educational contribution.

(Ibid., p. 7)

The reference above to measuring failure jars with what I and, indeed, Burgess himself came to consider as appropriate practice. Burgess, working with Betty Adams, later undertook significant theoretical and practical work on the processes of recording and recognizing student achievement (see, e.g., Burgess and Adams, 1985; Adams and Burgess, 1992).

With regard to accountability, in the School for Independent Study, students' individual programmes of study were validated by an external validation board, after first being validated internally (see Stephenson, 1981, pp. 150–3). The outcomes of students' studies were then validated in much the same way as other higher education qualifications in the United Kingdom, that is, through a process involving external examiners and an assessment board (ibid., pp. 154–5). Academic procedures and standards were overseen by the Council for National Academic Awards, which accredited the qualifications. Detailed proposals for developing similar practices in secondary schools are set out in Burgess and Adams (1985).

Burgess went beyond Karl Popper in exploring the implications of Popper's epistemology for the curriculum and summative assessment. Though as a young man Popper worked as a school teacher in Vienna (Popper, 1992a [1974], section 1; Hacohen, 2000, chapter 3), as a professional philosopher he did not attempt to publish a detailed and fully coherent educational theory. There are, however, a fair number of references to educational matters scattered throughout his works. For example, writing of university education, he referred to 'the myth of the subject' (Popper, 1985a [1956], p. 5, and see the first quotation at the head of this chapter, taken from the same page). Speaking about the education of children in an interview, he was critical of the national curriculum in England: 'What is being taught does not follow the interest of the teacher or the interest of the children. And these, I think are more important than the actual content of what is being taught' (Popper quoted in Bailey, 1995, p. 186). But it is not clear that Popper conceived of problem-based student-initiated curricula – 'What is valuable is that the child learns to interest himself in this or that subject' (Popper quoted in Bailey, ibid.) – and nowhere in print did Popper flesh out a means of realizing his educational dream (see the second quotation at the head of this chapter from Popper, 1992a [1974], p. 40). His critical view of the function of schools is evident in his suggestion that their only purpose is 'to get the children out of the way' (Popper, 1999, p. 48).

The totality of Burgess's educational writings presents a conception of curriculum, summative assessment and institutional structures which shows how Popper's (oft-quoted) dream can be realized in a way that is consistent with both Popper's epistemology and his concept of an open society (in addition to the publications cited above and below, see, e.g., Burgess, 1981, 1985a, 1986, 1992, 1999, 2000; Burgess and Adams, 1980; Adams and Burgess, 1980, 1989). Burgess's prose is packed not only with contextual detail but also with general educational principles which today's reader can reinterpret for her own situation.

3 A stumbling block in the way of Popperian curriculum development

My own formal studies worked out well. I received my MA, despite the aforementioned limitation of my dissertation. As a prospective PhD student, I met Burgess in 1978, and this marked the beginning of a 30-year collaboration. First, with the benefit of many convivial and thought-provoking conversations, supported by my reading of Burgess (1977 and 1979, in particular), in my practice as a primary school teacher I was able to adapt, exploit and develop (see Chapter 7) the principles I had initially encountered in 'Choice is not enough – go for responsibility' (Burgess, 1975). My research towards my doctorate included not only theoretical studies but also action research undertaken during a six-year period (1981–87) as a teacher of children in the age range of 7 to 11 years at a state-funded primary school in a social priority area of Inner London.

Naïvely, I had thought the world was on its way to becoming full of Popperians, or at least post-Popperians, and that Burgess's ideas, as exploited in the School for Independent Study (in addition to Burgess, 1977, see Stephenson, 1980, 1981, and Cross, 1988), would become common currency. I had not anticipated a widespread resistance to engaging with Popper's philosophy (for discussion see Burgess and Swann, 2003). Nor had I foreseen a massive increase in central government control of education in England and Wales, as made statutory in the Education Reform Act (ERA) 1988, and the direction that UK higher education policy was subsequently to take. ERA 1988, among other things, gave the Secretary of State for Education a vast number of new powers, which various incumbents of the post have not been loath to exploit. With the introduction of the national curriculum, which to all intents and purposes made the rigorous and sustained adoption of a problem-based approach to education illegal in state-funded primary and secondary schools in England and Wales, I left primary school teaching. I was awarded my doctorate (Swann, 1988) and I joined the ranks of education academics in 1989 – after 17 years of full-time employment as a school teacher (in primary schools and, briefly, in support services).

ERA 1988 destroyed 'a uniquely rational and humane form of educational administration' (Burgess, 1989). It was an outcome of ideological changes in English politics which accompanied a sustained period of Conservative government (as discussed in Wragg, 1988). In debate, the failings of one particular school were often cited as evidence that radical change of the kind introduced by ERA 1988 was needed. But in the same way that 'one swallow does not a summer make', so too William Tyndale Junior School (in London), as the famously problematic school in question (see, e.g., Auld, 1976), did not represent the wealth and variety of innovative and good educational practice that was going on in English and Welsh schools prior to the statutory changes brought about by ERA 1988. There were, of course, weaknesses in the system – as the case of William Tyndale Junior School highlighted – but there were at that time alternative and better ways of developing formal education. Most importantly, there still are.

It is worth noting that the prescription of a national curriculum and the associated emphasis on examination results flew in the face of evidence compiled by John Raven (1977) from large-scale studies undertaken in Great Britain and the Republic of Ireland. He found that students (at secondary school and of sixth form age in full-time further education) and their teachers alike rated 'self-initiated competences and qualities of character' as the most important goals of education, above 'academic knowledge content' (ibid., Part III). Raven found there was 'substantial agreement between pupils, parents and teachers that many of the most important objectives of education receive only scant attention in the classroom' (ibid., p. 95). Goals shared by the students, parents and teachers who were surveyed were those summarized by Raven as 'self-motivated, pro-active, rather than reactive characteristics'. He continued, 'They are quite different from the sort of reactive characteristics most commonly taught and evaluated in classrooms' (ibid.). ERA 1988 did nothing to address this discrepancy between aspiration and practice in schools in England and Wales. Indeed, sooner or later it served to curtail virtually all the educational initiatives that, if expanded, had the potential to improve schools along the lines that Raven and the majority of survey respondents had conceived.

As an academic, at various times during a 20-year period, I supervised student school experience placements in nurseries and primary schools and taught education studies to pre-service teachers and others (in England), spent a month working in a HighScope nursery for one of my 'recent and relevant' experiences, taught research methodology and qualitative methods at the master's degree and doctoral levels (in England and New Zealand), and engaged in funded empirical research (in England and Scotland). But I never again had an opportunity to develop student-initiated curricula with large groups of students. In the absence of opportunities to develop student-initiated curricula in practice, I have spent time developing the argument in its favour. I also refined my account of how the practice of developing student-initiated curricula, as a significant element of a broader Popperian approach to teaching, could be tested as part of a science of education (Swann, 2003a, and Chapter 9 of this book).

The School for Independent Study, despite its acknowledged success, was dismantled in 1991. And, as indicated above, one function of ERA 1988 and the aftermath has been to severely constrain educational innovation in the state-funded sector – other than those initiatives that chime with the ideology of central government, an ideology that with New Labour administrations (1997–2010) became increasingly authoritarian.

Another consequence of ERA 1988 and the aftermath – which includes an intensive centralized summative assessment regime, linked to national league tables – is that school and college leavers join the jobs market or universities having previously been constrained from expressing and fully developing independence of thought and judgement, and from reflecting critically on established social norms and currently accepted ideas. Moreover, their experience of formal learning from the early years onwards has been heavily directed towards success at externally conceived tests and examinations, rather than towards solving individually or collaboratively conceived problems. Of course, many elements of this state of affairs preceded the introduction of ERA 1988; but the deadening grip of central government has served to repress creativity, criticality and personal initiative much more systematically and 'effectively' than hitherto. Even worse, the value of the individual student, and indeed the value of the teacher, have been made subordinate to the value attached to measurable success according to a limited range of largely pedestrian standards (for an account of the emotional effects of this, see Thorne, 2001). Despite the best efforts of many who work in education, the system treats people – students and teachers alike – as means to various ends. As Jenni Russell, writing in the *Guardian* newspaper (2009), put it,

> The chief business of schools is no longer to produce educated people, but education statistics. For the first few years of Labour, the vast majority of the population could be impressed by those. But as more children went into the system, and more school-leavers emerged from it, the faster it became apparent to parents, students, employers and universities that there was a disastrous mismatch between the claims made by the figures and the reality of bored[,] stressed and puzzlingly under-educated teenagers emerging from it.

Despite the booster rhetoric of politicians and their appointees (and despite some nominal improvements in examination and test results), England's lengthy period of central control of the school curriculum failed to deliver hoped-for improvements in learning. On a more optimistic note, there are signs that as they see the judgements of others fail, school teachers in England – particularly teachers of younger children – are regaining confidence in their own professional judgements.

4 Some undesirable consequences of prescribed curricula

There is nothing wrong with wanting students to learn specific ideas and skills. The trouble is that most of us can list a great many things we think other individuals and groups, particularly children and adolescents, should learn. And although each of these things may be potentially valuable and appropriate, when assembled as a prescribed curriculum, undesirable consequences may ensue. The scale of such consequences will depend on the specific circumstances, including the proportion of the student's time devoted to prescribed curricula. Also significant is the extent to which teaching and learning are part of a process of social selection that influences post-school opportunities, wealth and status (see Chapter 5, section 7). But regardless of the extent to which, in a particular context, formal education is used as an instrument of selection, I would argue that the intensive use of prescribed curricula has five generalized consequences that conflict in the long term with the promotion of learning:

(i) *Learnt dependency:* Babies and toddlers engage in self-initiated and self-directed trial and error-elimination. This, for example, is how they learn to walk and talk. They may need to be helped and encouraged, but walking and talking are things children practise spontaneously – they do not do these things only at the behest of an adult. In general, much of a child's early trial-and-error activity can be construed as play (Petersen, 1988). It is entered into for its own sake – there is no extrinsic goal – but it would nevertheless seem to be a crucial aspect of the child's development. After entering formal education, this self-initiated activity is usually increasingly curtailed rather than cultivated. Curriculum developers may argue that their curriculum will enable students to develop greater independence, and various components of it may indeed have that potential; but the overall package, by virtue of being conceived and initiated by persons other than the students, constrains their development as fully autonomous learners. One of the significant things that most school students learn is dependency, in particular dependency with regard to the direction and content of their planned programmes of learning.

When students become apathetic, disaffected or rebellious, it is usually viewed as evidence that they cannot be trusted to take responsibility for their learning. These traits tend to be perceived as personal failings or inadequacies rather than a consequence of the way they have been treated in school. When teaching, schooling and education fail to lead to hoped-for learning and desired developments in society as a whole, the route to improvement may be construed as an intensification of the same – a more detailed and time-consuming prescription for what students should be taught. Instead, teachers, educationists and education policy makers should, I suggest, consider the possibility that restricting autonomous activity has negative consequences in respect of the attitudes, motivation and behaviour of children and adolescents, with implications for the kind of society they subsequently contribute to and help to develop.

(ii) *The marginalization of student preferences:* In the context of compulsory education, when students are reluctant to engage with the prescribed curriculum, the teacher's task becomes that of manipulating the students' will and interest, usually on the understanding that it is done 'for their own good', 'for the good of the school' or 'for the good of society' (as raised in Chapter 5, section 5).

Teaching becomes manipulative and coercive; instead of doing things *with* the students, things are done *to* them.

Even when students are prepared to try to learn what is expected – either out of interest or because of the promise of rewards or the threat of sanctions – this does not mean they are exercising preference. There may be many things not included in the prescribed curriculum that they would prefer to learn about or become able to do, including things that they, if given the opportunity, would decide they need to learn about, or to do, in order to develop as individuals. Some of the preferences of some students may be deemed by the teacher, school or society as a whole to be undesirable (or too expensive to address), but many student preferences are marginalized merely because they are not shared by, or were not imagined by, those responsible for curriculum development. I stress that it is one thing to say that some interests are undesirable and should not be pursued (e.g. bullying, torture and the dissemination of pornography), and quite another to specify what should be pursued.

After a long period of not being allowed to exercise preference, students may lose touch with the kinds of things they would prefer to do, and, even if this does not occur, the opportunity to develop their preferences will be stifled by the need to spend time on one or more of the options that have been determined by others. What they learn is to subordinate themselves to others, not in the spirit of collaboration but in order to fit into the education system. There are often penalties for those who fail to conform or meet expected predefined standards. This amounts to oppression.

(iii)   *Inadequate and inappropriate criticism:* Admittedly, in the context of prescribed curricula, some students become competent in the subjects they are taught. But often they remain incredibly naïve about crucial aspects of day-to-day living. A prescribed curriculum leads teachers to ignore – that is, leave unchallenged and unexplored – a wide range of assumptions the students bring to the classroom. Ideas relating to everyday experiences are sometimes grouped to become the subject of personal, health and social education (PHSE). PHSE may enable students to reflect on and address their own experience and it may challenge some of the assumptions they bring to the classroom. It may function in this way, for example, when 'circle time' approaches are adopted. But circle time is a method, not a curriculum. When PHSE becomes just another element of the prescribed curriculum, its content is more likely to become inflexible and to focus more on students as a generic group than on the experiences and assumptions of individuals.

Much of the criticism that children and young people experience focuses on their interactions (or lack of interaction) with prescribed curricula. As discussed in Chapter 5, section 7, if the teacher is under pressure to get the students to achieve what has been prescribed, she may be inclined to chide the students for the limitations of their performance. Although challenge and criticism are integral to learning, the criticism that aids learning is that which challenges ideas rather than the person. (But even criticism of this kind is not always appropriate – see Chapter 3, section 3; Chapter 5, section 2; Chapter 7, section 3.) Criticism that focuses on the person tends to undermine self-esteem and self-confidence and inhibit trial and error-elimination.

(iv) *The perpetuation of negative values:* People learn not only in response to what they are told and shown, but also in response to what they experience and observe on their own initiative. Students may be told about the importance of respect for persons and the development of learner autonomy, and about the potential value of diversity, and they may learn to espouse similar values. But if what they experience in person or see happening to others exemplifies a lack of respect, a preoccupation with conformity and the coercive and manipulative treatment of people, and if the practices in which these negative values are embedded are not challenged, then for many students these values will become taken-for-granted aspects of the human condition.

(v) *Loss of faith in formal education:* What students experience in school on a day-to-day basis is often a mix of boredom and confusion. Of course, there will be some things that students need to learn (see Chapter 7, sections 7 and 8), and there is clearly a role for teachers in stimulating students to consider ideas beyond their previous experience (see Chapter 5). But when a teacher introduces ideas and activities that are not a direct response to a student's expressed interests, or cannot be related in the student's mind to something that she perceives to be important, then the student may become bored or confused.

As a way of dealing with a diet of 'unwanted answers to unasked questions' (Popper, 1992a [1974], p. 40), some students for much of the time, and nearly all students for some of the time, 'turn off'. Some, particularly in secondary schools, engage with the teacher but in an adversarial way (they are disruptive). Some students consistently make a sustained effort to make sense of and 'take on board' what they are given, particularly in light of the penalties for not learning what is expected. They learn a number of (alleged) facts (often uncritically) and disparate skills, but these are not properly integrated, and this learning is primarily undertaken with the aim of pleasing the teachers, keeping out of trouble, and passing the examinations – instead of learning for the students' own purposes. For many students, the totality of what they learn in school does not make sense to them. They are not encouraged to reflect critically on the experience of schooling, so their negative experiences are viewed by them either as the result of their own limitations or are attributed to the nature of formal education. When such students enter higher education, they may be surprisingly lacking in confidence and/or be more inclined to view their chosen course of study purely as a means of gaining the specified qualification – the idea of learning for transcendence is missing and/or they have lost faith in the potential value of formal education.

The negative consequences of the use of prescribed curricula have been acknowledged and discussed by various teachers and educationists. One does not have to have a Popperian view of learning in order to make the above general observations and share the values these observations imply. But a Popperian view of learning, by shedding a different light on sociological and psychological issues, adds to the weight of argument in favour of making piecemeal, but nonetheless fundamental, changes in the way decisions about curriculum content are made. Quite simply, Popperian evolutionary epistemology supports the idea that formal teaching and learning should be problem-based rather than subject-based; more radically, it proposes that all learning takes place through the activity of the student and that, despite what may seem to be the case, nothing in the way of information is transmitted from teacher to student. And, following Popper, analogies and metaphors which present the educational process in terms of teacher transmission or delivery and learner receipt or absorption can be supplanted by a logically coherent and biologically credible account of what happens when learning takes place, one in which the concepts of expectation, preference, criticism and creativity are crucial (see Part 1 of this book).

Teachers, educationists and policy makers who defend national prescribed curricula often advance the argument that a national prescribed curriculum works in favour of equal opportunity. But such an argument ignores the significance of the student's preferences and expectations in her learning. When we acknowledge the central role of the student in her learning, we can see that a national curriculum in fact works against equality of opportunity because, given that children's and adolescents' expectations, preferences and values are varied, the practice of offering all school students the same curriculum means that some get a curriculum more suited to their requirements than others (Swann, 2000a).

Other common arguments in favour of national prescribed curricula include those relating to (a) school and teacher accountability, (b) progression when moving from one year group to the next and (c) ease of transfer if a student moves from one part of the country to another (see, e.g., Department of Education and Science/Welsh Office, 1987, pp. 2–5). The first of these can be dealt with by proposing a model of accountability that is not dependent on a common curriculum for all children and adolescents (see my Chapter 10, section 9); (b) and (c) can be entirely dissolved by the sustained use of student-initiated curricula – because planned learning is consistently dependent on the individual student, not the age cohort. Of course, national curricula are more generally introduced with the explicit purpose of raising standards. These standards are specified, and people are encouraged to work towards them. If standards are subsequently seen to rise, claims will be made that educational provision has improved. However, in working towards specific standards, overall levels of achievement in the broader sense are depressed; the idea of achieving specific standards deflects people from trying to achieve in the broader sense.

The effectiveness of a national curriculum is unlikely to be tested properly, not merely because those responsible for its design have a vested interest in its apparent success, but also because, by being applied nationally, the scope for empirical comparisons between different approaches to the curriculum is limited. The imposition of a national curriculum restricts the opportunity to develop and test alternative approaches, at least within the state-funded sector.

5 In support of student-initiated curricula

Some readers may view the degree of coercion and manipulation that often accompanies the use of prescribed curricula as a necessary price to pay for an approach to education that has proved effective in transmitting culture from generation to generation and is necessary to maintain coherence and stability within social structures. Such readers may believe that the only alternative to the intensive use of prescribed curricula is a laissez-faire approach that will precipitate a descent into anarchy. Or, when the reader has heard of student-initiated curricula, she may believe that their use results in egocentric individuals who lack basic skills and are unversed in the ways of society.

But, as mentioned at the end of Chapter 5 and as apparent in the quotations from Burgess in section 2 above, the development of student-initiated curricula should not be equated with a laissez-faire approach – as will be made even more clear in Chapter 7. Expecting students to take responsibility for the content of their formal programmes of learning does not mean they can do whatever they like, and the teacher does not have to abdicate responsibility for what ensues. Teachers can still be held to account for what takes place in their classrooms and institutions, though it would be preferable for the system of accountability to be problem-based rather than objectives- or target-based (see Chapter 10). And objectified knowledge, rather than being neglected, as is sometimes assumed, is construed in the context of student-initiated curricula as a crucial resource with which students are encouraged to engage not only as users but also as evaluators and contributors.

As acknowledged in the introduction to Chapter 5, the consequences of adopting any particular strategy or practice are a matter for empirical investigation. However, with regard to criticisms of the use of student-initiated curricula, I point out, first, that it is moot whether society actually is coherent and stable. Second, insofar as there is a degree of coherence and stability, one may still propose that our existing society might benefit from piecemeal change towards giving students the opportunity to exercise preference with regard to the focus of their learning in education institutions. Third, in my experience and that of Burgess and many others who were involved in the School for Independent Study, pessimistic expectations about the effects of student-initiated curricula were not fulfilled. The use of such curricula did not result in a narrowing of the curriculum or a general failure on the part of students to acquire social and other basic skills. Indeed, the opposite was true. For most students, the development of student-initiated curricula discouraged complacency and inertia, fostered sustained effort, and led to increased confidence, understanding and capability with regard to a range of socially relevant endeavours, including, in the case of the primary school students, literacy. In the case of students at the School for Independent Study, higher standards of achievement were evident in the relatively high proportion of students who gained First Class Honours degrees (see, e.g., *The Guardian*, 19 September 1989, pp. 27–31, 'First-class degrees: 1989', noting that NELP had been renamed Polytechnic of East London by this time). And the formal programmes of learning that students created, in both primary and higher education, though different from those that teachers and external curriculum developers might have conceived, were not foolish or inappropriate. These curriculum initiatives did not fail in educational terms; their demise was brought about by changes in the political ideology of the country in which they were developed (as discussed in section 3 above; for a rather different view, see Robbins, 1988, conclusion: 'Arresting the "great betrayal"').

The use of student-initiated curricula is consistent with the idea that all learning involves trial and error-elimination. The overall task of the teacher is to encourage and support the student's self-initiated and self-directed (including self-evaluated, self-monitored and self-regulated) endeavours in a safe environment. As a general principle, the teacher must strive to foster self-confidence on the part of students (see Chapter 5). She will also need to provide access to appropriate resources and to encourage in students a willingness to reflect critically on ideas – their own and those of other people. The teacher is clearly required to constrain behaviour that militates against the development of an environment conducive to learning. Bullying and behaviour that is racist, homophobic or sexist, for example, must be challenged and curtailed. Most importantly, the use of student-initiated curricula discourages learnt dependency, and coercive and manipulative practices on the part of the teacher are minimized.

6 Contrasting Popperian views

I must here acknowledge that Popperian educationists present neither a single view of the curriculum nor a single view of what teachers are for, that is, their role and purpose. This is not surprising, given that Popperians in general emphasize different aspects of Popper's philosophy, interpret his theories in different ways and have been influenced by different experiences and values. And, as indicated in section 2 above, Popper himself did not present a detailed and coherent educational theory and there is no public record of his view of student-initiated curricula, though it can be noted that rather than speaking of *starting* with the interest of the child, he spoke of *stimulating* the interest of the child – 'So what you should do, beyond the 3Rs is do your best to stimulate the interest of the child' (Popper quoted in Bailey, 2001, p. 27). But he was clearly against the practice of giving 'unwanted answers to unasked questions' (Popper, 1992a [1974], p. 40), and he described the best teacher as 'the teacher who can allow for the different interests of the children in the class' (Popper quoted in Bailey, 2001, p. 27).

It has also been suggested that Popper's idea of a world of objective knowledge is 'harmonious with the notion that much of that which is to be learnt requires (an appropriate form of) transmission' (Terry McLaughlin, personal communication, 2004). This is a view shared not only by non-Popperians but also by some theorists who have been influenced by his philosophy. But this was not the position Popper adopted, and such a view is inconsistent with his theory of learning. It can be argued, following Popper, that the process underlying individuals' interactions with objectified knowledge is no different from the process that underlies their interactions with physical phenomena and non-linguistic social phenomena. Of course, at the societal level, ideas are passed on within traditions; but this is not to say that there is any direct transfer of ideas at the level of the individual. The ideas that are passed on are often modified, intentionally or unintentionally, and, I would argue (see Part 1), they always have to be recreated by each generation of individuals.

The approach to the curriculum advocated by Popperian educationists such as myself and Burgess can be contrasted with that of Popperians and Popper-influenced educationists who view the purpose of education in terms of the continuing development of existing traditions of objectified knowledge. The development of objectified knowledge, rather than the development of the individual, seems to be their primary concern. This notion of the purpose of education is accompanied, conceptually at least, by what Richard Bailey has termed 'the criticalist curriculum' (2000, pp. 192–7, 199–206). The criticalist curriculum is a means by which children are introduced to 'the best that has been known and thought in the world' (ibid., p. 194). Criticalist curricula differ from conventional school curricula in that critical discussion is a crucial element – students are encouraged to criticize the ideas presented to them. Students, by being initiated into the practice of critical discussion, become better able to reassess and facilitate the development of their cultural heritage. But only on the basis of someone else's decision about the canon – criticalist curricula are prescribed curricula, and as such they risk the consequences described above.

In advocating the use of student-initiated curricula, I reject the idea that the primary purpose of education, and therefore the principal role of the teacher, is to transmit and develop existing traditions of objectified knowledge. Rather, I view the purpose of education as the open-ended – though not unconstrained or unevaluated – development of the individual, and I regard formal education not as a contract between teacher and society but as a contract between teacher and student (with the implication of long-term social benefit). I am not suggesting that the contract for a child's learning is between the teacher and the parent; the contract is, I stress, with the child. However, the teacher should endeavour to work with parents, as appropriate, to support the child's learning. My knowledge and personal experience of working with student-initiated curricula has given me no reason to believe that students, including young children, cannot, in general, be trusted to pursue their own learning aspirations. At times constraint will be needed – I am not proposing anarchy. But, as already stressed, it is one thing to acknowledge the need to curb or curtail certain learning aspirations on the grounds that they are morally unacceptable or have overly demanding resource implications, and quite another to try to prescribe what is to be learnt on the assumption that what students are inclined to plan for themselves (and then achieve) with regard to learning will invariably be inappropriate or inferior.

7 Three challenges

Social development and growth in objectified knowledge are dependent on the learning of individuals. Of course, progress requires collaborative action and a recognition of human interdependence, but to bring about a better world – to achieve improvement rather than mere change – we need individuals who are confident, creative, critical and fully formed as autonomous learners. To this end, individuals need to have the opportunity to make decisions and be responsible for the outcomes. And for democracy to develop, we need socially minded individuals who are not susceptible to manipulation and coercion.

Of those who reject the development of student-initiated curricula in the education of children and adolescents, in favour of some kind of traditional or criticalist alternative, I ask,

   (i)   How does the curriculum approach that you favour challenge – and therefore facilitate the development of – the expectations of the students that influence their everyday lives?
   (ii) How does it help students to deal with their learning problems, that is, what they want to learn but cannot learn or will have difficulty learning without the kind of support and challenge that teachers and education institutions can provide?
   (iii) How does it encourage individuals to engage in and develop their own self-initiated programmes of learning – that is, to become fully autonomous lifelong learners?

It seems to me that an approach to the teaching of children and adolescents that does not satisfactorily address these questions is ripe for a rigorous re-evaluation in light of the issues and arguments I have raised above and the kinds of strategies, practices and concerns discussed in the chapter that follows.

7 Developing Student-Initiated Curricula

[T]he 3Rs . . . are, I think, the only essentials a child has to be taught; and some children do not even need to be taught in order to learn these. Everything else is atmosphere, and learning through reading and thinking.
                    —*Karl Popper,* Unended Quest: An Intellectual Autobiography

Introduction

Following my critique in Chapter 6 of the intensive use of prescribed curricula with children and adolescents, this chapter offers a set of ideas about how to introduce, support and manage curricula that originate with the students themselves, that is, student-initiated curricula. I provide generic principles for use by teachers working with students of any age, but the substantial illustrative discussion derives from my work as a class teacher in a state-funded primary school in a social priority area of Inner London between 1981 and 1987. The children I taught were in the age range of 7 to 11 years. In accordance with conventional practice in England, classes contained children of a very similar age (i.e. members of a year group). As it was a primary school, each class had a class teacher who was responsible for most of the class's teaching during the course of a year.

As discussed in Chapter 6, the basic elements of my approach to teaching drew not only from the philosophy of Karl Popper but also from the educational theory of Tyrrell Burgess and my knowledge of the School for Independent Study at what was then North East London Polytechnic. The rationale and functioning of the School for Independent Study, which operated from 1974 to 1991, are well documented in Burgess (1977) and John Stephenson (1980, 1981). I again stress that the development of student-initiated curricula, both at the School for Independent Study and in my primary school classroom, was acknowledged to be highly successful in educational terms. The curtailment of these initiatives was, to a significant degree, a consequence of the increased centralized control of formal education policy and practice in England.

The illustrative commentary is intended principally for teachers working with whole classes of students, but the ideas could nonetheless be modified for use with individual students or small groups (including those being taught by parents-as-teachers working outside state-funded education). What I propose could be adopted when planning an entire formal curriculum (as was the case at the School for Independent Study), or substantial parts thereof (as in the case of my primary classroom). Even in England, despite the demands of the national curriculum, student-initiated curricula could be developed in almost any school, at least on a limited basis – such as one day a week, every afternoon, or two weeks a term.

Readers who are developing or plan to develop student-initiated curricula cannot avoid addressing for themselves the problem of how to do so in their specific context and with their particular students. In Chapter 10, I offer a problem-based methodology for professional development and action research that has been designed for and adopted by individuals and groups of teachers who wish to pursue the improvement of their educational practice. The issue of teacher and school accountability is also addressed in that chapter. Assuming either the absence of a national curriculum or the feasibility of suspending it where one is in force, in Chapter 9 I outline a proposal for research by means of which a hypothesis about the educational implications of evolutionary epistemology, including the use of student-initiated curricula, can be tested.

Elements of what follows are not original; in particular, many activities of the kind described in section 5 have been widely adopted in English schools. In general, I would hope that readers who are professional teachers will respond with 'I do this' to many of the practical ideas that follow. But I suspect that very few teachers are currently engaging in the full range of practices set out in sections 1 and 2 below, and these practices are crucial to the overall approach. The total package of ideas and its theoretical background are distinctive.

For clarity, I should perhaps stress that what I am proposing is neither subject-centred nor child-centred; rather, it focuses on the *student's learning problems*. The approach is structured and involves significant interventions on the part of the teacher. Some teachers and educators may be inclined to reject such a structured approach to the curriculum and to teaching in school, favouring instead one that is largely non-interventionist. I acknowledge that such an approach to teaching may work well with students already able to operate as fully autonomous learners in a range of problem areas. But for the majority of students – those who, in order to progress, require encouragement, support and/or challenge with regard to at least some of their learning – the adoption by the teacher of a largely non-interventionist approach would represent an abdication of responsibility.

1 Formulating learning problems

The teacher's first broad task is to help the student to formulate her (or his) learning problems. Learning problems (not to be confused with learning difficulties) are *practical* problems (see Chapter 3, section 5) of how to bring about developments in one's personal knowledge, understanding and/or capabilities. Of particular concern are those developments requiring notable effort, planning, time, other resources and/or support.

When working with older students, or younger students who have experience with a problem-based methodology, it is useful to encourage students to formulate their learning problems in the form of 'How can I . . . ?' questions, as a means of specifying, in terms that are clear but not immutable, what it is they want to become able to do, become better at and learn more about. However, in my teaching of young children (in classes I taught for two years at most), I felt it appropriate to work with children's broader expressions of their learning aspirations – as evidence of their learning problems – and I did not insist on the use of 'How can I . . . ?' questions.

Helping students to formulate learning problems is often not straightforward or easy. As Burgess states, 'It would not be enough to have a discussion one morning and think that has settled the matter' (Burgess, 1975, p. 6; see also my Chapter 6, section 2). School students may have particular difficulty in formulating their learning problems because they have not previously been given the opportunity to do so. When asked a question about what they wish to learn, they may interpret this as a 'test', whereby they have to work out what it is the teacher really wants them to say or do. Also, the expression of the most significant learning problems is often accompanied by feelings of discomfort – the student may become more acutely aware of a frustration, or fear a failure to solve the problem, and so on. Formulating learning problems can be demanding, both intellectually and emotionally. In general, the teacher should try to anticipate impediments to the formulation of some learning problems. The removal of impediments will require skill as well as understanding on the part of the teacher, and it should be viewed as a continuous process rather than a short-term goal.

The adoption of student-initiated curricula does not rule out a two-way exchange between teacher and student; it is not inconsistent with a sharing of interests and problem contexts. But the teacher who intends to support the development of student-initiated curricula must recognize that she cannot control what the students' learning problems will be. The teacher's problem and the student's problem are always different, though they may share an understanding of a problem situation. The teacher needs to be aware that students may wish to focus on problems that she considers to be peripheral, but which nonetheless lead to more profound learning. For example, a child may spend several weeks studying dinosaurs, and in the process greatly improve her ability to read and write.

Because the youngest children I taught were initially unreceptive to the explicit idea of wanting to learn, I found it more productive to begin by asking them what they wanted to do. For a number of reasons, including manageability in a whole-class setting, I asked students to write down their ideas. I gave them headings of the kind 'What I want to do in school' and 'What I hope to do [today/this week/this term/this school year]'. I also provided sentence openings for them to use to help them to express their ideas: 'I want to . . .', 'I would like to . . .', 'I hope to . . .', and so on. What they then produced were *statements of desired activity*.

The initial aspirations articulated by the students tended to be mundane – a continuation of the things they had already been doing in school. This was to be expected and was not a cause for concern. Students need to feel confident about the process; as mentioned above, when first asked what they want to do, they may think they need to work out what the teacher wants them to say. It is important that the teacher responds to the students – as far as possible and insofar as it is appropriate to do so – by meeting their requests and being seen to do so by the students. In general, when developing student-initiated curricula, students need to know that there is a direct relationship between what they write and what transpires. They need to experience, and come to assume, responsibility. When students recognize the relationship between what they write and what they then do, they will tend to flex their imagination.

As discussed in Chapters 5 and 6, one of the teacher's principal responsibilities is to encourage confidence on the part of students. One way of doing this is to ask them to reflect on their existing capabilities. I would ask my students at various times to write sentences under the heading 'What I am good at, what I can do'. The sentence openings I offered included 'I am good at . . .' and 'I am able to . . .'. At other times, I invited groups of students to make posters to illustrate 'Our skills, talents and good qualities'. These activities resulted in *statements of capability*. There is an enervating tendency in formal education to focus on the negative, to concentrate on what the individual cannot do or has failed to demonstrate. Also, as stated above, the formulation of the most significant learning problems is often accompanied by feelings of discomfort. To counteract social negativity and difficulties intrinsic to some learning, encouragement to self-affirm may be crucial. Interestingly, none of the students I taught appeared to overestimate their capabilities – quite the opposite.

The students were also encouraged to write *statements of desired learning*. The older children wrote under the heading 'What I want to learn, what I want to become better able to do', and the sentence openings I offered included 'I would like to learn more about . . .', 'I would like to learn how to . . .' and 'I would like to become better able to . . .'. With the younger children, these sentence openings were mixed in with those suggested for statements of desired activity. Interestingly, in a class of 11-year-olds, some students seized on the idea of 'becoming' and wrote statements about what they wanted to become in a broad sense as adults. This reinterpretation of what I had asked them to do turned out to be productive in respect of developing their planned learning.

One of the significant features of the approach I adopted was the amount of writing and reading required of the students. They were given support, as appropriate, for both activities, but regardless of their literacy level, they were expected to produce their own ideas, read my response (seeking help to do so when necessary) and sometimes read each others' plans. As these activities were integral to the process of their self-initiated planned learning, students were strongly motivated. I used 'learning diaries' with all of my classes. This was an important means by which a student could communicate her ideas to me. I also wrote in each student's diary. For instance, with regard to organization, I made comments about when the required resources would be available and with whom the student might work. Although each student wrote a set of learning aspirations, in order for this approach to the curriculum to be manageable in a classroom setting, the activities by which the learning was brought about were often undertaken in groups. Within any one day a student might work individually or with others on her own programme of learning and collaborate with others to enable them to fulfil theirs.

2 Selecting learning problems, planning learning and fulfilling plans

The teacher's second broad task is to identify which of the students' learning problems can be addressed within the specific environment, with the help of the teacher, other teachers and students, and by using existing resources or by involving individuals and agencies from outside the learning environment.

Some of the students' learning aspirations may be inappropriate or incapable of being addressed by the teacher(s) and the institution. A student may wish to pursue learning that is morally unacceptable, or not feasible because of resource limitations. When a student's learning proposal is rejected, the arguments underlying this decision should be made clear. Many judgements with regard to the curriculum involve values extrinsic to the general question of what promotes and what inhibits learning. What counts as morally unacceptable, for example, involves judgements of this kind. But, as a general principle, the problems that are the focus of the curriculum should be negotiated between the teacher and students, and as far as possible the curriculum should be based on student preference. This does not prevent the teacher from making suggestions, or prevent her from asserting the importance of some things rather than others, or stop her from vetoing the students' proposals (though one would expect there to be good reason for doing so). Some ideas which at first seem impractical or even impossible may be addressed in a modified form. For example, in one of my classes a student who wanted to become a book publisher was enabled to develop a school magazine. Skiing and snorkelling are two of the aspirations I was unable to support practically, but in these and similar cases I tried to validate the aspiration and explain why it could not be pursued at that time.

The teacher's third broad task is to help the students to plan their learning, paying attention to their learning problems; their skills, talents and achievements; and available resources, including time and expertise. Explicit attention to what happens when learning takes place may usefully form part of the discussion.

Depending on the circumstances, at this stage the teacher may also help students to critically evaluate their learning programmes by encouraging them to state in advance what would count as failure or success. As a teacher of undergraduate students of education (on a conventional modular programme), I found that many students were well able to engage with and benefit from such a process in respect of their plans for education research projects. At the School for Independent Study, the learning plans of undergraduate students were subject to formal validation (see Chapter 6, section 2), but in my practice with primary school children, short- and long-term plans were developed simultaneously, and there was no formal procedure for validation. In general, although I encouraged children to think about what they would need to do to be successful, I did not encourage them to formulate in advance criteria by which their overall learning plans could be judged. (They were, however, encouraged to evaluate their learning and its products, and supported in this endeavour – see section 5 below.)

The teacher's fourth broad task is to support the students in the fulfilment of their plans, offering additional resources (when available) and critical discussion. What this involves will very much depend on the students, their learning problems and the specific context in which they are working.

The students in the classes I taught developed diverse programmes of learning, some of which I would not have anticipated in advance. Learning programmes included, in addition to the one mentioned above, performance arts projects, often culminating in shows given for parents and/or other children; small business enterprises, such as making badges to sell; conventional historical projects; and teaching projects whereby a child would teach a small group of peers or younger children, having planned for this teaching, often by studying a particular topic for a number of days in advance.

Some children developed non-standard programmes for developing their abilities as readers. One boy who had previously shown little interest in reading spent a fortnight doing almost nothing else. He sat near a friend, who was a very competent reader, and he asked him for help with words he could not decipher. By the end of the fortnight he had developed from being one of the less able readers in the class to being one of the more capable readers. Similarly, another boy took it upon himself to choose from the reading books available (which were colour coded according to level of difficulty) only those that were long, contained few pictures and were extremely challenging for his level of reading ability. I must admit to trying to encourage him to read books that I thought would be more suitable, but he was adamant that he was reading what he wanted to read. During timetabled sessions devoted to books and reading, of which there were three or four a week (see section 7 below), he sat near me and asked for help with words he could not read or about which he was unsure. This student, who had previously been assessed as having limited reading ability, made very significant progress during the course of the year – a development noted by the head teacher when she conducted the annual end-of-year reading tests.

When students are self-motivated and take responsibility for their learning, an important aspect of the teacher's role is to allow them the freedom to follow their own initiative. When a child asks, 'Can I make a puppet, Miss?' the best response is often to say 'Yes'. The teacher's task is then to make resources available and provide assistance, as appropriate. In general, I strove to help students to take as much responsibility for the content of their learning as possible. I would stop myself from doing some of the things that I had previously seen as the teacher's task, which often meant that the students had to take responsibility for the mathematical aspects of non-mathematical projects. For business enterprises, for example, the students were expected to work out costings. In respect of another activity, I recall that on one occasion I was preparing the backing sheet for a large display, to be made by students, that was to be put up on the wall in the school hall. Two students were dispatched to measure the board in the hall and bring back accurate measurements. This was a genuine task, which the students fulfilled successfully – I had not taken the measurements in advance and, as I made clear to the students, if their measurements were wrong the display would not fit the board.

Concepts and ideas traditionally associated with science as a school subject were also integrated into self-initiated learning programmes. For example, students learnt how to make an electrical circuit using batteries, wire, bulbs and a switch, in order to give their model animals eyes which lit up. As a teacher, I saw it as part of my role to look for opportunities to extend the students' self-initiated learning, but not to force it. If the students had not wanted their model animals to have eyes which lit up, they would not have had to have them. Similarly, if they had not formulated the idea of making model animals, they would not have made them. Neither electrical circuits nor model animals were on my agenda. But neither did I adopt a 'discovery learning' approach, whereby children learn by trial and error-elimination without instructional procedures on the part of the teacher. I was inclined to pose thought-provoking questions or offer direct pieces of advice if I thought this would save students from needless struggle or the risk of major disappointment. When making models, for example, students were given clear guidance as to which adhesives would be most effective for bonding the materials they were using. So it can be said that I gave instruction, but I tried to do so largely in situations in which the underlying sentiment was 'Given that you want to achieve X, it will be helpful for you to engage with what I'm saying and showing'. Students are more likely to engage in the trial-and-error processes that are necessary in order to benefit from instruction when they believe the content of the instruction will be directly meaningful to them.

In general, everyone – myself included – was expected to support the learning programmes of every student in the classroom. As I saw it, one of the most important aspects of my role as the professional teacher in the classroom was to create a learning-conducive environment of the kind described in Chapter 5, section 4.

3 Challenge and criticism in learning

Before moving on to consider the next broad task of the teacher in the development of student-initiated curricula, it may be useful to say a little more about the function of criticism in learning and, in the section that follows, more about the role of the teacher in performing this function.

It has been argued in Part 1 that there is no learning without trial and error-elimination, which means, among other things, that there is no learning without a process in which the individual's expectations are challenged by experience, actual or anticipated. For humans, the challenges that stimulate learning include not only those that are external in origin – for example, if the ground on which we are walking gives way beneath our feet – but also those we create for ourselves in our mind's eye, that is, in our imagination (e.g. when asking oneself, 'In order to catch the 09:17 train, what's the latest time I can leave home?'). Learning can be construed as a process of 'imaginative criticism' (Popper, 1979 [1972], p. 148; see also my Chapters 3 and 5) whereby a challenge, whether external or internal in origin, to one of our existing sets of expectations provokes us both to be critical of what we had hitherto accepted as 'the case' and to replace the old set of expectations with a new set, which we create from our imagination. The challenge, and the criticism it provokes, may be so severe that the process leads to the replacement of the original set of expectations, but often what is created is merely, but not unimportantly, a modification.

'Imaginative criticism' can be used to describe all learning, human and animal, but the facility for imaginative criticism is extraordinarily heightened in humans. It is heightened not least by our facility for the development of complex description and argument, and by our ability to create and engage with objectified knowledge, that is, linguistically formulated problems, theories, expectations, hypotheses, assumptions of fact, values and arguments. When our expectations are objectified – that is, when they are externalized in speech or writing or some other form of expression – they take on an independent form. Criticism can be offered of objectified knowledge without there being any implied criticism of the person who created and/or expressed it. Criticism as construed here is a force for good. It means, for example, that we can help each other to eliminate some of our mistaken expectations before they have a deleterious effect on our well-being; in the extreme, our objectified ideas can 'die in our stead' (Popper, 1979 [1972], p. 244). There is also often an interim stage between unformulated subjective expectations and objectified knowledge, that is, when we create symbolic representations – descriptions, arguments, maps, music, visual images, tools, and so on – in our mind's eye.

As an illustration, if I leave my travel plans to instinct, I could leave home too late to catch the bus that will enable me to reach the railway station in time to catch a designated train. Alternatively, I could put into a linguistic form my subjective expectations about how to catch the train. I would then be in a position to review my plan critically, and I might realize that if I leave home five minutes earlier than anticipated, I would be more likely to catch the bus that will bring me to the railway station in time. As in this example, the set of expectations put in a linguistic form may not be fully objectified in the sense of being spoken or written down; but the descriptive plan of action, and the internal argument the individual engages in about it, require the internal objectification of subjective assumptions. I might then fully objectify my plan by putting it into spoken words to check it with someone else. That someone else might challenge the plan with criticism, such as 'The bus often turns up earlier than scheduled in the timetable, so it might be best to allow for this possibility.' I might then engage in further imaginative criticism and revise my plan (or not, if I decide that the challenge is ill-founded).

It does not always matter if we miss a designated train – if, for example, we are merely going sightseeing or shopping. Perhaps, in such a circumstance, we might not wish to devote time and effort to trying to ensure that we catch a particular train. But if we have an appointment, such as a job interview, the consequences of missing the train could be very significant and detrimental. In general, some of our practical problems are more likely to be solved satisfactorily if we think about proposed solutions in advance of action, if we critically review alternative strategies and expose our conjectured solutions to the critical scrutiny of others.

The way in which our proposals are criticized by others makes a difference to how we feel about ourselves and how inclined we then are to expose our ideas to critical scrutiny in the future. If the above comment about the unreliability of the bus timetable were accompanied by, 'I'm surprised you didn't know this. Other people know this. What's wrong with you that you haven't learnt this already?' it might serve to undermine the confidence of the recipient of the comments. The comments might provoke feelings that are more distressing than those experienced by missing the train. And even if the remark about the unreliability of the bus timetable were given without any implied personal criticism, the person who received the criticism of the travel plan might feel annoyed by the response or find it in some other way off-putting. Even well-meant criticism is not always welcome.

4 The teacher's role in challenge and criticism

Given the centrality of challenge and criticism in learning, the teacher – whether or not she is supporting the development of student-initiated curricula – is obliged to pay attention to the issues that challenge and criticism present for teaching and the creation of a learning-conducive environment, particularly given that individual students will respond to challenge and criticism differently, and any one student may respond differently at different times and in respect of different kinds of problems.

As argued in Chapters 5 and 6, in light of an evolutionary analysis of learning, good teachers foster student self-confidence; provide access to appropriate resources; and encourage students (of all ages) to reflect critically on their own ideas and actions, as well as those of other people. The teacher's task is not only to help create a safe place in which students are permitted and encouraged to engage in exploratory activity and to provide organizational support and resources, but also to promote criticality and offer challenges and criticism. One of the teacher's principal tasks is to create situations in which her students' assumptions about themselves, the world and their place in it, are challenged.

Challenge and criticism for the teacher are a matter of professional judgement. Challenges can assume a variety of forms, including 'Can you say more about this?', 'You are mistaken' and 'No, you mustn't do that!' With regard to when and how to criticize, there are no hard and fast rules, though I have suggested as an overriding principle that the value of criticism is to be judged by its effect in a particular circumstance, such that a specific criticism, even if valid, may be inappropriate if it ultimately serves to stifle creativity and inhibit subsequent trial and error-elimination (see Chapter 3, section 3; Chapter 5, section 2). I have also pointed out that criticism is not only to be conceived in terms of explicit statements of disapproval or rejection. It is also embedded in thoughts such as 'I could try something else' or the question 'What else might I do?' Indeed, it is implicit in any unstated or even unconscious degree of dissatisfaction that leads an individual to decide to do something rather than nothing, or to do one thing rather than another. I stress that, for the learner, the more subtle forms of criticism may be more motivationally powerful; for example, for the teacher to ask, 'What additionally (or alternatively) might you do?' may be more productive than saying, 'This is not good enough'. As also stressed earlier, criticism must not be personalized; ideas and behaviours, not the students themselves, are the only appropriate focus for criticism.

These last points are well known to many professional and lay teachers (including parents), but, as discussed in Chapter 5, section 7 (see also Chapter 6, section 4), when under pressure to bring the student's performance up to an externally conceived standard, the teacher may be inclined to see a student's non-achievement of the standard as a failure of the student. This may then be communicated to the student. In order to work effectively with student-initiated curricula, the teacher needs to develop a mindset that is different from the one that tends to develop in the context of the intensive use of prescribed curricula. The mindset needs to be different also from that which tends to prevail when teacher performance is judged according to the extent to which students meet prescribed standards.

Popperian teachers, that is, teachers who are familiar with and largely agree with Popper's evolutionary epistemology, may be inclined to see criticism as their key instrument in the support of student learning. Burgess, as a Popperian educationist, challenged this view of teaching insofar as he argued that confidence is essential if an individual is to accelerate her learning – confidence comes before criticism (see Burgess, 1977, p. 160 – and my Chapter 5, section 2). Without a degree of confidence, we do not freely explore, we do not conceive/create symbolic representations in our mind's eye, and we do not objectify our ideas to the point of exposing them to the critical scrutiny of others; we try to minimize the risk of discovering error and specific limitation. So although as a species 'our great instrument for progress is criticism' (Popper, 1979 [1972], p. 34) and as individuals we can suffer from too little criticism, at least in respect of our ideas (as distinct from us as persons), the teacher's first responsibility when faced with a student is not to undermine the student's self-esteem and self-confidence. And, almost invariably in my experience, the teacher will need to be proactive in finding ways to foster the student's self-confidence.

I am not suggesting that students must be protected at all costs from the experience of failure – to the point, for example, that they cannot enter competitions in case they do not win and cannot take examinations in case they do not pass – rather that many individuals experience too much personalized failure too soon, an impediment to long-term learning. For example, many children acquire a great deal of emotional baggage around learning to read. 'I'm not yet able to read' can become, implicitly, 'I'm incapable of becoming a reader' (see Chapter 3, section 2). This is more likely to occur when the message, explicit or implicit, that the student has received from her teachers is 'You are a failed reader'.

The following account of an aspect of a 7-year-old girl's learning programme provides an illustration of how a teacher might exercise her role in respect of challenge and criticism in the context of student-initiated curricula. The student's learning problem was 'How can I make a hand-sewn pencil case?' Paper patterns were made and altered, stitches were sewn and unpicked. This work was undertaken entirely by the student with minimal help from myself as the teacher. On her own initiative and through her own efforts, through trial and error-elimination, the student progressed from 'no hand-sewn pencil case' to 'hand-sewn pencil case'. At the end of the project, although I could see that the pencil case was significantly flawed (the stitches were so large that the pencils could slip through them), I acknowledged her achievement and offered no criticism. This student already had an appropriately critical attitude to her work in general; specific criticism from me would have served merely to diminish her immediate sense of satisfaction and achievement.

The student initiated another sewing project shortly afterwards. During the planning stage, I asked her if there was anything she had learnt from the construction of the pencil case that would be applicable to the new project. Her reply demonstrated both her awareness of what she had learnt while making the pencil case and criticisms that had subsequently occurred to her. She embarked on her second sewing project with the intention of using smaller stitches.

I do not know whether this particular student needed me to ask her to reflect on her own learning in advance of embarking on her second sewing project, but the fact that I did may have been useful to her and, as a general principle, reflecting on relevant past learning in this way can be useful when embarking on new projects.

There are, of course, some students for whom a challenging attitude is, on occasion, helpful in promoting learning, for whom 'If you really want to produce a pencil case you will have to take more care' or 'I cannot make sense of this – more accurate spellings must be used in order for me to understand it' are necessary in order to encourage progress. However, even when a critical response is appropriate, tact and sensitivity should be shown; the proffered criticism should not come across as an outright dismissal or a personal attack. In general, although criticism is central to learning, most children, adolescents and older students require some acknowledgement of the positive features of their endeavours in order to cope effectively with direct criticism from teachers in respect of errors or specific limitations.

For the most part, students in my classes freely presented their work to me for feedback. Providing feedback was an explicit part of my role. A teacher who took one of my classes when the children transferred to the next year group found their habit of requesting feedback disconcerting. He initially saw it as evidence of dependence; he thought students exhibited more independence if they completed their work and then put it away without reference to the teacher. I stress that the most desirable situation, which I think was often achieved in my classroom, is for students to work for themselves, that is, to be independently motivated, and to freely present work to the teacher (and, at times, each other) with a view to eliciting supportive and constructive feedback.

5 Evaluating and recording learning achievement

The teacher's fifth broad task is to help the student to evaluate her learning. Linked to this is the teacher's sixth task, that of helping the student to compile a record of some of her achievements resulting from learning. The idea of recording progress and achievements implies that work is evaluated according to standards. In the context of student-initiated curricula, the emphasis is on supporting students to develop and work with their own conceptions of standards. These standards will nonetheless be developed in a social context, and it can be expected that students will be influenced by cultural expectations without necessarily being constrained by them.

It is widely recognized that good teaching involves encouraging students to reflect on their learning. Teacher-initiated questions and discussion that encourage such reflection are part and parcel of working with student-initiated curricula. Some indication of what this involves has been given above in the discussion of my response to the 7-year-old student who designed and made a pencil case. When working with student-initiated curricula, the teacher should encourage students on a more formal basis to take stock of and record what they have been learning. With older students, their records of learning may include a statement of the initial learning aspirations – their formalized learning problems – and an account of where trial solutions were found to be successful, where they were less than successful and what was learnt from the experience. Such a record could also include an outline of learning problems that have developed from the work undertaken. At the School for Independent Study, student achievement was formally examined and accredited at this stage in the curriculum process. With young children, the teacher's initial aspiration may be merely to encourage a habit of reflection and a fairly simple process of valuing and collecting work and recording progress.

As mentioned in Chapter 5, supported by the discussion in Part 1, it is not always easy to judge whether or not learning has taken place, and, indeed, the true nature and scope of learning may be impossible to assess. Most learning is also very much an incremental process. While learners are often characterized as people who have 'become able to . . .' or have 'come to understand that . . .', more often learning is marked by changes that are less clear cut, whereby learners have 'become better able to . . .', 'developed their understanding of . . .', 'become more knowledgeable about . . .', 'developed a more critical attitude towards . . .', and so on.

As a primary school teacher, I encouraged my students to write *statements of learning achievement*. Under a heading such as 'What I have learnt, what I have become able to do' or 'What I have learnt in school this year', students would write statements using sentence openings of the following kind: 'I have become able to . . .', 'I have become better at . . .', 'I have learnt how to . . .', 'I have learnt that . . .' and 'I have learnt more about . . .'. I discussed with students the distinction between 'I have learnt how to . . .' and 'I have become better at . . .' as I found they tended to undervalue or disregard development that was rudimentary. I noted in particular that students whose progress with reading was comparatively slow tended to become disheartened about their potential to succeed. It is important for such students to recognize that they have made progress, even though they are not yet fully fledged readers.

The students' statements of achievement were added to folders which constituted their learning profiles – their personal record of work for the school year. These folders belonged to the student, contained a selection of work chosen by the student and included the learning diary and the student's written evaluations of her learning. Students were encouraged to reflect on the content of their profiles as evidence of their development and progress, and to see their achievements as an outcome of their efforts.

In addition, sometimes, towards the end of the school day, I would ask students to write a reflection on their work earlier in the day. I devised session evaluation sheets that invited students to reflect not only on what had gone well and what had been achieved but also on what had not gone well, and why, and what had been learnt from the process. The use of these evaluation sheets was not, however, a regular occurrence – I did not want reflection-on-learning to become a chore; rather, the purpose of such worksheets was to encourage reflective thinking, and it was a convenient tool for doing so in the context of class teaching. I also encouraged peer-evaluation in relation to work produced.

For many years and in various publications (Swann, 1983, 1999c, 2006, 2008) I have suggested that, given an evolutionary analysis of learning, an additional evaluative stage would be appropriate in the context of student-initiated curricula, whereby the teacher critically discusses with students the scope of their learning problems after they have been addressed, considering to what extent the formulated problems were well-conceived, whether better problems could have been formulated and what factors (if any) can be identified to improve future problem formulation. I pointed out that, in my experience, this was the most difficult step to apply satisfactorily. Although I still think the proposed practice has potential value, it is so often not appropriate for the specific student that I no longer include this practice as one of the highlighted steps in the procedure for developing student-initiated curricula.

The pursuit of formal qualifications can be accommodated in the context of student-initiated curricula, and this is so even when there is no available formal qualification in independent study of the kind that was developed and offered in higher education at the School for Independent Study (see Chapter 6, section 2). The decision to pursue formal qualifications should, however, be made by the student in the context of her broader preferences and aspirations; that is, the formal qualifications should be deemed by the student to be desirable in order to achieve some longer-term aim and/or as part of a programme of learning that is significantly more than a curriculum designed to achieve a set of qualifications. Context and student involvement are all-important here. What is wrong with many secondary school students' experience of schooling is that success in examinations has become the raison d'être for studying (see the second quotation from Popper at the beginning of Chapter 6), with nearly all planned learning being directed towards the achievement of specific qualifications, each with a syllabus that dominates teacher and student activity for a lengthy period of time (see my critique of prescribed curricula in Chapter 5, section 6, and Chapter 6). (For relevant discussion in relation to higher education, see Pratt and Cocking, 1999, on 'Making modularity work'.)

My knowledge of the learning programmes of students who undertake formal learning at alternative education centres – such as the South Downs Learning Centre (www.thelearningcentre.selfmanagedlearning.org.uk) – has led me to speculate that the intensive development of student-initiated curricula at the secondary school level would result in students pursuing individually fewer but collectively more varied formal qualifications than is current practice, at least in England. As implied above, students' qualifications would be part of their broader records of achievement and would better reflect the students' particular interests and aspirations. Qualifications would not be gained, as in conventional schooling, at the expense of the opportunity to develop as fully autonomous learners. Broadly, there is anecdotal and fragmentary evidence to suggest that students who study for qualifications that are integral to their self-initiated and self-directed learning plans tend to be highly focused and motivated, and often make speedier and better progress towards formal qualifications than would normally be expected.

6 Illustrating the role of criticism in learning

To help students understand the role of criticism in learning and to see how they can use critical reflection to enhance their own progress, I developed a staged procedure for use with whole classes of students. I have subsequently developed the procedure in different ways and have used it as part of a successful interview for a job, as an illustrative activity in workshops with academic colleagues and both undergraduate and postgraduate students of education, and as part of a series of prototype research instruments for evaluating learning how to learn with primary and secondary school students (Swann et al., 2003). The account below is of the version used with one of my own classes of 8-year-old students.

As the first step in the procedure, the students were asked, 'What do you think the new houses in [name of local street] look like? Try to draw Anne's or Julia's house as best you can.' The houses, similar to each other, were the homes of two of the students in the class. The houses were familiar to many of the students as they were friends of the students who lived in them. Also, the class passed these houses every week on the way to the local library. The discussion that accompanied these first drawings, undertaken in the classroom, focused on the nature of learning and on building construction and its representation, rather than on aesthetic values or how to represent qualities of homeliness. The planned stages of the procedure were outlined so that the students knew broadly what to expect.

The practical problem that the students were asked to address was that of how to represent one of the specified houses using visual imagery (P_1 – see Chapter 3, section 1). Each solution (*TS*), that is, each drawing, implied expectations or hypotheses (*TT* – see Chapter 3, section 5) concerning what the house looked like. At the second stage in the procedure, the students took their first drawings and tested them by looking at the houses (on the next trip to the library) and considering how the drawings could be improved (*EE* → P_2). This activity was accompanied by discussion about points of construction. With this particular version of the procedure, due to recent heavy snowfall and the coldness of the weather, there was at this stage no writing or drawing undertaken in the street. Rather, there was only spoken discussion such that all students were encouraged to develop their expectations about the construction of the chosen house, and errors and limitations in the initial drawings were discovered by the students with a view to eliminating them when making a second drawing back in the classroom.

In the classroom, all students made a second drawing in light of what they had learnt by empirically testing their initial drawing. I expressed the idea that the new drawing could encapsulate some of the student's learning, and each child produced a piece of writing about some aspects of what she had learnt. Making learning explicit in this way attaches value to learning and makes both learning as an activity and the content of learning more concrete and therefore more robust and susceptible to development. My specific encouragement was to produce statements using the openings 'I have learnt that . . .' and/or 'I am able to . . .' about aspects of what had been learnt – as evidenced in particular in the difference between the first and second drawings. In general, as will have been apparent in earlier sections of this chapter, when encouraging young students to write about their learning I found it useful to give them sentence openings. In developing ideas about learning, with young and mature students alike, the writing of complete sentences rather than phrases is to be encouraged so that students are challenged to form and express complete thoughts.

The next step in the procedure was to sketch the houses in the street in situ and, in light of the work that had already taken place, to make on-site decisions, some of them expressed in spoken and written form, as how best to represent features of the buildings. The drawings produced by the students provided evidence of developments in their expectations about the buildings. And, again, some mistaken expectations were eliminated, and more details of the buildings were observed and made explicit in the drawings – limitations were reduced. Back in the classroom, the students were asked to make written statements about the activity and about their learning.

With regard to the defined activity, that is, the representation of a house with particular reference to its construction, the last drawing of each student was the best. This evaluation was made and noted by many of the students. Nevertheless, all the pieces of work, not merely the final drawings, were explicitly valued and presented as part of the contribution of the class to the school centenary project. Each piece of work was an end product, but each set of pieces of work existed as an illustration of a process of learning. The procedure had been accompanied throughout not only by discussion of the structure of the houses but also of the significance each step of the procedure was intended to have in respect of the students' learning. The students were encouraged to recognize the value of their starting points, to identify a way of testing their initial expectations and skills so that these could be improved, and to reflect on the evidence of their learning by comparing pictures and by formulating statements about some of the learning that had taken place.

When I developed a similar version of this procedure for illustrative purposes with undergraduate student teachers in Liverpool, the students made drawings in the seminar room of the city's distinctive Catholic cathedral. These were then annotated – highlighting errors and limitations – at the site of the cathedral. In all subsequent versions, the entire procedure was conducted indoors using photographs as substitutes for the outdoor observation or, in one version, using mirrors to check and develop self-portraits. In these later versions of the procedure, only two drawings were required: one was made at the start of the activity before the observation and was then annotated in the context of the observation of the photograph(s) (or mirror image); the photographs (or mirrors) were then placed out of sight and the second drawing was made; the photographs (or mirrors) were reintroduced after the second drawing had been completed. Photographic subjects have included Tower Bridge, London; the London Eye; the parliament building in Wellington (for a presentation in New Zealand); and the shape and structure of spiders. I stress that it is essential that the first drawing be undertaken out of sight of the subject of the drawing. Some students may need encouragement to draw something that is unfamiliar to them or, in some cases, not known to them ('It's like a Ferris wheel' proved useful for a student who had not seen the London Eye). The teacher can view any student concerns about the apparent difficulty of the task as an opportunity to discuss the idea that observation is expectation-laden.

With a procedure of this kind, the students who make the most visible progress between the first drawing and the last may not be those who otherwise demonstrate the highest levels of achievement. Those students who are generally less confident and skilled in representational drawing may produce a set of drawings that shows significantly more development (i.e. greater evidence of learning during the procedure) than those whose confidence and skills were initially more advanced. The latter students are not disadvantaged by the procedure and the former students are potentially empowered by it. Useful though the procedure is, I would counsel against using it on more than two or three occasions with any one group of students. It illustrates the potential of self-directed criticism as a means of developing expectations, but it should not be employed as a substitute for providing students with opportunities to engage in self-initiated and self-directed trial and error-elimination.

7 The 3Rs

In the introduction to this chapter, I indicated that the development of student-initiated curricula is not an all-or-nothing matter and that it is better for students to have at least some experience of developing student-initiated curricula even if for the most part a prescribed curriculum prevails. Suppose, however, that teachers and students are not required to follow any kind of prescribed curriculum: is there anything that must be taught?

Popper provided an answer to this question in his intellectual autobiography – see the quotation at the head of this chapter, with the 3Rs referring to reading, 'riting and 'rithmetic (1992a [1974], p. 12). Elsewhere, in an interview, he remarked that

> the three R's ought to be taught with whatever pressure is necessary. But beyond that, that is a different question. Beyond that the pressure should not be put on. For example if a child doesn't like to learn History, he won't learn it, even if you exert pressure. In other words, it is necessary for the future of the child to know the three R's. It is a real need, and if they don't learn [the three R's], the teacher has really sinned on the child.
>
> (Popper quoted in Bailey, 2001, p. 26)

I support Popper's advocacy of the importance of the 3Rs, and while it does indeed seem to be the case that some individuals become literate and numerate without much obvious teaching, most of us need to have quite a lot of teaching in order to become proficient in these respects. I would also argue that, while it is possible to learn to read, write and do basic arithmetic without developing as a fully autonomous learner, it is very difficult to develop full learner autonomy without acquiring these capabilities. (Individuals who have impaired sight or other disabilities that prevent them from using the conventional means for engaging with or creating written words and other symbols can, of course, benefit from technological developments that facilitate activities that are comparable to the use of written forms. But this is not a case of neglecting the 3Rs; rather, it is the development of compensating abilities.)

Although in my own primary school teaching I was able to organize much of the week on the basis of student-initiated curricula, the 3Rs were not only taught through my support for student-initiated curricula but also in the context of teacher-initiated activities. I often taught specific (usually short) lessons, mainly on aspects of mathematics but also on reading and writing.

In addition to taught sessions in which I had specific learning outcomes in mind, I timetabled a one-hour session three or four times a week on books and reading. During these periods a range of books – non-fiction and fiction, including picture books – was available for all students to select from and read. Students were permitted to read in pairs and sometimes in threes. They could talk about what was in the books, but I insisted that there was no writing or drawing during this time. The reason for this was that some students were not spending much, if any, time on reading at home. Without books-and-reading sessions, opportunities for sustained reading for pleasure could have been largely overwhelmed by student-initiated activities and other teacher-initiated activities (see below).

It should be noted that I worked as a primary school teacher before the time when classrooms commonly had computers and internet access. Were I to be teaching in a primary school now, I would extend books-and-reading sessions to include the use of information technology. And I would hope also to be in a position to teach touch-typing in addition to handwriting skills.

Despite the importance of the 3Rs and notwithstanding my teacher-planned literacy and numeracy lessons and books-only periods in the timetable, I have a concern about Popper's reference to the use of 'pressure' (ibid.). If it means persistent encouragement and skilled support over a substantial period of time, then I am all for it. But the experience of pressure can be counterproductive. For example, some children become disheartened when they do not learn to read as quickly as they expect to – a negative state of affairs that is compounded when parents and/or teachers express disappointment with the child's reading progress. Some children have more difficulty than others in learning the 3Rs in the early stages, and some have lives outside school that offer little or no support for literacy and/or numeracy. Given these factors, it is important that the development of literacy and numeracy is not treated as if it is the primary focus of childhood education; rather, becoming literate and numerate should be treated as *part* of the process of developing greater autonomy as a learner. It is vital, for example, that children who do not learn to read as quickly as their peers are nonetheless given the same general learning opportunities. They may need extra support for learning to read, but care must be taken so that any time spent in this way should not seem like a penalty for their 'failure'. In general, it is important not to restrict a child's educational opportunities and, therefore, her intellectual development merely because she has some specific difficulties.

8 What should also be taught

I also have a concern about the quotation from Popper at the head of this chapter (Popper, 1992a [1974], p. 12): he seems to undervalue the importance of learning through spoken engagement. Perhaps spoken engagement is subsumed by the idea of 'atmosphere', but, clearly, spoken engagement is not highlighted as a specific stimulus for learning. Elsewhere, when describing his educational dream, he attributes to the teacher the role of stimulating students to 'pose problems and discuss them' (ibid., p. 40). One may assume that spoken engagement is involved, but practical trial-and-error activity is not mentioned. In general, Popper seems to have favoured a rather bookish view of learning in school (understandably so for a man of his generation and given his personal interests); practical problems are largely marginalized in favour of theoretical problems, and the potential for learning through spoken engagement is not stressed.

In light of my own experiences as a teacher, I propose that there are a number of things in addition to the 3Rs that should consciously be taught, except when they have already been learnt or are already being learnt without specific teaching.

First, students must learn how to behave in a way that makes possible the development and maintenance of an environment that is learning-conducive for all students. *A minimum standard of good behaviour* is required for the development of student-initiated curricula. Behaviour management is almost invariably an issue for teachers working with groups of children and adolescents. It is important to view behaviour management in terms of what the students need to learn and develop – ways of conducting themselves and understanding – rather than seeing the achievement of desirable behaviour as an outcome of manipulative activity on the part of the teacher. In my classroom, there were rules in respect of behaviour that the students were required to learn (i.e. to practise), and opportunities and sanctions were used to discourage and prevent behaviours that were unacceptable (such as violence or name calling) or undesirable (such as behaviours which inhibited the learning of other students). The exclusive and explicit purpose of sanctions was to maintain the efficacy of the learning environment, not to punish the student. I found, however, that the use of student-initiated curricula helped to minimize disruptive behaviour – most students for most of the time acted as highly motivated members of a learning-conducive mini-community. Even students who in other circumstances presented disruptive behaviour were well-integrated into the learning community of the classroom.

Second, students need to develop – that is, learn – *social skills and understanding and a degree of personal awareness* in order to develop full learner autonomy. Autonomy does not mean isolation. Human communities are communities of interdependent individuals. For such communities to develop and for objectified knowledge to grow, we need independently minded people who can function effectively with others and in the company of others. In my teaching of children, I organized regular sessions of whole-class games and other activities designed to encourage personal and social development (I drew on and adapted ideas from, for example, Brandes and Phillips, 1977). This was necessary because many students lacked confidence and were unused (outside school) to collaborative endeavour.

Third, oral communication skills often need to be taught, specifically skills required for the development of *descriptive and argumentative language* in the context of spoken discussion. It may not be appropriate to do this in a rigid or highly structured way, but it is something the teacher needs to keep in mind in her responses to the students when supporting the development of student-initiated curricula. My classroom was not a particularly quiet environment. Students were encouraged to talk (quietly) about their work, and conversation that was not directly work-related was not discouraged if it seemed likely to be conducive to their general state of well-being. (It is important not to allow conversations to proceed when one or more students are engaged in any form of verbal bullying.)

Fourth, although the development of *self-confidence* may not be something that can be taught, it can certainly be encouraged and, as discussed in Chapter 5, sections 2 and 3, and section 4 above, it must be learnt in order for the student to be proactive in the pursuit of learning.

Fifth, becoming a fully autonomous learner is a learning process, and the development of *full learner autonomy* in general requires a degree of teaching. In Chapter 5, section 3, I described a fully autonomous learner as someone with the ability and inclination to make independent and critically informed decisions regarding the timing, location, method, purpose and content of her planned learning. Being critically informed will usually mean having knowledge that has developed in a social context or tradition in which ideas are challenged and explored. *Full* autonomy as a learner is more than the ability and inclination for self-initiated and self-directed activity towards learning; it implies the ability and inclination for independent thought and action that takes cognizance of ideas that exist and are developing outside of the self, that is, in the external world of objectified knowledge. (In defining full autonomy in this way, I have been influenced by the distinction between personal and critical autonomy made by Kathryn Ecclestone, 2002, chapter 2.) Full learner autonomy may develop naturally through 'atmosphere, and learning through reading and thinking' (Popper, 1992a [1974], p. 12), but for many individuals, any such natural process is stifled by elements of their schooling. Schooling does, of course, promote more limited (but not unimportant) forms of learner autonomy, including what Ecclestone calls procedural autonomy, which results in, among other things, 'Confidence with procedures, systems, and the technical language underpinning particular subjects' (2002, pp. 36–7). As far as the development of learner autonomy is concerned, schooling often takes a lot away and gives a little back. In my experience as a teacher in higher education, the development of full learner autonomy was something that for many undergraduate students required specific teaching, not least in respect of developing informed criticality.

Sixth, *learning about learning* is potentially conducive to learning (see Chapter 5, sections 2 and 3), and, as illustrated in section 6 above, it is possible for a teacher to devise procedures that are specifically designed to encourage learning about learning. In general, the teacher can and should foster learning about learning in the context of a range of the students' trial-and-error activities.

9 Teacher attributes

Many of the personal qualities needed to introduce, manage and support the development of student-initiated curricula are the same as those associated with teaching prescribed curricula. In particular, it is important for the teacher to respect the students and have the patience and skill to be able to communicate with them effectively. Being broadly well-informed – knowledgeable – is a valuable asset, and one that will almost inevitably develop if the teacher has an attitude of service towards the students. Also important are self-confidence and high expectations of what students can achieve with appropriate opportunities over a period of time. In a classroom setting, when working with a large group of children or adolescents, it is essential that the teacher has the will and presence to command attention and respect. The effective management of plenary discussions requires a range of skills on the part of the teacher in order that students are enabled to talk to and listen to each other and so that sustained thought is encouraged. The ability to manage time and other resources effectively (and flexibly) is also very important in a classroom setting. With regard to the education of children, as indicated above, their teachers will almost invariably need to have developed skills and understanding for teaching the 3Rs.

In my experience of working with student-initiated curricula, there were no extra demands in terms of time – although my time in the classroom and in preparation for teaching was spent somewhat differently from what is required when teaching prescribed curricula (see earlier sections of this chapter). In general, working with student-initiated curricula made my experience of teaching less stressful and more enjoyable. The students were better behaved, more socially responsible and more highly motivated towards learning; the work undertaken, being more varied and challenging, was more intellectually stimulating for me. However, in order to create and sustain a learning-conducive environment, I realized that it was important to extend my understanding of human development and applied individual and social psychology beyond the level that had previously been required. To this end, I undertook (1980–83) the part-time, one-year foundation course and two-year diploma course in counselling skills at South West London College. It was nationally renowned at that time for operating as a self-directed learning community; that is, each year group, with its course tutors, developed their own programmes of learning (the curriculum was, however, student-initiated in a rather different way from that outlined in this chapter). Although teachers do not need to pursue a counselling qualification in order to introduce, manage and support the development of student-initiated curricula, and there are significant differences between teaching in the context of education and the kind of teaching (in the broad sense) in which counsellors engage, there are nonetheless useful ideas, skills and practices that educationists can draw from the field of counselling. In addition, for teachers of older children and adolescents, there is much of value to be learnt from the field of youth work.

As a student of counselling skills, one of my particular interests was the development of educational relationships. As a teacher developing student-initiated curricula in the context of action research, I did not set out to produce a definitive list of such skills for teaching; rather, I formulated a list as an outcome of posing and addressing 'What do I do and how can I improve it?' However, of the skills I identified as pertinent for my professional development, the following are some that would seem to be crucial for any teacher working with student-initiated curricula: listening and giving good attention to the whole person, maintaining appropriate boundaries, forming contracts, articulating ideas in speech (as noted above), sharing knowledge, checking out, and challenging (as noted earlier). In addition, the teacher needs specific skills when assisting in *problem formulation*, including the following: encouraging, reflecting back, synthesizing, remembering, prompting and reformulation. Insofar as empathy can be learnt, empathizing should be added to the list.

The above-mentioned skills are also valuable for teachers working with prescribed curricula, but in the context of student-initiated curricula, the overall demands on the teacher will be slightly different. Information about 'the whole person' comes from a variety of sources: from what the student says, how she sounds, the intonation of her voice, facial expressions, body movements, patterns of responding over a period of time, and so on. Although it can be impertinent not to accept what a student says at face value, to attend only to what she says may be to ignore other relevant information. In a situation in which the teacher is attempting to work with student preferences, it is particularly important to consider the whole person; a student may say 'I do not want to . . .' while conveying 'I am afraid to . . .', or say 'This is boring' when 'This is very difficult' might be a more accurate description of what the student is experiencing.

For group and class teaching, I would further argue that practising equity is essential, such that over a period of time all students receive broadly similar amounts of attention from the teacher. Practising equity can be more difficult in the context of student-initiated curricula as the teacher will often need to balance out her attention over the course of a week rather than during a day or a single lesson. Giving attention does not necessarily mean talking to the student. The teacher may decide not to intervene when a student is working but merely observe the student and learn for future reference.

Drawing on psychodynamic psychology, I found the concept of transference pertinent – providing the underlying process is not presumed to be one of induction (see Chapter 4). An unexceptional example of transference in the classroom is when a child calls the teacher 'Mum'. This most often occurs when a child is focusing on her work and spontaneously seeks interaction with the teacher. In calling the teacher 'Mum', she is to some degree identifying the teacher-figure as a mother-figure. Often children and teachers are embarrassed by this kind of error, but it is a natural and understandable mistake. A similar example is when a female teacher is accidentally referred to as 'Sir' or a male teacher referred to as 'Miss'. Although these examples do not raise anything particularly problematic for classroom learning, impediments to the effective development of the teacher-student educational relationship may arise when a student transfers (non-inductively, of course) qualities to the teacher which she has learnt to expect from people she already knows or has known, and when these qualities are inappropriate in the new context. For example, a child may have learnt to expect to be punished when she is seen to have made a mistake and then wrongly expects a similar response from her teacher. This is an impediment to learning in the classroom, unless the teacher can discourage the transference and assert the distinctiveness of her teaching role whereby she views the discovery of a mistake as a valued stimulus for learning. Other inhibiting transferences may occur when students have previously been discouraged from expressing certain interests and assume, wrongly, that the teacher will discourage the pursuit of these interests in the context of student-initiated curricula.

Generally speaking, the teacher should discourage transference on the part of the student by not being reticent and by 'making herself real to her students' through the honesty of her interactions with them in her role as teacher. If the teacher thinks that transference is leading a student to hold back from expressing specific preferences, the teacher may usefully make statements of the kind 'I don't mind if you . . .' and 'You know you can . . . if you want to'.

The idea of counter-transference, though less clear-cut than that of transference, can be useful when considering some of the teacher's responses to her students. A good teacher will not want her students to pick up on and adopt any negative or otherwise inappropriately limiting expectations that she might have in respect of learning. A teacher's counter-transference may, however, be of the kind which arises more directly as a response to the behaviour of the student and may be relevant to the student in her dealings with others. For example, during an informal small group discussion, when I found myself getting annoyed with a student who was talking to me in a bossy manner, I realized this way of talking might be a significant factor in the difficulties she was having with her peers. I was then in a position to talk to the student about a possible cause and effect in the context of her classroom relationships.

I do not want to give the impression that exceptional levels of skill and knowledge are necessary in order to introduce and support the development of student-initiated curricula. Skill and knowledge deficits on the part of the teacher are to be expected and can be reduced through a willingness to learn and engage in professional development activities, such as those discussed in Chapter 10. Note also that the skills and qualities I have identified above are not, in themselves, sufficient. The most important teacher attribute in respect of student-initiated curricula is a deep-seated commitment to fostering the development of full learner autonomy. This means relinquishing to the students some, perhaps much, of the power traditionally assigned to teachers in education institutions. It means giving up the need to try to control students' learning. The teacher must refrain from trying to mould students according to her own image or the image of what she or others consider to be ideal. There are, as I have indicated previously, learning and behaviours that teachers may rightly wish to prevent, and there are others they may wish to discourage; but the idea of *proscription* need not lead to *prescription*.

Part 3
Developing Teaching

Research and the Development of Teaching

Chapter Outline

[I]f we produce many competing ideas, and criticize them severely, we may, if we are lucky, get nearer to the truth. This method is the method of conjectures and refutations; it is the method of taking many risks, by producing many (competing) hypotheses; of making many mistakes; and of trying to correct or eliminate some of these mistakes by a critical discussion of the competing hypotheses.

—*Karl Popper,* The World of Parmenides:
Essays on the Presocratic Enlightenment

Introduction

Part 3 of this book addresses the problem of 'How can teaching best be developed and improved?' It will become apparent that my proposed solutions to this problem attribute value to research of various kinds. Research is a way of finding things out and developing new and potentially better ideas and practices. Teachers who are intent on developing their teaching are strongly advised to take an interest in relevant research – not least as critical evaluators and potential users of the research output of others. I also promote the idea that professional teachers should be encouraged and supported to undertake action research on their own practice as part of their programmes of professional development.

In this chapter, drawing on Karl Popper's evolutionary epistemology, I discuss some knowledge issues that are relevant to education research and the development of teaching. In Chapter 9, I propose a Popperian science of school teaching as a means of developing our understanding. Chapter 10 is concerned with method in the improvement of practice, specifically the professional practice of teachers. In Chapter 11, in light of an evolutionary analysis of learning, I relate issues of fact and value to address the question of what teachers are for, that is, what their role and purpose are in respect of promoting learning.

Aside from the discussion of science and action research, this book does not provide practical 'how to . . .' guidelines for education researchers. For a set of Popperian principles for good research practice in education, see John Pratt and Swann (2003, pp. 178–93). For a Popperian discussion of policy research that is applicable to education, see Pratt (2003).

1 Popperian epistemology and the growth of objectified knowledge

Key features of Popper's evolutionary epistemology as it applies to the growth of objectified knowledge are summarized below (and see the quotation at the head of this chapter from Popper, 1998, p.152). The content of (iv) was discussed in Chapter 1, and the other ideas were discussed in Part 1 in the context of the growth of subjective knowledge, that is, with reference to learning. The remaining sections of this chapter and Chapter 9 amplify the content of these summarized features.

(i)   We inhabit a shared reality that includes not only physical phenomena but also other people, objects and processes that are the consequences of individual, social and cultural activity. We can attempt to represent the shared reality by means of descriptive language, and we can discuss these descriptions through the use of argumentative language. There are, in short, facts about our reality that we can attempt to ascertain and may be successful in ascertaining.

(ii) What we believe to be the facts – that is, the outcomes of our attempts to represent our shared reality – are always conjectural. There is no certain knowledge, and the idea of foundational knowledge (known truths on which other knowledge is built) is highly problematic, not least because ideas that appear to be secure (i.e. reliable and dependable) may in fact be erroneous.

(iii) The pursuit of truth is not the pursuit of certainty. Although certainty is unattainable, we can pursue truth – that is, try to gain knowledge of the facts – and sometimes attain it.

(iv) Questions of fact and questions of value arise together in situations but can nonetheless be differentiated. A question of fact – that is, a question about whether or not something is the case – can be distinguished from whether or not we, or others, like or dislike the particular fact (or alleged fact) or whether or not it is in some objective sense good.

(v) Science is concerned with the pursuit of truth, that is, concerned with matters of fact about reality. Scientific theories are universal theories and statistical theories which have been so formulated that they are susceptible to falsification. Scientific knowledge comprises falsifiable theories, and formulated problems and arguments which relate to such theories.

(vi) Non-scientific theories are an important part of our knowledge, and they may be susceptible to criticism by means of argument even though they are not susceptible to refutation by reference to empirical evidence.

(vii) The idea that knowledge advances through a process of induction is a myth. There is no growth of knowledge without the discovery of error (or specific limitation) – a new expectation or hypothesis is a creative response to such a discovery. Regardless of how it seems at the time, knowledge progresses only as a consequence of discovering mismatches between expectation and experience (actual or anticipated) and trying to resolve them – a process of trial and error-elimination.

(viii) Given that all knowledge is conjectural, and all attempts to justify particular claims to knowledge are (for logical reasons) futile, no claim to knowledge is warranted by seemingly compelling evidence or good reasons. In the growth of knowledge, evidence and reasoning facilitate criticism, not justification.

(ix) A useful distinction can be made between the three worlds with which we engage: physical objects and events (world 1), subjective experience (world 2) and objective knowledge (world 3). The world of objective knowledge (or *objectified* knowledge, as I call it) is a human construct that is no less real than the other two worlds. It is comprised of formulated problems, descriptions, hypotheses, explanations and arguments. These ideas are embedded in products (books, musical scores, paintings, films, etc.), social practices and institutions. Ideas in world 3 are in the public domain and can be criticized, modified, developed and perhaps destroyed by anyone who has access to them.

2 Knowledge of reality

We are not only *in* a real world, a shared reality, we are also *of* it. In light of evolutionary epistemology, we can see that there is a sense in which all living things have conjectural knowledge of reality in the form of inborn and, in some cases, learnt expectations (see Chapter 2). Human knowledge, like that of other species, has its roots in how we came to develop and why we have avoided extinction. What is distinctive about our expectations – our knowledge of reality – is that we are extraordinarily more adept than any other species at making our expectations explicit by means of descriptive language, and, unlike any other species, we can argue about the truth of these descriptions. We can also discuss the validity of our arguments and the merits of our preferences and their underlying values.

Practitioners – such as teachers – engage in activities which involve a large number of complex ideas, many of which have been learnt through practical trial and error-elimination and are not fully articulated. One of the most important characteristics of implicit 'craft' knowledge of this kind is that, in principle, it can be made explicit, critically evaluated and utilized by others – indeed, there is a strand of education research, on teachers' thinking, which sets out to do this (see, e.g., Brown and McIntyre, 1993, and Swann and Brown, 1997).

So humans have not only an ability to learn – that is, to modify inborn dispositions – but also an ability to encapsulate many dispositions in a form that can be accommodated in the world of objectified knowledge. And, as already stated, ideas in this objectified domain can be criticized, modified and developed by anyone who has access to them. The world of objectified knowledge has a degree of autonomy; it is generated by us, but has an independent existence. As an illustration, I can formulate and publish a written argument, then forget about it for a decade; when I reread the argument, I may have to relearn it in order to understand it. It is my argument, in that I constructed it, but it has become detached from me to the extent that I have to reread the article in order to re-engage with its content. Even when I re-engage, it may still be the case that there exists someone who understands my argument better than I do. In short, not only do we interact with the natural world (landscape, other species, etc.) and the human world (involving consciousness of oneself and others), we also engage with theoretical constructs, including assumptions of fact, values, explanatory theories, and arguments (see Popper, 1979 [1972], chapters 3 and 4, and my Chapter 3, section 5). As illustrated in Chapter 7, section 3, we can use internally objectified expectations to engage in private trial-and-error thought experiments.

This discussion has, so far, left open the nature of the relationship between a description (which may have explanatory elements) and the reality that the description is about. Epistemologically, the only satisfactory position is to regard the description as a (trial) representation of an aspect of reality. The description (which is in itself real) is *about* something without being the thing it represents. Representation does not imply reproduction – assuming that it does leads to unnecessary epistemological difficulties (for further discussion, see Hammersley, 1998). Some critics of this form of realism equate it with a belief in certain or secure knowledge. They suppose that 'knowledge of reality' refers to ideas about reality which are certainly, or almost certainly, true. If we adhere to the idea of certain or secure knowledge, then the realism I am proposing is indeed problematic, not least because there is no independent way of checking the truth of our knowledge against reality. However, if we abandon this idea of foundationalism and its attendant concern with verification and justification, then the objections to the idea that we can have knowledge of reality pale into insignificance. We cannot *justify* our knowledge by checking it against reality, but we can *test* it against reality. Provided that knowledge is regarded as representational rather than reproductive, and provisional and fallible rather than certain or secure, then it need not be contentious to say that we have knowledge of reality.

3 Limitations of evidence

As stated in the introduction to this chapter, research is a way of finding things out and of developing new and potentially better ideas and practices – a means of advancing knowledge. The term 'research' also implies some kind of systematic investigation, with outcomes that are presented in a publicly accessible form, for discussion and use by others. As intimated above, I would further suggest that research in the physical and social sciences and research that relates either directly or indirectly to education or social policy and practice are concerned with facts and theories about facts – though this is not to deny that value issues are also important, particularly in research related to education or social policy and practice. Research that is empirical (that which utilizes observation and experience or experiment) and research that is historical (that which involves the study of the past) are concerned with the production not only of argument (the focus of philosophical research) but also of evidence. There are, however, various conceptions of evidence, and the way it is used varies significantly across different research projects. This is true not only across different fields of enquiry but also within the field of education research. Given the prevalence of the widely discussed idea of evidence-based practice, the topic of evidence merits some consideration here.

Suppose you read a report of a research project that appears to have been well designed and in which the conclusions seem to be consistent with the evidence presented. Would you believe that the research findings are secure – that is, reliable and dependable? Were the findings to be replicated in similar studies, or seemingly confirmed by evidence of a different kind from elsewhere, would this make them even more secure? Insofar as the findings have practical implications, do they constitute a basis for making practical judgements? The answer that many researchers and policy makers in education would give to these questions is yes. In particular, it is widely assumed that the growth of knowledge involves the accumulation of evidence – presented as research findings – that supports generalized theories. An increase in confirming evidence, particularly that which has been sought under controlled conditions, makes belief in the truth of a theory more reasonable and the theory less subject to doubt. Generalizations are considered to be more secure the greater the extent to which they are justified by argument and evidence, the production of which is thought to be the raison d'être of research.

As discussed in Part 1 of this book, Popper's philosophy contests that assumption and its justificationist epistemology. Following Popper, while accepting that evidence is crucial to research endeavours, I question the role widely attributed to it, not least because our perceptions of evidence are always expectation-laden and fallible. It is worth remembering that there was considerable evidence to support the idea that 'the Earth is flat'. This idea was reasoned, seemingly consistent with what was observed, and false. In the remainder of this section and the one that follows, I revisit some of the ideas that were discussed in the context of learning in general in Chapters 2 and 4. Here my concern is with research as a particular exemplification of learning. Although the points I raise are not new, they are often overlooked.

First, it is a commonplace of post-Humean philosophy that no number of true singular statements of the kind 'This is a white swan' will establish the truth of the universal theory 'All swans are white'. Nonetheless, many people are still inclined to believe that when a phenomenon has been observed on many occasions, this justifies the conclusion that it is universal. According to this view, if, in a specific type of situation, a particular teaching practice, X, and a particular set of learning achievements, Y, have occurred together, then in comparable circumstances the teaching practice will be accompanied by a similar set of learning achievements. It is often further inferred that there is a causal link between X and Y. Logically speaking, however, there is no reason to assume that the future will be like the past, and any explanatory theory about the link between X and Y is not made more secure by multiple observations in which X and Y occur together.

Of course, at a practical level, we have to assume some regularities, but this is not to say that those we take for granted are made more secure by the proliferation of supporting evidence. We are often inclined to believe that future occurrences will match current expectations, but any such expectations we may have – including those formalized as theories – are not objectively strengthened by our subjective attachment to them. (Except, of course, in the case of self-fulfilling prophecies, whereby we bring about what we expect to occur.) The discovery of evidence that seems to support a universal theory or other expectation may be comforting, but the theory (or other expectation) is not strengthened by such a discovery, though our confidence in it may be (such psychological confidence should not to be confused with epistemological confidence – see the discussion of the role of so-called confirming evidence in Chapter 4, section 3).

Second, what we observe in any situation is dependent not only on what is there but also on our expectations, explicit and implicit (as discussed in Part 1; see also Popper, 1979 [1972], appendix 1). Often we see what we expect to see and fail to notice what we consider to be unimportant. Sometimes we fail to observe something because we would prefer that it did not exist. Even if our intention is to observe a situation with an open or unbiased mind, we cannot do so because expectation-free observation is impossible. Observations are made rather than received; they are selective, and there is always scope for distortion and error. Even when two or more people think they have observed the same thing, and have agreed what that thing is, they may still be mistaken.

Third, there is an extension of the second point: we cannot know everything there is to know about a situation. Even if our knowledge is sound – and we cannot know whether this is so – it will inevitably be limited. Those aspects of a situation about which we are currently ignorant may be of great importance. For example, a teaching practice may have the desired effect of increasing students' measured achievement at reading, but it may also have the unintended consequence of discouraging reading for pleasure.

Given that evidence is fallible and that so-called confirming evidence has no cumulative value other than to make us feel more confident, it is prudent not to construe the purpose of research as the pursuit of argument and evidence that will lead to secure knowledge. We can instead view research as a systematic attempt to speed up the development of *conjectural* knowledge. To regard research in this way does not preclude us from using the outcomes of research when making decisions about which one of a set of competing conjectural theories to exploit in practice (as discussed in section 5 below). And it makes no difference whether the research we conduct is classified as scientific. It may be believed that the conclusions of a scientific study are justified more strongly than those of any other type of research, but such a belief is mistaken (Miller, 2006a, chapter 7); the arguments against the pursuit of secure knowledge apply no less to science than to other types of research.

4 Appropriate use of evidence

As discussed in Chapter 4, section 2, Popper, in one of his most significant contributions to the philosophy of science, drew attention to an asymmetry between the verification and falsification of a universal theory (see, e.g., Popper, 1972a [1934], section 6). While no number of true singular statements can verify or prove the truth of such a theory, one true singular statement can refute it. Therefore, although no number of true statements of the kind 'This is a white swan' will imply the truth of the universal theory 'All swans are white', the statement 'This is a black swan', *if true*, will refute it.

This argument is well known among professional philosophers and fairly well known among academic educationists, but the subtleties of Popper's philosophy and its implications are often misunderstood. What is often wrongly assumed is that Popper asserted falsification as a means of pursuing secure knowledge of what is not so. Note that I have italicized the words 'if true' in the above paragraph: 'This is a black swan' falsifies 'All swans are white' only if the phenomenon to which it refers is indeed a black swan rather than, say, a bird that has been misidentified as a swan. As mentioned earlier, our observations are fallible. I stress again that Popper was not a naïve falsificationist: he never suggested that falsifiable claims to knowledge can be refuted conclusively. Deciding whether or not a theory has been falsified is always a matter of judgement, and judgement is potentially flawed.

Although the discovery of another white swan adds no weight to the universal theory 'All swans are white', the observation of a black swan shows that something is wrong. What may be wrong is the universal theory (as in this illustration), in which case we should be inclined to modify or abandon it. Or our observation may be in error. Either way, the situation with regard to our knowledge is not as it was.

There are different ways of dealing with the disequilibrium engendered by an apparent refutation: (a) we might deny or ignore the claim that a black swan has been observed, (b) we might immunize our universal theory by saying, for example, 'If it's black, it can't be a swan' or (c) we might decide to empirically investigate the matter further. The last of these responses may involve a replication study in which further attempts are made to observe black swans under what appear to be similar conditions to those of the initial observation. A replication study, as conceived here, is not designed to *confirm* the sighting of what is thought to be a black swan, but is a more focused attempt to *challenge* the universal theory 'All swans are white'. For our knowledge to develop, (c) is clearly the best option, not because it will lead to secure knowledge (it will not) but because an investigation requires us to engage in self-directed trial and error-elimination. In such a process, the discovery of error or specific limitation is the spur to create something new. Discoveries of error (and specific limitation) encourage us to create new theories, new artefacts and new ways of doing things.

In this regard, humans differ from other animals. We alone have a well-developed ability to seek out error by adopting a critical attitude and by setting up test situations, that is, situations specifically designed to facilitate the search for error. We also differ from other animals in the extent of our ability to respond creatively when an error is discovered. Our facility for descriptive and argumentative language and, following from this, our ability to interact with and contribute to a world of objectified knowledge better equip us to create situations in which our hypotheses 'die in our stead' (Popper, 1979 [1972], p. 244; see also my Chapter 3, section 5). Not only are we an inherently imaginative species, we can also afford to be bold in our imaginings because, by engaging in thought experiments and critical discussion, and by the use of drafts, pilot studies and prototypes, we can weed out at least some of our ill-judged and erroneous ideas without allowing them to further influence our actions.

If one accepts this argument, an important role for research lies in the discovery of evidence and in the formulation of arguments that challenge existing theories and assumptions, including those that underlie current and proposed policy and practice. This is not to suggest that any evidence (or argument) should be treated as conclusive; what counter-evidence serves to do first and foremost is encourage us to reconsider our existing assumptions. Again I stress that nothing should be regarded as secure, neither our existing assumptions nor any arguments and evidence that appear to challenge them. Although Popper's philosophy is one of absolute scepticism – there are no secure grounds for belief, and there is no place for justification – as discussed in my Chapter 4 (and see Chapter 9, section 2), it nonetheless admits the value of pursuing the truth about our shared reality. By pursuing truth we may, so to speak, stumble upon it, though we cannot be certain that we have done so. The method of pursuit is imaginative criticism (Popper, 1979 [1972], p. 148), which requires both an inclination to challenge the given or the habitual and also the intention to create something new and potentially better. The outcome is progression (in the form of new conjectures) and perhaps, if things go well, progress (new conjectures that are better than our previous conjectures).

The distinction between progression and progress is important (see Chapter 2, section 3). There is no guarantee that what develops by means of imaginative criticism will be an improvement on what went before. The growth of knowledge involves progression, as in the development of a new expectation ('Not all swans are white'), but it may not result in progress, as in the development of a better one. If we learn something that is false ('The Sun revolves around the Earth'), our knowledge will have changed but not necessarily be improved. Criticism facilitates progress; it does not ensure it. Given that our knowledge is fallible and partial, we can never be sure that progress or improvement has been achieved, even though it may appear to us that it has. The idea of progress and improvement, like that of truth, is best regarded as a regulative ideal, a standard at which to aim (see the introductory section to Chapter 10 for further discussion of the concept of improvement).

5 Choosing between competing theories

This discussion so far begs the question of how, when the situation arises, to choose between competing theories – specifically how to decide which of a set of competing theories might be utilized when developing proposals for action (e.g. how to choose between contrasting theories about how to teach reading).

In this regard, Popper stressed that 'from a rational point of view, we should not "rely" on any theory, for no theory has been shown to be true, or can be shown to be true' (Popper, 1979 [1972], p. 21) and added, 'but we should *prefer as basis for action the best-tested theory*' (ibid., p. 22) (see also, Popper, 1974, section 14, partly reprinted in Popper, 1985b, sections ix and x). An unrefuted, tested theory is 'an evaluating *report of past performance . . . it has to do with a situation which may lead us to prefer some theories to others. But it says nothing whatever about future performance, or about the "reliability" of a theory*' (Popper, 1979 [1972], p. 18). To think otherwise is to accept induction, and induction, as Popper cogently argued, is a myth (see my discussion in Chapter 4).

In the penultimate quotation, Popper seems to have suggested that a tested theory, specifically a well-tested theory, is preferable to one that has not been tested or has not been tested so rigorously. If 'tested theory' is taken to mean a refutable theory for which refuting evidence has been sought – rigorous empirical testing – then his recommendation is problematic. First, when faced with two competing theories, one of which has been subject to rigorous empirical testing and one of which has not, there is no reason to assume that an untested theory must be worse (or better) than a tested one (Miller, 2006a, p. 124). Second, even when choosing between theories that have been subjected to rigorous empirical testing, there is no logical reason for preferring a theory that has been tested but not refuted to one that has been tested and refuted. It is overstating the case to infer that we should prefer the unrefuted theory; all that can be deduced logically from the evidence is that we should not prefer the refuted theory to the unrefuted theory. As Miller put it (following Howson, 1984, p. 144),

> All that may be derived from the empirical report that T_1 is refuted and T_2 is not refuted (together with a statement of our preference for truth over falsehood) is not that T_2 *should be preferred to* T_1, but that T_1 *should not be preferred to* T_2.
> (2006a, p. 127)

The details of the discussion above may seem of little relevance to practitioners – such as teachers, education policy makers and managers – who are, of necessity, usually obliged to choose between competing theories that have not been (and in many cases could not be) tested by the search for refuting evidence. However, when one reads more of the passage from which Popper's comment about preference has been drawn, it seems that he has assigned a broader meaning to 'tested theory' than that of a refutable theory for which an empirical refutation has been sought. He states that 'the best-tested theory is the one which, in the light of our *critical discussion*, appears to be the best so far' (Popper, 1979 [1972], p. 22). This quotation from Popper is drawn from a lengthy discussion about the effect that the results of *empirical* tests may have on our theoretical preferences, but the idea of choosing between theories in light of critical discussion has broader implications. We test theories by means of critical discussion, and such discussion may or may not refer to the outcomes of empirical tests.

I propose that in what might be described as an ideal situation, the practitioner will be able to choose between critically evaluated theories. And if a choice is to be made between theories of what is the case, then sometimes it will be between those for which refutations have been sought, if these theories are scientific in the Popperian sense of being refutable. In all circumstances, a rational decision would involve rejecting any theory that had failed to withstand criticism or had stood up to criticism less well than an alternative. This would not commit us to the view that the surviving theories are justified or secure, or that the criticism is secure; rather, we would merely make our decision on the basis of the available argument and evidence. These ideal circumstances presuppose the existence of prior critical thought and, in the case of empirically tested theories, prior research. But often the choices that face us are between theories that have not been subjected to rigorous criticism, or between some that have and some that have not – in which case, as indicated above, there is no reason to assume that a theory that has not been empirically tested and/or critically discussed must be less (or, perhaps, more) satisfactory than one that has been empirically tested and/or critically discussed.

6 To go boldly, or not

Research can do more than challenge current theories and assumptions; it is a means by which ideas that transcend rather than merely conflict with existing knowledge may be developed. It involves not only the search for critical evidence but also the creation of new problems, new theories and new arguments. At best, the outcomes of any research project or programme will include one or more of the following (modified from Swann, 2003b, p. 12):

(a) the revealing of a hitherto unrecognized mismatch between expectation and experience (actual or anticipated) that has far-reaching practical and/or theoretical consequences

(b) the formulation of a new and important problem
(c) the production of a new and better solution to an existing problem
(d) the development of a constructive way of challenging existing expectations.

This conception of research attributes value to intellectual boldness. Intellectual boldness is not to be taken to imply boldness in social practice. As Miller explained, 'Popper prescribes revolutionary thinking in science because its products, imaginative new theories, are easily relinquished if they are mistaken', and 'he proscribes revolutionary activity in society' because 'its consequences, which are rarely possible to foresee, are almost always altogether impossible to overcome' (1985, p. 12). Whereas caution is a virtue with regard to radical large-scale education policy initiatives, it is not desirable when developing hypotheses about the nature and effects of existing practices and about how these practices may best be developed. (Caution is, however, appropriate in respect of the ethical implications of devising ways of testing hypotheses.)

A tradition has developed in the physical sciences in which bold hypotheses are formulated and tested, but in education research there have been comparatively few projects of this kind. It seems that most education research projects are designed to address a set of research questions and are not designed to test a set of hypotheses. This is partly because hypothesis testing is widely construed to require a large quantity of data, but much education research is small-scale, and ideas about hypotheses formulation and testing are not well understood. The assumption that testing requires an abundance of supportive data is significantly different from the Popperian idea of testing as the search for refuting evidence. The latter, among other things, gives credence to the idea that a small-scale, rigorously conducted case study can cast doubt on a widely accepted theory or assumption. The Popperian researcher aspires to create a bold hypothesis which withstands rigorous attempts at refutation and/or rigorous criticism. And science is, at its best, a tradition of problem posing in which bold explanatory ideas about the world (and our place within it) are created and then tested by the search for refuting evidence.

If one assumes that discovering more white swans will strengthen the theory 'All swans are white', one will be inclined to search for white swans, not swans of a different hue. And although most people will accept that a theory is challenged by refuting evidence, they are often reluctant to view a refutation as a welcome stimulus for learning. Rather, a refutation is construed as evidence of failure to produce the secure knowledge that is desired. In such a climate, bold theorizing tends to be unwelcome. And what often happens is that generalizations, which are usually somewhat timid, are proffered at the end of a research project according to the amount of supporting data seemingly generated or identified through the research – the assumption is clearly, if not explicitly, that knowledge grows by a process of induction.

With regard to question-answering research, some questions are genuinely open-ended, that is, the researcher does not have an answer in mind. However, as discussed in Pratt and Swann (2003, p. 183), although there is nothing wrong per se with formulating interesting and consequential questions of what is the case and developing ways of answering them, it seems that question answering is often used in education as a substitute for hypothesis testing; the researcher has expectations about what the answers to the research questions might be, but these are not made explicit. For example, a researcher might set out to address 'What is the impact of our literacy programme on children's attitudes to reading?' It may be the case that she has no conscious expectations as to what the answer will be. But if she has, there is a danger that she will merely search for evidence that will confirm her unformulated expectations (implicit hypotheses). Of course, even when a hypothesis is explicit, the researcher may be tempted to search for – and therefore be more likely to find – confirming evidence. But, in general, an explicit hypothesis is more encouraging of a challenge, unless it appears to be a statement of the obvious. (But even those hypotheses that appear to be obviously true may in fact be false.)

While education researchers tend to be timorous with regard to theory development, education policy makers, particularly in England, have become increasingly willing to throw caution to the wind when it comes to introducing radical and far-reaching policy initiatives. As discussed in Chapter 6, section 3, the Education Reform Act 1988 gave the Secretary of State for Education a huge number of new powers with regard to the content, organization and conduct of education. As Tyrrell Burgess (1989) predicted, these powers are exercised through the 'deft use of councils and committees', which to a significant extent shield the Secretary of State and her (or his) Ministers for Education from taking responsibility for the consequences of government policy.

Perhaps unsurprisingly, research that challenges government policy is not welcomed by the government. Politicians in power tend to favour research with the potential to challenge the practices of teachers and education managers, rather than government policy makers' assumptions about the purpose, structure and administration of the education system. In such a context, and given a justificationist epistemology, one of the principal tasks for education researchers becomes that of finding out 'what works' in schools and classrooms. The job of education policy makers becomes that of devising the policies that will 'ensure' that teachers and education managers apply this knowledge in their practice (see, e.g., Blunkett, 2000, paragraph 63; the Organisation for Economic Co-operation and Development, 2003, p. 3, discussed in Swann, 2005).

If we could have secure knowledge of what works, then the boldness of the vision of politicians and their appointees might perhaps be commendable, though the intention to intervene in people's lives on a grand scale might still be criticized as authoritarian. Given that secure knowledge is no more than a chimera, large-scale social engineering – which is what many governmental policy initiatives are designed to bring about – should be embarked on with extreme caution. Piecemeal rather than holistic approaches are to be recommended (Popper, 1961 [1957], section 21, reprinted in Popper, 1985d, section II; see also my Chapter 10), with the function of research being both developmental and critical in relation to the assumptions that underlie social policy.

7 Practical and theoretical problems

The idea of applying in practice what is learnt through research is also problematic – more so than is apparent in much of the debate about evidence-based or research-based practice. As discussed in Chapter 3, section 5, there are two significantly different kinds of problems – practical and theoretical – and these require qualitatively different types of solutions. Although Burgess (e.g. 1977, 1985b), Pratt (1999) and myself are not the only educationists to distinguish practical from theoretical problems (see, e.g., Naish and Hartnett, 1975), researchers and other scholars mostly focus on the analysis of theoretical problems and their solutions rather than practical problems and their solutions. Practice, including policy-as-practice, is often thought to embody theory, but rarely is it analysed in terms of the question 'Which practical problem, or set of practical problems, is this practice designed to solve?' Problems of practice are rarely differentiated from theoretical problems, with the result that solutions to the former are often misguidedly sought in solutions to the latter (Burgess, 1977, pp. 133–4).

Practical problems are those of getting from one state of affairs to another (following Krick, 1969 [1965], p. 3). Their solutions – successful or not – require states of affairs that arise as a consequence of things having been done (or decisions being taken not to act, or when something happens that solves the problem). Further to my discussion in Chapter 3, section 5, practical problems can be formulated as 'How can . . . ?' questions. Answers to such questions can also be formulated in words, for example, 'By doing . . .' or 'By not doing. . .'. But the content of such a linguistic formulation is not a solution to a practical problem; it merely indicates what might be done. In contrast, theoretical problems are those for which the solution is a theory or set of theories. They include problems of fact ('What is so?', 'What was so?', 'What will be so?', and 'Why?'), as well as problems of value ('What is good?', 'What ought to be done?', 'What is aesthetically pleasing?', and 'Why?') and problems of logic ('What is valid?' and 'Why?').

A key difference between theoretical problems and practical problems is that the testing of solutions to the former involves addressing the question 'Is this theory true?' and/or 'Is this argument valid?', whereas the testing of solutions to the latter involves addressing the question 'What happened?' or 'What is happening?' Of course, solutions to theoretical problems can be useful insofar as they constitute relevant knowledge that can be exploited in practice or because they signal the need for caution in respect of a particular practice or proposal for action, but it is a major mistake to assume that solutions to theoretical problems can be directly translated into solutions to practical problems.

Practical problems include those traditionally referred to as engineering problems. A typical formulated engineering problem is 'How can we build a bridge across this river?' (though it should be noted that this presupposes an earlier problem, 'How can we cross this river?', and the chosen solution 'by building a bridge'). In order to solve the problem, the engineer will explore alternative solutions and exploit universal theories about bridge building. Although the best approaches to bridge building generally involve the exploitation of scientific theory, bridge building is not merely a matter of applying the outcomes of scientific research (Miller, 2006a, chapter 5). Indeed, bridges were being built long before there was any scientific research to exploit. Scientific knowledge is a valuable resource that engineers can exploit, but of itself it does not enable them to build a successful bridge. Neither the natural nor the social sciences can provide us with blueprints that will guarantee practical success. Practical problems can be messy and complex, and their solutions may be affected by multiple uncontrollable variables. Bringing about a desired state of affairs requires creative activity on the part of the practitioner, even though she will invariably draw on knowledge of various kinds, much of which will be implicit and/or taken for granted.

Teaching and education policy making are practical activities, and people who engage in them are necessarily involved in processes of practical trial and error-elimination, whether or not they are conscious of this being so. These processes may exploit the outcomes of education research, but they will always have unresearched dimensions, and these can have greater significance than politicians and other policy makers care to admit. Teachers and other educationists can, and generally speaking should, exploit ideas from research in their policies and practices. But they should be wary of accepting the outcomes of research uncritically, and they should also refrain from adopting the pervasive 'positivist' idea that everything that is important about teaching and learning can be unambiguously observed and measured. Research-*influenced* practice is, I would suggest, a better term and a better aspiration than evidence-based or research-based practice. And whatever the quality of the research, the improvement of educational practice requires practitioners to 'try it and see'. They need to formulate practical problems, and propose and critically test solutions.

How, then, should we choose between proposals for action, for example, proposals about the organization and conduct of teaching? My answer is that we should view a set of competing proposals for action as a response to a practical problem, addressing the following:

(i)   What is the problem that these proposals are intended to solve?

(ii) Whose problem is it? (For example: the teachers'? the students'? central government politicians'? etc.)

(iii) To what extent is the problem worthy of attention?

(iv) What are the cost implications (monetary or otherwise) of each of the proposals, that is, as tentative solutions to the problem?

(v)   For each proposal, if we act on it, is the problem unlikely to be solved?

(vi) For each proposal, what might be the unintended consequences, desirable or undesirable, of acting on it?

(vii) Do we need to look for a better way of doing things?

When addressing these questions, we should refer to evidence and argument that are relevant and available to us, then reject 'any practical proposal that does not survive critical scrutiny as well as others do' (Miller, 2006a, p. 124). After that, what we decide to do can be only a matter of guesswork. We have to try it and see. If practical improvement is what we desire, each of us – working individually, as a member of a group or as an agent of an institution – has to adopt a course of action and evaluate it. If we discover unexpected consequences (desirable or undesirable), we are then in a position to learn.

It should be noted that Popper also distinguished between practical and theoretical problems (see, e.g., Popper, 1992a [1974], section 29; 1992b, chapter 5 [1969]; 1994b, p. 11), but the distinction remained relatively undeveloped in his work. To quote from Burgess's (2002, p. 5) discussion of Popper's 27 theses on the social sciences, 'he [Popper] does not match the usefulness of practical problems for theory with an account of the part theory might play in the solution of practical problems'. Popper did, however, discuss the relationship between science and technology (see, e.g., 1979 [1972], pp. 352–3) and between social science and social engineering (1961 [1957], section 20).

8 Two types of research

Given that there are two significantly different types of problems, there is scope for two significantly different types of research: one focusing on the formulation of theoretical problems and the development and testing of theoretical solutions; the other focusing on the formulation of practical problems and the development and testing of practical solutions. The first type includes not only philosophical research but also scientific research and exploratory theoretical studies of various kinds. The second includes engineering research (now often subsumed under the label of scientific research) and, in social fields including education, what is often referred to as action research.

The distinction I am making goes beyond differentiating between theorizing about theory and theorizing about practice. Both of these categories of activity produce theory; either may produce theory with direct relevance to practice, though only the latter is specifically designed for this purpose. Action research and engineering research also produce theory, but the theory they produce is distinctively the outcome of the practical attempt to solve practical problems. (See Chapter 10 for further discussion of action research.) The idea of applied research is broader than that of engineering or action research. Applied research focuses on a specific practical problem, but not all applied research involves the development of a practical solution. Evaluation studies, for example, are concerned with evaluating, not creating, solutions to practical problems; an evaluation study may conclude with proposals for action, but the exploitation of these proposals in practice is not part of its remit. If we want to research practical problems practically, then we must engage in some kind of engineering research or action research.

I stress that, in saying there are two types of research, I am not implying that they are unrelated. Nor am I suggesting that engineering and action research have no theoretical dimension. When our ideas develop, this potentially affects what we are capable of doing and what we may wish to do. And when we do things and learn from the experience – when the things we do are shown to have unexpected consequences – this involves us in modifying our expectations, our implicit and explicit theories. Both kinds of research have implications for practice: they produce conjectural knowledge to which practitioners, such as teachers, can refer when they plan to act, act and evaluate action. Research of both kinds is required if the improvement of practice is our goal, and both are the better for being undertaken with a critical rather than a justificationist attitude.

9 Developing a Popperian Science of School Teaching

I hold that orthodoxy is the death of knowledge, since the growth of knowledge depends entirely on the existence of disagreement.

—*Karl Popper,* The Myth of the Framework:
In Defence of Science and Rationality

There is a reality behind the world as it appears to us, possibly a many-layered reality, of which the appearances are the outermost layers. What the great scientist does is boldly to guess, daringly to conjecture, what these inner realities are like. This is akin to mythmaking. . . . The boldness can be gauged by the distance between the world of appearance and the conjectured reality, the explanatory hypotheses.

But there is another, a special kind of boldness – the boldness of predicting aspects of the world of appearance which so far have been overlooked but which it must possess if the conjectured reality is (more or less) right, if the explanatory hypotheses are (approximately) true. . . . It is the boldness of a conjecture which takes a real risk – the risk of being tested, and refuted; the risk of clashing with reality.

—*Karl Popper, 'Replies to my critics'*
(*in* The Philosophy of Karl Popper, Book 1, *edited by P. A. Schilpp*)

Introduction

While it is true that assumptions of value – ideas about what is right and good – influence the way in which individuals and groups construe the nature and purpose of education, this should not blind us to the existence of assumptions of fact about how to promote learning and improve the conduct and organization of teaching in our institutions of formal education. The policy and practice of education and teaching are influenced no less by assumptions of fact than by assumptions of value. In this chapter, I show how a Popperian approach to science – a form of *post*positivism – has the potential to advance our conjectural knowledge of the facts about the organization and conduct of teaching. In the context of this discussion, I show how the set of principles and guidelines for teaching set out in Part 2 of the book, when supported by the approach to professional development advocated in Chapter 10, could be tested and developed as part of a science of school teaching.

This chapter builds on the discussion of learning in Part 1 and presupposes an understanding of the issues addressed in Chapter 8, 'Research and the development of teaching'. Note in particular that although my concern in this chapter is with a science of school teaching, I attach value also to other kinds of educational inquiry. There is clearly a place for action research, with its focus on practical problems (see Chapter 8, section 8; Chapter 10, section 6), and for a variety of theoretical studies, including philosophical, historical and ethical investigations, and exploratory empirical inquiries of various kinds. What science offers is the most rigorous means at our disposal for addressing 'questions of fact, and assertions about facts: theories and hypotheses; the problems they solve; and the problems they raise' (Popper, 1992a [1974], p. 19). How policy makers and other practitioners construe, respond to and use research is, of course, another matter entirely.

1 Positivism, postpositivism and empiricism

Science is often associated with positivism and with the so-called quantitative paradigm of positivist research (for a critique of the quantitative/qualitative dichotomy, see Pring, 2004 [2000], pp. 44–56). I would not mention the terms 'positivism' and 'positivist' were they not still so commonly used in discussions of science, specifically in the social sciences and education (with regard to the latter see, e.g., the widely read Cohen et al., 2007 [1980], chapter 1). Denis Phillips, writing two decades ago, highlighted limitations in usage:

> those philosophers to whom the term [positivist] accurately applies have long since shuffled off this mortal coil, while any living social scientists who either bandy the term around, or are the recipients of it as an abusive label, are so confused about what it means that, while the word is full of sound and fury, it signifies nothing.
>
> (1992b, p. 95, and 2000, p. 157)

Despite the above words, Phillips (1987, chapter 4; 1992b, chapter 7; 2000, chapter 9; and Phillips and Burbules, 2000, chapter 1) and many other theorists have tried to make sense of the ways in which 'positivism' is used, distinguishing in particular between Comtean positivism (the term 'positivism' being attributable to the 19th century French philosopher Auguste Comte), logical positivism (a philosophical movement that developed in Austria and Germany during the 1920s) and the use of 'positivism' in common parlance. While I acknowledge that the term is problematic, it seems to me that it is a convenient and not inappropriate label for the following set of ideas:

(i) Scientific knowledge is derived from the accumulation of data obtained theory-free and value-free from observation.

(ii) Anything that cannot be observed and in some way measured – that is, quantified – is of little or no importance or (in extreme versions of positivism) non-existent.

(iii) Science is the pursuit of foundational knowledge.

In addition, positivism in the social sciences includes the idea that

(iv) Scientific method is applicable not only to the study of natural phenomena but also to the study of human affairs.

Given this description of positivism, it can be seen that behaviourism as a learning theory (discussed in Chapter 4) has developed out of a positivist epistemology. I would further argue that positivist ideas have continued to thrive in government social policy, at least in the United Kingdom. Nonetheless, it is clear that many scientists are *not* positivists, and to define science as exclusively positivist is to ignore the diversity of scientific endeavour in both the natural and social sciences.

Sometimes the term 'positivist' is used to describe anyone in the social sciences and related fields who accepts point (iv) above, but this use of 'positivist' invariably fails to acknowledge the development of non-positivist science. Many scientists and philosophers think there are similarities of method between the natural and social sciences, but their conception of science is non-positivist; that is, they reject points (i), (ii) and (iii). Many of them could be described as postpositivists.

The term 'postpositivism' does not represent a unified school of thought, and there are significant issues about which postpositivists disagree. But the term usefully denotes a view of science which acknowledges that 'human knowledge is not based on unchallengeable, rock-solid foundations – it is *conjectural*' (Phillips and Burbules, 2000, p. 26). Postpositivists are united in their adherence to fallibilism – the idea that all scientific knowledge is potentially subject to the discovery of error and should therefore be regarded as provisional. The view of science presented in this book, and in this chapter in particular, can therefore be classified as a form of postpositivism, and in broad terms my thesis is compatible with that of Phillips and Nicholas Burbules when they argue that

> much educational research can be, and ought to be, 'scientific.' But we add the vital proviso that this position is reasonable only if the positivistic account of the nature of science prevalent in earlier times is replaced by a more up-to-date *postpositivist* account.
>
> (Ibid., p. 65)

'Positivist' is sometimes used incorrectly as a synonym for 'empiricist'. Traditionally, empiricism has been contrasted with rationalism. In modern thinking, however, these 'isms' have been modified to the point at which a coherent epistemology may be both empiricist and rationalist. Put simply, to an empiricist, knowledge and sensory experience are inextricably linked. Knowledge is thought to start with experience (naïve and classical empiricism) or be justified by experience (an implication of pragmatism) or be open to criticism by experience (the Popperian view). Rationalists, on the other hand, elevate reason above the senses in the development of knowledge (Cottingham, 1984, p. 6). Empiricists do not inevitably deny the importance of reason in learning (on the contrary), nor do rationalists deny the importance of sense experience. Although naïve and classical empiricists either reject or do not attribute importance to the idea of a priori knowledge (i.e. knowledge before experience), this is not true of modern empiricists. Similarly, whereas classical rationalists assert the existence of infallible a priori knowledge, modern rationalists regard such knowledge as fallible.

Although most positivists are empiricists, not all empiricists are positivists (and many are clearly postpositivists). There is no inherent conflict between empiricism and the idea that there are features of the world (particularly the human world) which are important yet not readily measurable or even directly observable. Karl Popper is, emphatically, not a positivist (see Popper, 1994a, chapter 3 [1970]). He described himself as 'a rationalist of sorts' (Popper, 1972b [1963], p. 6) in that he believed in a priori knowledge. However, he departed from classical rationalism in that he regarded such knowledge as conjectural and fallible. He was also 'an empiricist of sorts' (ibid., p. 406; see also p. 6) in that he argued that 'we learn from experience – that is, from our mistakes – how to correct them' (ibid., p. 406), but, as discussed in my Part 1, he nonetheless rejected the idea of pure observation and pure sense experience. Popper's variety of rationalism is now widely termed *critical rationalism*.

2 Rejecting justificationism

Although Popper's epistemology is clearly a form of 'postpositivism', the term 'postpositivist' does not imply full acceptance of Popper's falsificationist approach to science nor his complete rejection of justificationism.

Justificationism in science is the idea that

> a hypothesis has to pass tests, or be confirmed, or in some other way be touched with grace, if it is to be admitted to the realm of scientific knowledge; if it fails these tests, or is disconfirmed, or even if it fails to be confirmed, it is excluded. . . . For justificationists . . . the passing of tests is quite as important as the failing of tests, for it is precisely this that determines whether a hypothesis is admitted to the body of science.
>
> (As described in a critique – Miller, 1994, pp. 6–7)

Falsificationism, by contrast, is the idea that a falsifiable universal theory may be admitted to science, even if nothing is known about how it performs in practice. Once admitted, it must be subjected to testing – that is, to the search for refuting evidence. A refuted theory may either be rejected or, in some cases, modified.

Popper's anti-justificationism is best understood as a *sceptical* form of fallibilism (and by implication a sceptical form of postpositivism). In the words of David Miller, 'A *fallibilist*, in brief, is one who repudiates the quest for conclusive justification and certainty. A *sceptic* is one, like Hume and Popper, who repudiates also the quest for partial justification and probability' (2006a, p. 72). Miller goes on to distinguish pyrrhonian sceptics, who advise against making any judgements about the worth of hypotheses, from optimistic sceptics, such as Popper and others who proceed on the understanding that 'some . . . hypotheses are sometimes better than others' (ibid.).

At the heart of justificationism is the idea that an appropriate response to a claim to knowledge is to ask 'How do you know?' on the grounds that such claims should be accepted only if they can be justified or verified (Perkinson, 1971, p. 25). To ask 'How do you know?' – or, more formally, to ask for grounds for a particular assertion – is to call for reasons; it is also to call for the identification of an authority. What counts as an acceptable authority varies according to era, culture and ideology. Accepted authorities include, variously, religious texts, the senses, intuition, acknowledged experts, empirical evidence and common sense. Scientific rationality has traditionally been associated with a call for empirical evidence as the accepted authority, but such a view of science is no less justificationist, and no less problematic, than a claim to authority that refers to intuition, or a holy text.

Justificationism is problematic in a number of respects. In its purest form, it serves to undermine rationality, as the following critique by Henry Perkinson shows:

> no justificationist . . . can avoid falling into an infinite regress. For no matter what authority is appealed to, we can always ask that the authority itself be justified. In other words, if someone tries to justify a claim by producing 'evidence' to support it, and then justifies the 'evidence' by appealing to the so-called 'rules for evidence,' he can still be challenged to justify these rules for evidence. And until he does, the original claim remains unjustified. Moreover, no matter what authority he appeals to in order to justify the rules for evidence, we can ask him to justify that authority as well, and so on into infinity. And this simply means that we can never justify our claims. . . .

> There is one 'out' the chastened justificationist might take: he can become dogmatic. He can set up some authority as infallible. This might be 'the majority,' or the 'rules of evidence accepted by philosophers,' or 'ordinary language,' or 'normal sense experience' or some other authority. In this case he simply rejects all requests to justify his authority, since that authority is 'infallible.' But using this 'out' to avoid the infinite regress still results in a denial of rationality . . . since the chastened justificationist now winds up accepting his authority without its being justified.
>
> (Ibid., p. 27)

Partial justificationists may be less susceptible to the above critique because they at least acknowledge the fallibilist nature of knowledge, maintaining that

> even if scientific hypotheses cannot be proved by evidence, they remain open to partial justification, confirmation, empirical support, or something of that kind. Universal hypotheses cannot be made certain – if only because the evidence is not certain – but they can be rendered plausible, or probable, or reasonable.
> (As described in a critique – Miller, 2006a, p. 71)

However, as David Hume, Popper and others (e.g. ibid., pp. 71–6) have argued, the logical invalidity of inductive inferences is no less relevant to the pursuit of probability and to the concepts of plausibility and reasonableness (see also, ibid., pp. 153–8). Also, methodologically, one of the major problems with justificationism, whether full or partial, is that it stifles creativity because new ideas often cannot immediately be justified by reference to what has hitherto been acknowledged and accepted. Orthodoxy tends to prevail, and with it the growth of knowledge is undermined (see the first quotation from Popper at the head of this chapter – Popper, 1994a, p. 34).

Notwithstanding the now widely accepted view, quoted in section 1 above, that 'human knowledge is not based on unchallengeable, rock-solid foundations – it is *conjectural*' (Phillips and Burbules, 2000, p. 26), partial justificationism thrives in many areas of academia. The pursuit of certainty has been abandoned and with it justificationism in its purist form, but partial justificationism survives and the optimistic scepticism of Popperian falsificationists does not prevail. Even as fallibilists, Phillips and Burbules show an adherence to partial justificationism when they write,

> We have grounds, or warrants, for asserting the beliefs, or conjectures, that we hold as scientists, often very good grounds, but these grounds are not

indubitable. Our warrants for accepting these things can be withdrawn in the light of further investigation.

(Ibid.)

As discussed in my Chapter 4 (and see section 1 above), Popper developed a new form of rationalism, critical rationalism, which admits no grounds or warrants for knowledge. Critical rationalism has broken the link between rationality and justification, such that, with regard to science,

What is rational about scientific activity is not that it provides us with reasons for its conclusions, which it does not, but that it takes seriously the use of reason – deductive logic, that is – in the criticism and appraisal of those conclusions.

(Miller, 1994, p. ix)

Reason serves not to justify claims to knowledge, not even partially; rather, its role is in the criticism and, more broadly, the evaluation of such claims. In light of critical rationalism, one need not feel obliged to attempt to justify theories and beliefs, though one may feel obliged to defend them against criticism; defence should not be conflated with justification. The task of the scientist is that described by Popper in the second of the two quotations at the head of the chapter (1974, pp. 980–1, reprinted in 1985c, p. 122; and see my Chapter 8, section 6). The task is to create bold and empirically testable challenges to orthodoxy, challenges which are effective because refuting evidence, though sought, is not forthcoming.

3 Science, fact and value

For Popper and Popperians, the creation of testable universal theories is fundamental to science. Scientific knowledge is that body of objectified knowledge which comprises universal theories that have been formulated in a way that makes them susceptible to falsification, and formulated problems and arguments which relate to such theories. We pursue truth – that is, we try to advance our knowledge of the facts about the universe – by searching for and eliminating error and specific limitation in what we know.

This conception of science is no less applicable to the study of human social endeavours, such as education and teaching, than it is to the study of natural phenomena. Despite ethical constraints, and problems of reflexivity, whereby the researcher and the researched interact, there are nonetheless ways in which we can study scientifically the relationship between (a) educational structures (such as schools) and practices (such as teaching) and (b) those involved in education (students and teachers). We can also consider the implications of scientific studies of the behaviour and functioning of humans for the conduct and organization of teaching and learning within educational institutions.

The conception of science set out in this chapter (and, indeed, in the book as a whole) is compatible with the features of a social science discussed by Popper in his 27 theses on the logic of the social sciences (1992b, chapter 5 [1962]). For the social sciences, he proposed the method of '*objective* understanding, or situational logic' which 'consists in analysing the *situation* of the acting person sufficiently to explain the action in terms of the situation without any further help from psychology. Objective "understanding" consists in realizing that the action was objectively *appropriate to the situation*' (ibid., p. 79). This situational logic assumes not only the existence of a physical world but also a social world that includes social institutions as well as people. Popper further suggested that 'We might construct a theory of intended and unintended institutional consequences of purposive action' (ibid., p. 80; see also Pratt, 2003). 'Purposive action' refers to what individuals do, not only when they act purely for themselves but also when they act as agents of institutions: 'Institutions do not act; rather, only individuals act, within or on behalf of institutions' (Popper, 1992b [1969], p. 80).

It follows that we can develop scientific hypotheses not only about the intended consequences of action but also about unintended consequences – for instance, in the context of institutions, such as schools. An example of the latter, drawing on situational logic, would be 'In all situations in which school league tables, based on student achievement in standard tests, are introduced, 80 per cent (or more) of all the teachers involved become increasingly inclined to teach to the test, and for these teachers the learning of 90 per cent (or more) of all their students becomes narrower in scope and less profound.' By specifying '80 per cent (or more) of all teachers' and, for these teachers, '90 per cent (or more) of all their students', I have made the theory less bold and perhaps less susceptible to refutation than if I had merely said 'all teachers' and 'all students', but the theory has not necessarily been made less interesting. This theory is, however, merely illustrative – I am not for the purposes of this chapter asserting that it is true, though I am assuming that the stated consequence would be unintended. Note that, with regard to any action, both a theory about its intended consequences and a theory about its unintended consequences may be true.

I am aware that some people think that questions about education are pre-eminently questions of value, and, as noted earlier in the book, I do not deny that in education, as in other fields, issues of fact and value emerge together with problems (see Popper, 1992a [1974], section 40). Nor can discussion of such matters be divorced from the idea that whereas some trains of thought contain valid arguments, others do not. But it seems clear that we can pose questions – that is, formulate problems – in which the principal concern is with matters of fact, and these differ from questions in which the principal concern is with value or with logical validity.

We can, for example, formulate problems regarding the value of reading, and our solutions to such problems will relate to the way in which we construe the primary purpose of an education service and the schools that operate within it. Possible answers to the question 'What value is there in teaching children to read?' include 'To enable them to eventually become effective members of the workforce', 'To enable them to develop full learner autonomy' and 'So that their lives may be enriched by the pleasures of reading'. Although these answers are not necessarily incompatible, each presupposes a different set of values. In general, there is no single shared idea of what it means to be a reader; rather, there are overlapping sets of dispositions towards reading. Reading involves being able to decode and make sense of the printed word, but most of us have a broader understanding of what it means to be a reader.

Although we have value-laden ideas about the teaching of reading, this does not mean that no facts pertain to reading and how it is taught. The reasons why people do not consider it appropriate to hit or ridicule children when they misread a word relate not only to the idea of respect for persons; the use of violence and ridicule is, and is generally thought to be, ineffective in helping children to become readers. Answers to questions about which practices are most effective in helping children to decode and make sense of the written word – the emphasis placed on phonic awareness, whole word recognition, and so on – are hotly debated, and the judgements made by teachers, researchers, parents and politicians are based to a significant extent on expectations about what is so and why. Whatever value a teacher sees in the teaching of reading, the question 'If I don't teach phonics, can I be an effective teacher of reading?' cannot be answered satisfactorily without reference to matters of fact.

Similarly, we can formulate problems regarding the value of self-initiated and self-directed exploratory activity, such as 'What value is there in encouraging children and adolescents to engage in self-initiated and self-directed exploratory activity?', and our solutions will similarly reflect our ideas about the primary purpose of an education service and the schools that operate within it. Possible answers to the question include the following, mentioned above for reading: 'To enable them eventually to become effective members of the workforce' and 'To enable them to develop full learner autonomy'. As stated above, these answers are not necessarily incompatible, but they presuppose different sets of values. Although we have value-laden ideas about the merits (or demerits) of encouraging children and adolescents to engage in self-initiated and self-directed exploratory activity, this does not mean that no facts pertain. Indeed, facts of this kind are the focus of much of this book. In Parts 1 and 2, I have presented a philosophical argument in support of the (alleged) fact that when children and adolescents are prevented or discouraged from engaging in self-initiated and self-directed exploratory activity, their learning is inhibited in general and, in particular, they are handicapped from developing as fully autonomous learners. I have further alleged that the development of full learner autonomy is essential for the transcendent learning of which humans are capable. I also here maintain that, *broadly speaking, children and adolescents will engage in more of the kind of learning that leads to further learning, and to the development of full autonomy as learners, if their education institutions and teachers exploit the principles and practices set out and defended in Part 2 of this book, and the problem-based approach to professional development set out in Chapter 10.* In the penultimate section of this chapter I show how this italicized passage can be modified to form a hypothesis that can be tested as part of a Popperian science of teaching in schools.

4 Theoretical explanations

One of the principal purposes of science is the provision of theoretical explanations from which, given initial or boundary conditions, predictions are derived. Although, during the course of history, scientists and others have held different ideas with regard to what counts as an acceptable theoretical explanation, all such explanations (apart from those in which the major premise is statistical) nonetheless have the same logical structure:

> all consist of a *logical deduction*; a deduction whose conclusion is the *explicandum* – a statement of the thing to be explained – and whose premises consist of the *explicans* (a statement of the explaining laws and conditions). . . . . an explanation

is always the deduction of the *explicandum* from certain [that is, specific] prem-
isses, to be called the *explicans*.

(Popper, 1979 [1972], pp. 349–50)

Explanations for singular events – such as 'This child is absent from school'
or 'This group of children has made surprisingly good educational progress' –
comprise at least one *universal theory* and *a set of specific initial conditions*,
and, necessarily, involve making a *deduction* – though sometimes the universal theory 'is omitted as if it were redundant' (ibid., p. 351). (In the case of
explanations for general statements, initial conditions may not be required.)

A universal theory, such as 'All swans are white' or 'All 5-year-old children
enjoy stories about animals' (see Chapter 4, section 2), is a statement (or prop-
osition) which purports to describe an exceptionless feature of the world. The
term 'universal theory' may be used when describing all people, objects or
events in the world and when describing all members of a specific group. One
can formulate universal theories about, for example, 'all schools', 'all schools
in England', 'all children' and 'all 8-year-old children in England'. All universal theories are general theories, but not all general theories are universal.
'Some swans are white' and 'Most 5-year-old children enjoy stories about animals' are examples of general theories that are not universal.

An explanation presupposes the posing of a why question, such as 'Why is
this child absent from school?' or a how-did/does-this-happen question, such
as 'How did this group of children make such good educational progress?' The
creation of an explanation for a singular phenomenon involves, as implied
above, the formulation of a universal theory and a set of specific initial conditions (together constituting the *explicans*) to account for that which is to be
explained (the *explicandum*). As an illustration, a response to the question
'Why is this child absent from school?' might be 'The child is absent from
school because she has a temperature of over 38° Celsius.' This explanation
could be taken to assume that 'All children with temperatures over 38° Celsius
are absent from school' (universal theory) and 'This child has a temperature
of over 38° Celsius' (specific initial condition). From these two premises, it
can be deduced why the child is absent from school.

Popper emphasized the importance of using the two-valued system of logic,
in which a statement is declared to be either true or false (not to be confused
with the idea of *knowing* whether a statement is true or false) (see, e.g., Popper,
1979 [1972], pp. 55, 305–6). The two-valued system enables valid inferences
to be made which transmit the truth of the premises of an argument to the

conclusion or retransmit the falsity of the conclusion to at least one of the premises. If, to extend the above illustration, we take the universal theory 'All children with temperatures over 38° Celsius are absent from school' and the specific initial condition 'This child's temperature is over 38° Celsius', it leads to the conclusion 'This child is absent from school'. If the conclusion is false, and the child is not absent from school, then one or both of the premises must be false – the universal theory and/or the specific initial condition may be in error. It may be the case that children sometimes come to school with temperatures over 38° Celsius and/or that the child's temperature is not over 38° Celsius. This example can also be used to show that leading to a true conclusion, or to many, does not establish the truth of a universal theory: the child may be absent from school and have a temperature over 38° Celsius, but would have gone to school were it not for a heavy fall of snow that blocked the road.

Using the logical analysis above, it can be seen that not all explanations are satisfactory. It is important, for instance, to avoid explanations that are circular. For example, if asked to defend 'The child is absent from school because she has a temperature of over 38° Celsius' as a response to the question 'Why is this child absent from school?', it would not be satisfactory to respond by saying 'How can you doubt it, seeing that the child is absent from school?' The reasons given in defence of a hypothesis should be other than, and independent of, the *explicandum*. If it is possible to adduce only the *explicandum* itself as evidence, the explanation is circular (ibid., p. 351).

In general, a process of scientific investigation often begins when an observed feature of our environment clashes with an expectation or when we discover that two or more theories about our environment conflict. Consider the following example: 'It is surprising that after seven years of compulsory full-time schooling, many school-leavers in England are "bored[,] stressed and puzzlingly under-educated"' (the quoted phrase is from Russell, 2009, as discussed in my Chapter 6). One way in which such a disappointment can be problematized is by asking a 'Why?' question, that is, by seeking an explanation. In response to this specific disappointment, we can attempt to develop an explanation to account for the following speculation: 'These school-leavers have not developed, personally and intellectually, as well or as quickly as they might have done had their formal education been different.'

One explanation to account for the poor progress made by school students, as described above (the *explicandum*) is 'These school students have not developed, personally and intellectually, as well or as quickly as they might have done because their teachers have not practised in accordance with the insights of evolutionary epistemology.' In its boldest interpretation, this embodies the universal theory '*All normal children whose teachers do not practise in accordance with the insights of evolutionary epistemology fail to demonstrate greater educational progress than normal children whose teachers do*', and the following specific initial conditions: 'These are normal children' and 'Teachers are not practising in accordance with the insights of evolutionary epistemology'. 'Normal' is used here to mean 'typical', that is, to denote children attending mainstream schools.

A universal theory will require development in order to make it testable. I have included the idea of *demonstrating* progress in the universal theory formulated above, not because I have forgotten the importance of learning that is unobservable or unobserved, but because for the purposes of developing a science of school teaching, predictions about observable phenomena are required. In addition, it may be noted that I have substituted my earlier characterization of positive change, 'engage in more of the kind of learning that leads to further learning, and to the development of full autonomy as learners', as stated earlier in section 3, with 'greater educational progress'. The first characterization of positive change is subsumed in 'greater educational progress', and it leaves open, at this stage of the discussion, the issue of what else, for the purposes of testing, is to be deemed as educational progress.

5 Testing universal theories

A universal theory can be tested by using it to formulate a prediction. Given a falsificationist conception of science, the prediction, which is essentially a falsifiable hypothesis, is tested by the search for evidence which contradicts it. In order to test the hypothesis 'There does not exist a situation in which a child with a temperature of over 38° Celsius will attend school', one or more researchers might search for children with temperatures over 38° Celsius who are at school. (Note that it would not, of course, be appropriate to falsify the hypothesis by dragooning a child with a high temperature into school!) If evidence which contradicts the hypothesis is found, the hypothesis may be judged to have been falsified. Of course, the nature of the error may not be obvious. We might question whether the universal theory is false and whether the research (or elements thereof) has been misconceived, badly set up and/or poorly conducted. Clearly, given the arguments set out in Chapter 4, knowledge of children who have temperatures of over 38° Celsius and who have stayed at home in no way constitutes evidence in support of the theory.

Putting the matter simply, a scientist uses a universal theory about how the world is to predict that, under a set of specific conditions, a particular circumstance can be anticipated. The theory is subjected to criticism that, crucially, involves checking to ascertain whether or not the prediction is fulfilled. For this process to be scientific in the Popperian sense, the prediction must be sufficiently precise for there to be a risk that counter-evidence could be discovered. If it is not sufficiently precise, the process is mere soothsaying. The best predictions are specific, inconsistent with at least some prior expectations, and fulfilled. Note, however, that if the prediction is fulfilled, it may not be for the reasons suggested. Nothing is proved in science; there is no scientific verification.

The fact that no theory can be proved to be true did not lead Popper to relativism, even with regard to choosing between unrefuted – that is, unfalsified – scientific theories. In discussion of how best to choose between theories competing within a problem situation, Popper introduced the idea of critical preference (Popper, 1979 [1972], chapter 1). The pursuit of truth is maintained by searching for and eliminating false theories, and this is supplemented by the idea of 'growth of informative content'. For a theoretician, any theory with a great deal of informative content is interesting, even prior to testing (which involves the search for falsifying evidence): bold theories, those which entail a large number of consequences, are preferable to theories which predict or imply little. A bold theory is nonetheless required to stand up to tests, to be subjected to the risk of refutation. But even when such a theory is refuted, the act of refutation can lead to more learning than if a theory with fewer consequences is falsified. Boldness is a virtue in that a bold prediction, if fulfilled, is more challenging of our expectations, and thus potentially more stimulating of the growth of knowledge.

It is important that refutation is not evaded by 'immunizing tactics or stratagems' (Popper, 1974, p. 983, reprinted in 1985c, p. 126), though some kinds of auxiliary hypotheses are valid (Popper, 1992a [1974], p. 42; 1974, section 8, reprinted in 1985c, section IV). An immunizing stratagem makes a theory less testable – for example, by introducing a degree of vagueness – and is undesirable because it limits the potential for learning (see Popper, 1974, section 6, reprinted in 1985c, section II; 1979 [1972], p. 30). Specificity is a virtue, and a modification that makes a universal theory more specific may be necessary and desirable even if it makes it less falsifiable, for example, 'Doing X is always the best way of achieving Y, *except when . . .*'.

So, the task of science is to produce bold universal theories that expose themselves readily to refutation but which turn out to be, given the way the world is, difficult to refute. The refutation of a theory does not automatically lead to a new theory (in the same way that David Hume's criticism of the theory of induction did not readily lead to a replacement). Refutation, in the first instance, leads to a new problem, and any subsequent theory is a product of the imagination in the context of that problem. Also, as emphasized in earlier chapters, the falsification of a theory requires us to make a judgement in light of the evidence and argument available, and our judgement may be incorrect. Popper did not suggest or imply that the search for refutation is an alternative means of achieving certainty. The discovery of falsifying evidence is itself a conjectural business.

6 Proscriptive hypotheses and technological prohibitions

In discussing explanatory theories, Popper makes a recommendation which I exploited in my classroom research (Swann, 1988) and which I have explored theoretically both with regard to testing the theory of teaching set out in Part 2 of this book and in the approach to professional development advocated in Chapter 10 (see Swann, 1999c, and section 7 below). The recommendation is useful in the development of theory:

> There is a way of formulating scientific theories which points with particular clarity to the possibility of their falsification: we can formulate them in the form of prohibitions (or *negative existential statements*) . . . It can be shown that universal statements and negative existential statements are logically equivalent. This makes it possible to formulate all universal laws . . . as prohibitions.
>
> (Popper, 1979 [1972], pp. 360–1, and for earlier related discussion, see 1961 [1957], section 20, and 1972a [1934], section 15)

In the context of classroom research, a proscriptive hypothesis (what Popper called a prohibition) may be derived from a (preferably bold) explanation as to why, for example, student achievement is not greater than it is. The universal theory might take the form 'All 8-year-old children whose teachers do not exploit [specified set of ideas] fail to demonstrate greater progress in respect of [specified competences] than 8-year-old children whose teachers do'. This universal theory, accompanied by the condition 'This [specified set of ideas] is not being exploited by teachers of 8-year-old children', can be used to create an explanation for specified limitations in the progress of 8-year-old children.

When the above universal theory is formulated proscriptively, it challenges the researcher to look for situations in which the prediction fails: '*There does not exist* a situation in which 8-year-old children whose teachers practise in accordance with [specified set of ideas] will demonstrate progress in respect of [specified competences] that is equal to or less than 8-year-old children whose teachers do not.'

Of course, what is considered to be a worthwhile competence is value-laden, but this does not stop us from testing the application of various theories vis-à-vis predicted outcomes. The value of using proscriptive hypotheses can be understood only by reference both to the idea that the discovery of error (or inadequacy) is the basis for the growth of knowledge of the facts, and to the idea that secure knowledge is a chimera.

With regard to the technological application of science or, rather, its exploitation, the negative existential statements formulated by scientists can be reformulated as technological prohibitions (Popper, 1961 [1957], pp. 61–3) or as statements of advice which may, if true, be useful to engineers or other practitioners when they set out to create a desired state of affairs – be it, for example, a bridge across a river or literate children. Technological prohibitions are of various kinds, including 'You cannot achieve X by doing Y', 'You cannot achieve X without doing Y', 'You cannot achieve X by doing Y without also causing Z' and 'You cannot do Y without causing Z'. As an illustration of the last kind of prohibition, one of the universal theories mentioned earlier could take the form 'You cannot introduce school league tables based on student achievement in standard tests without 80 per cent (or more) of all the teachers involved becoming increasingly inclined to teach to the test, and without the learning of 90 per cent or more of students taught by these teachers becoming narrower in scope and less profound.'

As an illustration of a statement of advice regarding teaching, imagine that the following universal statement were to be tested and not refuted: 'In England, there does not exist a situation in which normal children whose teachers practise in accordance with the national curriculum and the related guidelines on the teaching of literacy will demonstrate progress in respect of literacy that is equal to or less than normal children whose teachers do not.' We might then formulate an advice statement of the kind '[In England] you cannot find a more effective and efficient way of achieving X [literate children] than by doing Y [practising in accordance with the national curriculum and the related guidelines on literacy].' If the theory were to be refuted – such that we have evidence that is consistent with 'There is a more effective and efficient way of achieving X than by doing Y' – we would have rigorous empirical evidence to support allowing schools to adopt a different approach to the curriculum and/or to literacy. Of course, refutation of the prediction would not constitute evidence that a particular alternative approach would be more successful. Let us suppose, however, that the theory were to be refuted, then modified in light of the nature of the refuting evidence. The result might be an advice statement of the kind 'You cannot find a more effective and efficient way of achieving X than by doing Y, *except when . . .*' (see the penultimate paragraph of section 5 above). The modified theory, if true, would be preferable to a false theory or no theory. Although modifying a theory in this way makes it less bold, it may make it more useful to the practitioner. I stress, however, that neither the natural nor the social sciences can provide us with a blueprint that will guarantee practical success (see Chapter 8, section 7).

7 Testing this book's theory of teaching

The previously stated universal theory 'All normal children whose teachers do not practise in accordance with the insights of evolutionary epistemology fail to demonstrate greater educational progress than normal children whose teachers do' can be made more specific about 'the insights of evolutionary epistemology' by replacing this phrase with 'the principles and guidelines set out in Part 2 and the problem-based approach to professional development set out in Chapter 10 of *Learning, Teaching and Education Research in the 21st Century: An Evolutionary Analysis of the Role of Teachers*'. Using the modified theory to make a prediction formulated as a proscriptive hypothesis has led to the following:

> There does not exist a situation in which normal children whose teachers practise in accordance with the principles and guidelines set out in Part 2 and the problem-based approach to professional development set out in Chapter 10 of *Learning, Teaching and Education Research in the 21st Century: An Evolutionary Analysis of*

the Role of Teachers will demonstrate educational progress that is equal to or less than the progress of normal children whose teachers do not.

The bold hypothesis above requires further modification if it is to be tested. Although my broad theory is not confined to a particular age of student or size of class, the proscriptive hypothesis below represents a step towards a formulation for testing in a specific research project. Other formulations are conceivable; this particular hypothesis has developed out of my empirical research with 7- to 11-year-olds, who were taught in classes of 25 or fewer (normal at that time for primary schools in social priority areas of Inner London). The detailed practical illustrations in Chapter 7 on developing student-initiated curricula relate particularly to this age group. The hypothesis specifies students in the age range of 7 to 9 years as, in England, research to test the hypothesis would be most practical for children in this age range. Note also that the teaching and learning approach I am advocating must be adopted consistently for a period of at least two years; hence the new hypothesis specifies a two-year period.

Class L: a class of between 20 and 25 children, taught for two years from the age of 7 to 9 by a teacher who practises in accordance with the principles and guidelines set out in Part 2 and the problem-based approach to professional development set out in Chapter 10 of *Learning, Teaching and Education Research in the 21st Century: An Evolutionary Analysis of the Role of Teachers*. Class N: a class comparable to Class L but taught at the same time, and for a similar period, by a teacher who does not practise in accordance with the principles and guidelines set out in Part 2 and the problem-based approach to professional development set out in Chapter 10 of *Learning, Teaching and Education Research in the 21st Century: An Evolutionary Analysis of the Role of Teachers*.

Hypothesis: there does not exist a situation in which, at the end of the specified two-year period, children in Class L will demonstrate educational progress that is equal to or less than the progress of children in Class N.

As mentioned earlier in this chapter, given the nature of the Popperian theory of learning presented in Part 1, I have some qualms about evaluating approaches to teaching purely by reference to short-term outcomes that are pre-specified and observable. The 'kind of learning that leads to further learning, and to the development of full autonomy as learners', cannot be summed up by a set of specific competences, attitudes and 'bits' of knowledge and understanding. Though it is possible to demonstrate that individuals have learnt by focusing on short-term changes, it is not possible to account for all learning in this way. The assertion that teaching which exploits my universal theory has greater long-term benefits than other approaches is important, but there are considerable practical difficulties in empirically testing for long-term effects (there would, for example, be many uncontrollable variables). Predictions of measurable short-term benefits are, however, more readily testable. For the purposes of testing, the proscriptive hypothesis therefore has to have a rider regarding what counts as 'educational progress', which in this context refers broadly to the kind of learning that leads to further learning and to the development of full autonomy as learners:

> 'Educational progress' here refers to improvements in self-confidence, social skills, attitudes to learning, literacy and the use of oral language – as measured in standardized tests given to Class L and Class N children.

The children would be tested prior to the start of the two-year project and then again at the end, perhaps after a holiday period but before further experience of classroom teaching. The range of specifiable improvements included in the rider to the hypothesis is, of course, value-laden and rooted in the philosophy from which the theory has developed. To test the theory in terms of, for example, England's national curriculum attainment targets and related summative assessments is not being proposed. The detail of the specified improvements would also be value-laden; for example, literacy would be assessed according to the ability to use language effectively rather than analyse its structure. With regard to confidence, some pre-existing standardized tests could be used from the field of educational psychology. With regard to attitudes to learning, new tests would possibly need to be devised, including tests which attempt to access attitudes conducive to the development and exercise of full learner autonomy.

In any specific context in which the hypothesis is tested, thought would need to be given to potential unintended and undesirable consequences and to how such consequences might be identified and addressed. For example, at the end of the two-year period, Class L children's numeracy skills should not compare unfavourably with those of the children in Class N, though how this would be evaluated would be problematic. Note also that I am assuming that educational progress would be averaged for both classes. Such averages might, however, mask significant differences in spread.

I am not denying that there would be other considerations to bear in mind. Setting up medium- to large-scale research to test the hypothesis would be both complicated and financially expensive, not least because of the difficulties in constructing a valid test and the need to involve a number of examples of Class L and Class N. The practical experiment would require not only the involvement of comparable classes (taking into account, for example, socioeconomic factors), but also prime Class L and Class N exponents of the art of teaching. It would not be a fair test if one of the teachers in the pair were a weak exponent of her (or his) chosen approach. However, pairs of teachers working in schools with parallel classes could, on their own initiative, undertake small-scale research (amending the hypothesis as necessary for slightly larger classes of student and slightly older children). In England, for example, a pair of teachers could compare the approach advocated in the hypothesis with one that strongly adheres to central government policy. Such research in state-funded schools would, however, require the suspension of the national curriculum for all children in Class L.

8 Some general implications

In general, with regard to the pursuit of improvement in educational practice in schools, a science of school teaching would be of use to education practitioners (including teachers, policy makers and managers) *only* if it was construed as a critical process of the kind described in this chapter and in Chapter 8, and if the limitations of any technological prohibitions derived from such a science were acknowledged. Anyone who desires a science that will provide reliable and sufficient knowledge about what works will find my account of science unpalatable. But in light of a Popperian epistemology, it is clear that such a desire cannot be fulfilled. Science is best construed as a means of challenging some of our assumptions about what is so; it can facilitate the discovery of erroneous theories. When theories fail, we are often inspired to create new and potentially better ones. The value of science, both as a means of advancing knowledge and of helping us to improve practice, lies only – but not insignificantly – in the method of criticism.

Formulating a scientific problem, developing a universal theory as a trial solution, and devising a means by which this solution may be tested all involve a high degree of creativity. It is unreasonable to expect a novice researcher or a researcher new to a specific field of enquiry to be able to create a theory that is bold, refutable and able to resist refutation (though we should not exclude the possibility that she might do so). But researchers have to start somewhere. The basic process, beginning with a problematized disappointment and proceeding to a tested theory, is appropriate for adoption not only by experienced researchers but also by at least some novice researchers with an interest in investigating a question of what is so and why.

The development of a Popperian science of school teaching would not necessarily require large-scale experiments. One well-conducted case study has the potential to cast doubt on existing expectations. Whatever the nature of the research strategy and the scale of the experiment devised to test an educational hypothesis, the task of testing will be problematic. (A particular challenge would be that of dealing with threats to validity – for relevant discussion, see Phillips, 1999, pp. 187–8.) It is nonetheless possible to devise ethical and rigorous tests with the potential to challenge, and challenge constructively, existing expectations about the organization and conduct of teaching in schools. Discovering error and limitation in existing knowledge is a preliminary to creating new knowledge.

My expectation is that empirical research of the kind I have outlined (including my specific hypothesis relating to the theory of teaching set out in this book), if conducted rigorously, would in the long-term provoke significant developments in practice and outcome. Experiments are potentially risky for those involved, but leaving things as they are is risky too. Many of the assumptions that influence teaching practice have not been rigorously tested – that is, they have not been *critically* tested. With reference to the organization and conduct of teaching, there are many theories and assumptions about matters of fact that could be but have not been formulated in a way that makes them susceptible to refutation and whose truth is assumed. It may be to our detriment that such theories and assumptions are not tested in the critical sense outlined here, that is, as part of a science of school teaching.

10 Improving Our Practices as Teachers

Institutions do not act; rather, only individuals act, within or on behalf of institutions.

—*Karl Popper*, In Search of a Better World:
Lectures and Essays from Thirty Years

Introduction

This chapter addresses the practical problem 'How can we improve our practices as teachers?' In formulating this problem, my use of 'improvement' rather than 'change' is deliberate and intended to be significant. This chapter is not about change. Change is inexorable; we cannot avoid it even if we want to. Of course, we can set out to instigate a particular change, and our efforts in this regard may be rewarded; but the new state of affairs we help to bring about may not constitute an improvement – not even according to the standards which we ourselves would apply. The road to improvement is uncertain, and we may think we are going in the right direction only to find later that we have been mistaken. As argued in Chapter 2, section 3, it is important to distinguish progress from progression: progression involves moving from one state of affairs to a *different* one; progress involves moving from one state of affairs to a *better* one. When we move forward, there is progression, and some things may seem clearly to have improved, but this does not mean there has been progress or an overall improvement. Even when our endeavours achieve apparent success with regard to what we explicitly wanted, invariably there are unintended consequences, one or more of which may be undesirable – possibly even to the point that, with knowledge of the full range of consequences, we would say that the overall outcome had been disastrous.

Change can be evaluated according to the question 'What is different now from then?', a question of fact about what happened, whereas a judgement about improvement involves both fact and value, such as 'What is different now from then?' *and* 'Is this better?' It may be thought, therefore, that change can be evaluated more objectively than improvement and that change is a more appropriate concept for a general discussion of method. But observations of social and personal change are not only invariably expectation-laden (see Chapter 2 for relevant discussion), they are inevitably also made against a background of values. And, when individuals and groups pursue specific changes, improvement is usually anticipated – people set out to change things for the better. They may talk about change, as is often the case in public debate, but what they want is improvement. For some individuals and groups, improvement seems too problematic a concept to mention. First, it implies that things are not currently as good as they might be, the acknowledge-ment of which may be accompanied by a sense of personal discomfort and/or lead to social difficulties. (Hence in some circumstances, individuals may be best advised to talk about *enhancing* their practice rather than improv-ing it.) Second, what one individual or group regards as an improvement, another may view as a deterioration. For the most part, in this chapter I leave unanswered the question of what is to count as better teaching, and focus instead on improvement as a regulative ideal bounded in context by the values of the individuals or groups who are engaged in its pursuit. The crux of my argument is that regardless of how you construe improvement – and bearing in mind that there is never any guarantee of success – one method of pursuing it is likely to be more effective than another.

Most methods of pursuing improvement involve some kind of system of planning and evaluation (or review), but there are significant differences of approach with regard to planning for action and, as a corollary to this, differences in how the consequences of planned action are evaluated. Generally speaking, systematic approaches to planning can be divided into two broad categories: objectives-based and problem-based. Objectives-based approaches are used in many countries in the planning and evaluation of education policy at macro- and micro-levels, including the planning and assessment of learning, and curriculum development in general. In countries such as the United States, Australia and South Africa, 'outcome-based education' (OBE) presumes the efficacy of working with objectives in that the desired outcomes of the educational process are defined in advance and teachers and students then work towards them. In England, the adoption of an objectives-based approach is compulsory – at least at the level of documentation – at all levels across a range of state-funded endeavours, including state-funded education.

The terminology associated with objectives-based planning has changed over the course of time. 'Targets' and 'goals' have supplanted 'objectives' in some contexts, and 'intended learning outcome' is widely used as a synonym for 'learning objective'. Somewhat confusingly, the terminology of this approach to planning is defined differently by different theorists and practitioners, though, broadly speaking, objectives and targets are said to be more specific than goals. For the purposes of the discussion that follows, 'objectives' has been adopted as a generic term that encompasses targets and, where appropriate, intended learning outcomes.

Of course, teachers and other practitioners tend to work with a composite of methods, and my account of objectives-based planning and evaluation is an imprecise picture of what actually takes place. The thrust of the argument, drawing on situational logic (see Chapter 9, section 3), is that planning and evaluation practices which adhere to the objectives model tend to incorporate specific flaws, particularly in complex situations in which significant learning is required. These flaws are less likely to occur when a problem-based method is adopted. It follows that in the context of my proposal in Part 2 (that schools and classrooms should be places where teachers encourage and support the development of student-initiated curricula), the adoption of a problem-based methodology for the teacher's professional development is not an optional extra. I would go so far as to say that in the longer term the successful support and management of student-initiated curricula requires of the teacher the adoption, privately if not publicly (where the appearance of objectives-based planning is compulsory), of a problem-based approach to professional development (see the hypothesis for testing my theory of teaching in Chapter 9), rather than an objectives-based approach.

1 Who plans, and why

All humans engage in planning. The planning may be undertaken by individuals, pairs or groups, and may or may not be documented. It may be comparatively trivial, such as making a shopping list, or more profound, as in planning to get married or planning an undergraduate degree programme. The plan may not be designed specifically to advance learning, but merely to get something done; even so, learning may take place. Planning to cook a meal, for example, often necessitates a change from 'not having all the ingredients' to 'having all the ingredients'. While the process of securing the ingredients may result in ad hoc opportunities for learning, learning may not be an intended outcome. However, when a meal is based on a new recipe, the planning will either explicitly or implicitly involve some expectation of learning.

Planning inevitably arises from some kind of evaluation – at a minimum there is the evaluative thought, conscious or unconscious, that 'a plan is needed in this situation'. But often planning is undertaken more carefully than evaluation, in part because the need to plan in some detail may seem more pressing than the need to evaluate, and because to evaluate thoroughly (i.e. to look for evidence not only of success but also of failure) is to risk feeling uncomfortable. In general, people plan for two main reasons. First, they want to improve a current or anticipated state of affairs or achieve a specific state of affairs in the foreseeable future. In the former instance, they judge the current or anticipated situation to be deficient or problematic and wish to bring about an improvement, though the precise nature of the improvement may not be specified or known ('there must be something better than this'). In the latter, the desired state of affairs is also regarded as an improvement, although the idea of improvement may not be explicit. In both circumstances, there is a belief that planning is necessary to achieve desirable change. Second, people make plans because they are obliged to do so (for instance, by their employers). A formal requirement to make plans may be regarded as intrinsically worthwhile, viewed cynically as a bureaucratic activity, or perhaps a bit of both.

There are sound reasons why teachers, including student teachers, are encouraged to plan for their teaching. Some of the reasons associated with the 'delivery' of a prescribed curriculum are not relevant to the support and management of student-initiated curricula, but many reasons are relevant in both contexts. In my experience of student-initiated curricula, careful planning of time and resources was essential in order for all students in the class to have the opportunity to pursue their learning aspirations (see Chapter 7). Through planning, the teacher can maximize the time available for positive learning, and a degree of planning is essential for the maintenance of order when working with a class of potentially boisterous children or adolescents. For the teacher, planning is also a crucial part of the process of professional development. Teachers can, and arguably should, plan to expand and deepen their professional knowledge and increase their professional capabilities.

Although, generally speaking, planning is a good thing, one can have too much of it. Planning should not be so detailed and intensive that there is little or no room for spontaneity; for the same reason, plans should not be followed inflexibly. One should have plans but be prepared to change them according to what transpires. Planning at the individual level is best construed as an activity that can serve creativity and help us to avoid making mistakes that would be detrimental to the well-being of ourselves and others.

2 The ubiquitous approach to planning

According to the objectives model of planning, the first stage in any planning process should involve the formulation of one or more aims or broad goals. These are determined by answering a question of the kind 'What am I (or we) trying to achieve?' The result is a description of a desired future state. The next stage involves the formulation of a series of objectives which, if met collectively, will result in the achievement of the aim(s), the specified desired future state. Objectives are more specific than aims, although some people's objectives are so vague or broad that they are indistinguishable from other people's aims. In general, policy targets, curriculum objectives and intended learning outcomes are associated with measurable, or at least clearly demonstrable, achievements. Once objectives have been formulated, the courses of action that follow are evaluated according to whether or to what extent the objectives have been met. The link between the objectives and the initial aim(s) is not usually reconsidered at the evaluative stage.

The impetus for objectives-based planning and evaluation in teaching originated in the United States in 1956 with the publication of the *Taxonomy of Educational Objectives, The Classification of Educational Goals, Handbook 1: Cognitive Domain*, written by educational psychologist Benjamin Bloom (who was also the editor) and four associates (Bloom, 1956). And even today Bloom's taxonomy is probably still the most widely discussed formulation of cognitive goals.

In the late 1960s and early 1970s, debate about 'instructional objectives' focused on the relative merits of non-behavioural and behavioural objectives, the latter being demonstrable and measurable by reference to specific changes in student behaviour (see, e.g., Popham et al., 1969). As an illustration, 'To further the class's understanding of Hardy's "The Darkling Thrush"' is a non-behavioural objective, whereas 'At the end of a forty-five-minute lesson on Hardy's "The Darkling Thrush" the class will be able [to] detail the images which conjure up a landscape of winter and death' is a behavioural objective (Cohen et al., 1996, p. 61). Objectives may also be distinguished according to vagueness or specificity – as in, respectively, 'The students will develop an understanding of events leading up to the second world war' or 'The students will put in chronological order six events leading up to the second world war'.

In the United Kingdom, Bloom's classification of cognitive goals was probably more talked about than exploited in schools, but elements of it have been widely used in further and adult education (for an early example, see Technician Education Council, 1976), and in higher education it is sometimes recommended in the development of new courses and modules (see, e.g., Butcher, 2009). During the 1970s, educationists and teachers who favoured the use of objectives in curriculum planning often felt obliged to argue in support of this practice, referring not only to Bloom (1956) but also, for example, to Ralph Tyler (1949), John Kerr (1968) and James Popham et al. (1969). The controversial nature of objectives-based planning was usually acknowledged, and arguments against the use of objectives – such as those in Lawrence Stenhouse (1975) and Robert Dearden (1976) – were given serious consideration, even if they were ultimately dismissed (seemingly for ideological reasons). From the early 1970s, the formulation of objectives was increasingly favoured by curriculum organizers and examining bodies, and by the end of that decade public debate about the validity of objectives-based planning and evaluation had largely ceased. Despite later critiques by authors such as Geva Blenkin and Vic Kelly (1987), it became a widespread but rarely discussed assumption that objectives provide the only sound basis for education planning. As stated in the introduction to this chapter, in England, professionals at all levels are obliged to work with objectives, although it is possible to employ one or more different methods and present one's plans and achievements as if the objectives model has been consistently adopted.

The arguments that have been used in support of objectives-based planning and evaluation include the following, all of which will be challenged in section 3:

(i) Objectives-based planning and evaluation is the only rational approach. Choosing not to adopt the objectives model is to act irrationally.

(ii) The alternative to the use of objectives is a laissez-faire approach which often results in chaos.

(iii) We need to know where we are going.

(iv) If our objectives are clear, we are less likely to be sidetracked by trivial ad hoc suggestions.

(v) Objectives-based planning helps us to focus on important and worthwhile achievements.

(vi) The formulation of objectives is consistent with democratic principles. For example, outcome-based assessment, in which the outcomes sought are pre-specified for the students, makes the teaching and learning process transparent; consequently the assessment of student achievement is fairer and more equitable, because students (and their assessors) know the criteria against which the work is to be judged.

(vii) Practitioners can be guided in their work by means of objectives set by policy makers. This results in higher standards of performance and greater consistency within and between institutions.

(viii) The use of objectives is consistent with creating and maintaining systems of accountability. People know what they are required to do and achieve during a specific period, and it is relatively straightforward to assess whether the objectives have been met.

3 Against objectives

While the objectives model of planning and evaluation can support the achievement and review of goals in situations that are fairly straightforward, its use in more complex situations is, as indicated earlier, highly problematic.

Ten specific criticisms are outlined below. The epistemological assumptions embedded in the criticisms have been explored in Part 1 and Chapters 8 and 9 of this book and are not revisited in this section. The numbered points refer to the content of the above list in support of objectives, but the order of the supporting points has not been followed systematically. All refer to personal and social practice in general, apart from the last, which focuses more specifically on learning.

(i)   The two initial arguments in support of objectives-based planning and evaluation are erroneous because, quite simply, there are other rational options that are clearly distinguishable from a laissez-faire approach. Later sections of this chapter discuss one such option. When it comes to planning and evaluation, and improvement in general, the idea that the choice is between using an objectives model or adopting a casual approach is a myth, albeit a persistent one.

(ii) The objectives model fails to address the open-ended nature of human endeavour and, in particular, personal and social change. Although we may wish to know where we are going, this knowledge is rarely available except in the most general terms. Even when it appears to be available, our expectations may be mistaken. Therefore, when advocates of objectives-based planning ask, 'How do you know where you are going if you haven't formulated aims [broad goals] and objectives [targets]?' a valid answer in all but the most mundane situations is, 'You don't – but you can have some idea of where you are (through problem formulation), of where you and others have been (by being aware, where applicable, of previously tested ideas, practices and strategies), and what you are travelling with (a method).' The future, unlike the past, is open; people cannot, with any degree of certainty, know what will take place.

The formulation of objectives is often construed as a matter of expressing ideas that are latent, the assumption being that we all have objectives, even if they are merely implicit. But while we may all have broad aims, associated with our preferences, it is not true to say that we all have objectives, be they implicit or explicit. In the words of Stenhouse, 'We do not *have* objectives: we choose to conceptualize our behaviour in terms of objectives – or we choose not to' (1975, p. 71).

(iii) Although the use of objectives can help people to avoid being sidetracked by trivial ad hoc suggestions, it tends to encourage a blinkered view of what will be possible and successful in practice. Most crucially, the unforeseen consequences of action often go unacknowledged within the planning and evaluation process. Planners should be mindful that the unintended consequences of policy are often more far-reaching than those which are intended. This is particularly true of social planning. (For a critique of far-reaching objectives as a form of utopianism, see Popper, 1961 [1957], of which sections 20, 21 and 24 are reprinted as

1985d, and 1972b [1963], pp. 358–63; Little, 1981.) Rather than using objectives, a method is needed which encourages us to make reflective judgements about ad hoc ideas (rather than dismiss them out of hand) and to discover and address unexpected and undesirable consequences of action.

(iv) Given the open-ended nature of human endeavour, it makes sense to begin our planning by focusing on the present rather than on a desired future state of affairs. A critical response to questions such as 'What am I going to do?' and 'What am I trying to achieve?' is 'Why do or try to achieve anything?' This may sound facetious, but a serious point is being made. Any action or desire to act is best understood in relation to its problem context. People formulate questions about what is to be done and what is to be achieved because of experienced or anticipated difficulties. The belief that good planning starts with the formulation of aims and objectives is mistaken; instead, it is important to focus initially on the problem context and the formulation of one or more pressing and/or significant problems.

When a plan is required in order to address a problem, the context should be scrutinized before launching a solution. Good planners will do this whether or not they are working with objectives. The objectives model does not, however, encourage such good practice. People are often inclined to concentrate on a solution, because acknowledging a problem can be uncomfortable. But in the context of a well-formulated problem, all proposed solutions can be critically discussed with regard to whether or to what extent they seem likely to solve the initial problem, and with what additional consequences. The evaluation of policy and practice is directed towards the questions 'To what extent has the problem been solved?' and 'Have there been unexpected consequences and, if so, what are they?' This is in contrast to evaluation within an objectives-based process, which tends to focus on the questions 'Have our stated objectives been met?' and 'If not, why not?'

(v) In general, when the objectives model of planning and evaluation is adopted, the task of implementing policy to achieve the stated objectives tends to take priority over the issue of whether or to what extent the aims and objectives were worthwhile in the first place.

(vi) In practice, objectives-based planning discourages the expression of contention. What frequently happens is that disagreement, having no legitimate outlet, is suppressed or sidelined. Instead, we need to find ways of legitimizing conflict and working with it, and in this regard a problem-based rather than an objectives-based methodology is enabling.

When a group convenes to develop policies and/or plans, trying to achieve a consensus about aims often results in the selection of the lowest common denominator of the group's ideas. This is why statements of aims are generally so banal (though they can turn out to be more controversial than their formulators anticipate). Focusing on aims means that the initial starting point for the group – a shared and often pressing problem – may be ignored.

(vii) It follows from (vi) that objectives-based planning tends to encourage mediocrity of vision because it provides no social mechanism by which bold and potentially valuable ideas may be discussed and subsequently tested.

(viii) The objectives model of planning – or, rather, the ubiquitous version of it – often results in lists in which the objectives are not prioritized, and there is often an unwitting mix of problems and solutions (as noted in Pratt, 1976) and/or different types of objectives (e.g. policy targets, teaching objectives and intended learning outcomes are listed together).

(ix) When objectives are set by one group of people for others to adopt, ideological and empirical issues are raised. For example, a national curriculum, by denying individuals the right to determine important features of their formal learning, is essentially authoritarian, where '"authoritarian" is taken to mean a discipline system with a dependence relationship in which one person is dominant and another or others dependent' (Meighan and Siraj-Blatchford, 2003 [1981], p. 209; see also my Chapter 1, section 6). Students are dependent on teachers, who in turn are dependent on policy makers. Teachers' professional judgements about curriculum content – for instance, in light of their students' individual learning problems – are supplanted by the decrees of politicians and their appointees (see my Part 2). And although outcome-based assessment can be used to make elements of teaching and learning transparent, and its assessment seemingly fair and equitable, it exemplifies the organizational form of authoritarianism whereby 'order is obtained through detailed organization, indicating a clear structure, giving full instructions and deciding ends and means in a systematic way' (Meighan and Siraj-Blatchford, 2003 [1981], p. 209).

This is not to suggest that practitioners should be unaccountable to their clients, their employers, taxpayers, and so on, but the model of accountability associated with objectives-based planning and evaluation is flawed: it constrains creativity and (despite any expressed intentions to the contrary) diminishes the practitioner's sense of responsibility (see sections 7 and 9 below for further discussion). The use of centrally agreed objectives may well result in greater consistency within and between institutions, and clarify what people are required to do and achieve during a specific period. It is, however, frequently not the case that overall standards of performance are improved by this means. Consistency and control are achieved at the expense of creativity and responsibility. Also, while it is proper to legislate against bad practice (for instance, to ban physical punishment from schools), it is not possible to plan for excellence by insisting that everyone follows identical guidelines.

(x) As suggested earlier in the chapter, the objectives model is particularly flawed when it is applied to learning – not least because of its failure to address the open-ended nature of human endeavour. Only the most basic learning can be planned in detail and predicted with accuracy.

For example, learning to play a musical instrument well requires interpretative skills that cannot be fully encompassed by a list of targets or intended learning outcomes (unless the intended learning outcomes are so broad that they are, to all intents and purposes, aims). In a guitar master class, the teacher helps the musicians to refine their technique and improve their understanding of the instrument and its potential. In the pursuit of excellence, there is no question of trying to make all students play in exactly the same way; rather, they are encouraged to interpret the music individually (see Stenhouse, 1975, p. 81).

Within compulsory education, learning objectives are generally devised by policy makers and teachers; thereby, major decisions which shape the experience of students are made without their involvement (with the implications discussed in (ix) above). This practice reflects misconceptions about the nature of learning. As argued in Part 1, although learning is often an unconscious process, it is never passive. Learning necessitates autonomous activity on the part of the learner, and it is always developed out of the skills, knowledge, values and attitudes which the learner brings to the situation. It is, of course, possible to encourage learning, and it is often possible to get people to do specific things through forms of coercion; but learning is something for which the individual learner is uniquely responsible. When we set learning objectives for others, we ignore important aspects of what would-be learners bring (desires and values, etc.) to the learning environment.

Moreover, the use of objectives usually focuses attention on performance rather than learning (see the discussion of behaviourism in Chapter 4, section 8). Performance is a product of learning (and other factors), but it is not synonymous with learning. We may assess students in accordance with our stated objectives, but what they learn in a broader sense is beyond our control and the scope of our assessments. (Their learning may even be contrary to our intentions.) The objectives model of education planning is associated with the idea that the assessment of educational provision is largely synonymous with the assessment of student performance. However, performance refers to what the student can be observed to do, and learning is merely inferred. The use of behavioural objectives focuses attention on readily observable events, and learning is then commonly treated as a linear process. These objectives, in particular, usually fail to address the development of attitudes, and they are not suitable for evaluating changes in long-term dispositions and potential.

This leads to the question 'If we do not use objectives how can we plan to promote learning?' Instead of asking, 'What educational purposes or objectives should the school or course seek to attain?' (Bloom, 1956, p. 25, following Tyler, 1949, p. 1), we should address the question 'What do the students conceive to be their most significant and/or pressing learning problems?'

4 Problem-based planning and evaluation

As discussed in Part 1, in light of Karl Popper's evolutionary epistemology, it can be seen that every instance of learning is the outcome of a process of trial and error-elimination in which a problem is created in response to a mismatch between expectation and experience, actual or anticipated, conscious or unconscious. The creation of a problem triggers the need for a solution, the creation of which brings with it a new set of expectations (which may or may not be explicit), and these too may subsequently be found to be flawed (i.e. erroneous or inadequate). Once an attempt has been made to solve a problem, the trial solution, whether it is successful or not, exists within the history of the situation; for instance, if we try to do something and fail, we may recognize what not to do in the future, even though we may remain unsure about what to do for the best. In Popper's words, 'All life is problem solving' (Popper, 1999, title of book and chapter 9; see also p. 100), but as I have argued, not all problem solving involves learning. And, clearly, not all organisms learn. Those that do are characterized by changes in disposition (i.e. changes in preference and/or expectation) which are not purely the outcome of genetic inheritance or haphazard organic change.

The problems that living things are mostly concerned with solving are practical problems (also sometimes called concrete problems by Popper; and engineering problems by Burgess, 1977, 1979). Practical problems are problems of how to get from one state of affairs to another: from hungry to not hungry, from bread to toast, from unable to read to able to read, and so on (see my Chapter 3, section 5; Chapter 8, section 7). Practical problems can be formulated as 'How can . . . ?' questions:

> 'How can I . . . ?' – used for a personal practical problem, such as 'How can I assuage my hunger?', 'How can I turn this piece of bread into toast?', 'How can I become a reader?' or 'How can I improve my professional practice?'
>
> 'How can we . . .?' – suitable for a group practical problem, such as 'How can we play this symphony better?', 'How can we better help these children to become readers?' or 'How can we make this institution more democratic?'
>
> 'How can . . .?' – used for general practical problems, such as 'How can classroom practice be improved?'

But the most important feature of a practical problem is that it is concrete and exists independently of its formulation. One can want to get from being hungry to not being hungry without putting the idea into words. This is mostly what happens; indeed, it is only humans who formulate their practical problems in language. And even for humans, only some of our practical problems are formulated, and only some need to be.

As discussed earlier in the book, a solution to a practical problem is embodied in a state of affairs that has arisen because something has been done (or something has happened to solve the problem). A solution to a practical problem always involves action (or inaction, when a decision has been taken not to act or when something happens that solves the problem). A solution to a practical problem can often be formulated in words, but the words themselves are not the solution. If our practical problem is 'How can we make this institution more democratic?', the solution requires a course of action that addresses this problem. The solution, the course of action, may or may not be successful – hence Popper and Popperians tend to talk about *trial* solutions. The test of a solution to a practical problem involves addressing the question 'What happened?' or 'What is happening?' An appropriate evaluation of what has happened or what is happening requires us to think about (a) the extent to which the course of action solved (or is solving) the practical problem it was intended to solve and (b) what were (or are) the unintended consequences, desirable or undesirable.

Theoretical problems, by contrast, are those for which the solution is a theory or set of theories. They include problems of fact ('What is so?', 'What was so?', 'What will be so?', and 'Why?'); problems of value ('What is good?', 'What ought to be done?', 'What is aesthetically pleasing?', and 'Why?'); and problems of logic ('What is valid?' and 'Why?'). The test of a solution to a theoretical problem involves addressing such questions as 'Is this theory true?' and 'Is this argument valid?'

Following Burgess (1977, p. 129), I do not talk about *identifying* or discovering problems; rather, I talk about *creating* them (see my Chapter 2, section 5). In my analysis, a problem involves a mismatch (explicit or implicit) between expectation and experience, actual or anticipated, that the individual desires to resolve. Any single mismatch can be turned into a number of different problems, all of which will be expectation-laden and value-impregnated. For example, 'The students didn't behave in the way I expected when I asked the question' can be formulated as a problem of 'how to change the behaviour of the students' or 'how to change the way the question is posed' or 'how to find a more effective way of eliciting the students' views'. It is misleading to say (as most authors do) that problems are identified; mismatches between expectation and experience are identified, but problems have to be created.

It is apparent that some of our practical problems are more likely to be solved satisfactorily if we think about proposed solutions in advance of action, and if we critically review alternative strategies and expose our conjectured solutions to the critical scrutiny of others. At the basic everyday level, when conscious thought is needed in the pursuit of improvement, it would seem that we will do well to analyse problem situations; formulate problems; and develop solutions and critically evaluate them, prior to action, after action, and, when both possible and appropriate, during action. We can also critically evaluate the problems themselves, that is, consider whether we might have formulated better ones. What we learn from our evaluations can be used to inform the decisions we make about future action.

When we reflect on a problem situation, it is useful to acknowledge what is good about it; we do not need to limit our thoughts to what is problematic. The benefits of recognizing the positive features of a situation are that it helps us to feel more energized about proceeding and it brings to the forefront of our minds a recognition of what we already have that is worth maintaining and defending. By means of the latter we are less likely to throw the baby out with the bathwater. It is often useful, too, to sharpen the focus of our endeavours by reflecting on what seems to be impeding progress (it may, for example, be a lack of knowledge), and by identifying which impediments are within our power to address. I am not suggesting that we should always refrain from reflecting on factors that we cannot control, rather that when practical improvement is our primary concern, we need to avoid having our attention diverted by what we cannot directly influence.

As mentioned above, when we decide to act, it is often crucial to consider not only how we will characterize a successful outcome but also what kinds of outcomes we would consider to be unintended and undesirable. When we evaluate action we will, it is to be hoped, be better prepared to identify unintended consequences (desirable and undesirable) as well as those that were originally intended. I find that in discussion, people invariably agree that identifying undesirable unintended consequences of action is an essential aspect of the evaluation of social policy and action; but in practice, such consequences are often overlooked. This is, as I have suggested in item (iii) of section 3 above, because the adopted objectives-based model of planning and evaluation allows the unintended consequences of action to go unacknowledged.

5 Distinguishing between problem-based and objectives-based planning

In discussions about problem-based versus objectives-based planning, it has been put to me that a practical problem is in itself an objective or an aim, because a state other than the present one is sought. For instance, the practical problem 'How can we construct a model bridge without the use of adhesives?' may be seen to imply the objective 'To construct a model bridge without the use of adhesives', and 'How can classroom practice be improved?' may be seen to imply the less specific objective or aim 'To improve classroom practice'. This objection can be countered in the following way.

In formulating a practical problem, attention is necessarily drawn to the current situation and what is wrong with it. Hopes or aims may be considered, but, in contrast to the objectives model, they are not the starting point of planning. The fulfilment of a hope and the achievement of an aim may or may not be possible, and there is no certain route to success; but by formulating problems and seeking to identify impediments to progress, there is the (uncertain and not predefined) possibility of *creating* a route. The problem-based approach encourages a critical consideration of hopes and aims, which may be modified and developed along with other ideas that an individual or group holds to be true or valid. (Note also that in the context of teaching, the formulation and presentation of an objective – in contrast to the formulation of a teaching problem – often implies that teaching to the objective is unproblematic, which invariably it is not.)

It has also been suggested that the term 'objective' may be applied to the linguistic encapsulation of a practical problem. However, as illustrated in this chapter, methodologies designed to address practical problems are very different from those associated with objectives. To call a practical problem an objective is to fudge this important distinction.

A further distinction between the approaches arises when ideas resulting from the use of a problem-based methodology are tested. A particular method or process may be developed and adopted, and, in seeking to test this method, statements about its possible consequences will be formulated. For instance, in seeking to make an empirical comparison between the use of problem-based and objectives-based approaches in the teaching of children, 'better spelling' might be highlighted as a desirable outcome of both. An exponent of objectives-based planning might then conclude that 'better spelling' was an objective of the problem-based approach.

This indicates a misunderstanding about both the nature of problem-based planning and the idea of testing a *process*. One of the ways that processes may be distinguished empirically is by their observable outcomes; however, the status of some of these outcomes may be that of a by-product. For instance, success in formal tests and examinations may be construed as a desirable by-product of better classroom practice, rather than as a goal of better classroom practice. Part of the evidence in support of a process lies in observable outcomes, but a process involves more than can be specified. There is, for example, more to better classroom practice than the achievement of better spelling. Moreover, treating 'better spelling' as a specified objective distracts attention not only from the more significant general problem but also from the difficulties of bringing about such a change and, most importantly, from the potential for unintended consequences.

If we wish to test problem-based processes, we must attempt to formulate ideas for the identification of *some* tangible results; these ideas can include both desirable and undesirable outcomes. But when desirable outcomes are formulated, they do not represent goals or objectives – their role is that of test statements. Individual practitioners may, of course, turn test statements into goals or objectives, but, in the context of a problem-based approach, this inclination should be resisted.

6 Professional development through action research

With regard to adopting a problem-based approach to the pursuit of improvement, I have so far discussed only what is involved day to day or at a rather basic level. When improvements in practice involve complex concerns, specifically those which require a significant degree of learning, then a more systematic problem-based methodology is needed. The adoption of such a methodology, when elements of what is learnt are put into the public domain, falls under the umbrella of action research. If what is learnt is not expressed in a written report or formal oral presentation, then I would suggest that it is preferable to refer to the process merely as one of professional development, without giving it the attribute of 'research'.

'Action research', as some readers will be aware, is a term that came into widespread use following the work of Kurt Lewin (1946). The term has various meanings but, in general, it 'denotes that a project includes both action to change a specific situation and also research designed to understand the situation better, or to monitor the change, or both' (Finch, 1986, p. 189). Accounts of action research generally make an explicit link between this approach and the desire to improve practice, and many accounts use the term 'problem' to describe the impetus for its adoption. Some authors, such as Wilfred Carr and Stephen Kemmis (1986), lay stress on the collaborative implications of the approach. This is evident in the quotation below, which also usefully delineates three areas of desired improvement that action research addresses – practice, understanding and the situation:

> There are two essential aims of all action research: to *improve* and to *involve*. Action research aims at improvement in three areas: firstly, the improvement of a *practice*; secondly, the improvement of the *understanding* of the practice by its practitioners; and, thirdly, the improvement of the *situation* in which the practice takes place. The aim of *involvement* stands shoulder to shoulder with the aim of *improvement*. Those involved in the practice being considered are to be involved in the action research process in all its phases of planning, acting, observing and reflecting. As an action research project develops, it is expected that a widening circle of those affected by the practice will become involved in the research process.
>
> (Ibid., p. 165)

As discussed in Chapter 8, section 8, given that there are two broad types of problem, I have argued that there are two broad types of research: research that is primarily concerned with practical problems and research that is primarily concerned with theoretical problems. I stress the word 'primarily' here. At no time have I suggested that theoretical problems have no bearing on research that focuses on a practical problem, or vice versa. It follows from my analysis that, when embarking on research, researchers should formulate and focus on the type of problem which provides the impetus for their work. If the impetus is a practical problem, then some form of action research is required. All action research addresses practical problems, even though these may be ill-defined.

Action research has been widely criticized for lacking rigour, but while action research, like any other approach to research, can be adopted without due concern for rigour, this is not to say that action research lacks rigour per se. Action research is a broad church – no particular methodological stance is involved (see, e.g., Somekh, 1995). However, insofar as action research is characterized as a process of trial-and-error that involves the testing of ideas and practices, it is compatible with Popperian epistemology, and the iterative dimension of many action research projects, whereby there are multiple phases of plan-do-review, is clearly consistent with an evolutionary analysis of learning.

My interest in action research first developed when I studied the Ford Teaching Project (see Elliott, 1976, as the final report of the project) as part of my research for an MA dissertation (Swann, 1976). The Ford Teaching Project operated on the assumption that teachers as individuals, working with each other and other educationists, could take positive and critically reflective steps to improve their own classroom practice. The project offered a welcome alternative to the idea, common at that time, that 'as a teacher I cannot effect significant improvement in my practice until the education system changes'. It acknowledged the potential power of individuals in institutions in a way that is consistent with the quotation from Popper at the head of this chapter (Popper, 1992b [1969], p. 80), and it offered action research as the key to empowerment.

John Elliott and Clem Adelman – respectively, the project's director and senior research associate – argued that 'teacher education should be very much concerned with initiating teachers into a tradition of reflecting about their practice in a way which tests and contributes to theory' (1975, p. 106). This had not been my experience of teacher education, neither at pre-service nor at in-service levels. And although I studied the Ford Teaching Project for my master's qualification, I did not concurrently exploit any of the methodological ideas in my own professional practice. I was working full-time and studying part-time and had assumed that the development of my theories about practice would be accompanied by improvements in practice. In the event, during the two years of part-time study, my attention was diverted from my teaching, and when the course was completed I became sharply aware of a massive gap between what I explicitly knew about learning, having studied Popper's evolutionary epistemology, and what was implied by what I was doing in the classroom.

Even when I embarked on my doctoral studies, and after I had joined the Classroom Action Research Network (later renamed the Collaborative Action Research Network), it took a while for me to realize that addressing the initial overarching research question 'How can classroom teaching practices be improved?' required me, as part of my studies, to research my own practice. Jack Whitehead (private communication) put the situation thus: 'there is no way of avoiding the implication in this question of actually attempting to improve one's own teaching practices and then to analyse the way in which this was or was not achieved.' While I would argue that it is possible to help others to improve their classroom teaching practices (see section 8 below for an example of how this can be done), a process in which a practitioner addresses a question of how to improve the kind of practice with which she (or he) is familiar seems to require at least some element of practical 'try it and see'.

I provide the above personal detail because my experience has aspects typical of that of many other teachers. As a lecturer in higher education who spent many years working with part-time master's degree students, I observed that many of those teachers and other professionals who began their research modules with a keen interest in improving practice subsequently embarked on a research project which focused on a theoretical rather than a practical problem. In some cases this was appropriate, but there were others for whom an opportunity to improve their own practice and situation seemed to have been lost due to a lack of understanding of the potential of action research. I stress again that I am not against developing theoretical knowledge. Pursuing improvements in practice through action research involves developing such knowledge, but the knowledge gained then serves the purpose of, or is a consequence of, an attempt to solve practical problems. In general, notwithstanding some centres of excellence, the understanding of action research seems to be patchy on the part of teachers of research methodology and methods, and, consequently, on the part of their students.

In my practice as a research supervisor, my first concern was to find out whether the research student was primarily interested in addressing a practical problem or whether her principal concern was with one or more theoretical problems. I then supported the student according to her response and in light of what was possible in the specific circumstances. Some practitioner researchers who have formulated an important practical problem may need to expand their knowledge first. For example, they may need to conduct a non-inductivist survey of colleagues' or students' (or clients') views or responses. In such circumstances, the research may need to be undertaken in two phases, the second being action research. When the first phase is extensive, it may require all the time and effort available for the research element of the course of study, and the action research phase is rightly shelved until later.

Although many practitioner researchers who undertake action research do so as part of an accredited course of study, the pursuit of a formal qualification is clearly not essential. The next section of this chapter is designed for use not only by research students but also by researchers and other professionals with the role of facilitating the professional development of others and by self-facilitating practitioner researchers. Note that although action research is well suited to professionals in full-time or part-time employment, it can be problematic for full-time students. When researchers cannot be party to a process of practical development, then the research they undertake will not be *action* research.

Action research is often, mistakenly, regarded as an alternative to case study; many students studying for a master's degree in education are encouraged to choose either action research or a case study when planning to undertake their research project. But all action research involves the development of at least one case study, although, of course, not all case studies involve action research. So there is a distinction to be made between an action research case study and a case study that does not involve action research. And although action research invariably involves an element of evaluation, action research and evaluation research are different approaches serving different purposes (see Chapter 8, section 8) – evaluation studies are generally concerned with evaluating solutions to practical problems in limited ways, whereas action research involves the attempt to solve a practical problem and evaluate the outcomes. Action research does not exclude the use of interview or questionnaire surveys, quasi-experiments or various other research methods; but their outcomes, in the form of knowledge developed, serve the process of addressing the overarching practical problem and are not ends in themselves. Action research is perhaps one of the most demanding and complex approaches to research, but its potential rewards are great in terms of improvements in practice, improvements in understanding and improvements in the situation (see the earlier quotation from Carr and Kemmis, 1986, p. 165).

7 A problem-based methodology for professional development

I devised the initial version of my systematic problem-based methodology circa 1990 for use by myself and my teaching colleagues at a college of education where I was employed. Later it was developed more generally for use by small groups of practitioners who wish to improve their professional practice (for earlier versions, see Swann, 1997, 1999b, 2000b, 2003b; Burgess and Swann, 2003; see also the references that follow in the next sentence). The methodology has been adopted by higher education lecturers (two related projects: Swann and Ecclestone, 1999a, 1999b; Swann and Arthurs, 1999), and teachers of students in post-compulsory education (sixth forms, further education colleges, community learning centres – as reported in Andrews et al., 2007, and Swann et al., 2011) and primary education (Barnes, 2008, 2009, 2010). I have twice used the full methodology to support the development of my own professional practice; on all other occasions I have facilitated (mostly working with a co-facilitator) the adoption of the methodology by others. The methodology was designed for use by a team of teachers (or other professionals) but has also been used by individual teachers who have posts of responsibility as team leaders (Barnes, 2008, 2009, 2010). When teachers have been willing volunteers, the methodology has been very well-received by them and significant positive outcomes have been reported. (I am aware that the methodology has been used in situations other than those I have mentioned here, but I have no further knowledge of what was done, by whom and with what consequences.)

Central to the development of the methodology is the idea of empowering the practitioner. The power to create social policy and practice brings with it a responsibility to critically evaluate the consequences of what has been created. In a society in which there is a plethora of top-down initiatives, practitioners can lose a sense of themselves as creative agents in the workplace. Instead, they may see their role largely in terms of responding to the initiatives of others. Responsibility for policy and outcome is diffuse. When things go wrong, policy makers blame practitioners for not implementing the policy correctly; practitioners blame policy makers for instigating the policy. There is blame and complaint, but often little progress. For progress, action and acknowledged responsibility for action need to be closely linked. Empowering practitioners means helping them to identify which aspects of their situation they can affect and encouraging them to formulate problems and create and test solutions.

Of the ten stages of the methodology (see below), the first seven can be addressed within a single two-and-a-half-hour session. The eighth requires a longer period of time – usually at least six months – after which the ninth stage is undertaken. When the methodology is being used within an action research project, as has mostly been the case, the tenth stage follows. The methodology was originally designed as a relatively low-cost approach to support professional development, and in all of the projects with which I have been directly involved, it has not been possible for the facilitators to provide much, if any, additional support outside of the workshops and communications relating to the workshops (see section 8 below). Alison Barnes, however, as an advisory teacher working for a local education authority, was able to provide significant support to the primary school 'gifted and talented' coordinators with whom the methodology was adopted (Barnes, 2008, 2009, 2010).

(i)   Address the question 'What is going well in the present situation and what do I/we anticipate will go well in the future?' (In other words, 'What do we want to defend, maintain and develop?') Accentuating the positive in this way may increase our confidence to act and can guard against the unintended consequence that a seemingly welcome development has involved the loss of desirable features that were taken for granted before the development took place.

(ii) Address the questions 'What is not going well?' and 'What do I/we anticipate may not go well in the future?' and, in light of this, 'What developments do I/we wish to bring about?'

(iii) Address the question 'What might impede the developments I/we desire to bring about?'

(iv) Address the question 'Which impediments fall within my/our sphere of influence?'

(v)   Given your answers to the earlier questions, formulate one or more practical problems using questions of the kind 'How can I/we . . . ?'

(vi) Make a list of the courses of action you might adopt in order to solve each problem and select at least one to adopt and test in practice. (Different members of a team may be able to test different solutions.) The cost implications (monetary and otherwise) of proposed solutions should be considered at this stage.

(vii) Decide how you will test the efficacy and worth of the solution(s) adopted. Be specific – use the following sentence openings: 'My/our solution to this problem will be successful insofar as it results in . . .', 'My/our solution will be a failure if it results in . . .' and 'Success and failure will be judged, at least in part, by . . .'.

(viii) Implement the chosen solutions, being mindful of the potential not only for desirable intended consequences but also for consequences that are unintended and potentially undesirable.

(ix) For each problem and each adopted solution, after allotting sufficient time for the solution to be tested properly, carry out a review by addressing the questions 'To what extent, if at all, has the initial problem been solved?', 'What unintended and unexpected consequences (desirable or undesirable) have arisen?', 'With the benefit of hindsight, might another solution have been preferable?'

and 'What new problems might now be formulated, and are they such as to require attention?'

(x) When the development process is part of an action research project, write a formal account of what has taken place and, in particular, what has been learnt.

The version of the problem-based methodology above is very open-ended with regard to the problem that the teachers or teacher are being supported to formulate. When the methodology is used in a situation in which the teachers (or other professionals) have agreed on an overarching problem in advance of adopting the methodology, such as 'How can we improve our formative assessment practice?', then I would suggest an amended version of stage (v) (following Barnes, 2008, 2009):

> In light of your answers to the earlier questions and given the overarching, practical problem '[overarching practical problem to be specified here]', formulate one or more practical problems using questions of the kind 'How can I/we . . . ?'

Barnes also introduced a new stage after stage (vii), making 11 stages in total, which worked well in the particular circumstances:

> Develop a timeline of how you will implement and test the strategies selected in response to [stage (vi)]. It should detail the timescales, actions, personnel involved and other significant events in the school during the timeframe that may have bearing on the outcomes.
>
> (Ibid., p. 5)

In summary, this problem-based methodology is a means of encouraging professional teachers to formulate their own meaningful problems that can potentially be solved by developing their own strategies and practices, then to create and adopt practical solutions and evaluate their effects on student learning. The adoption of such a methodology will inevitably raise ethical concerns. In particular, issues of confidentiality and anonymity will need to be addressed. There is little point in reflecting on practice if one reflects only on things that are going well, yet by exposing difficulties and weaknesses in practice there is always the risk of exposing oneself to hostile criticism. It is particularly galling if a disclosure of limitations in one's own practice is misused by people whose practices would not withstand a similar degree of scrutiny. In using the methodology, I would strongly recommend (as has been my own practice) that all practitioner researchers and facilitators agree from the outset to a specified set of ethical principles and procedures, including the principles of the institution in which the participants are working, the principles of the relevant country's educational research association (such as the British Educational Research Association, 2004) and the demanding principles for collaborative action research set out by Kemmis and Robin McTaggart (1988, pp. 106–8).

8 Facilitating problem-based professional development

In this section, I provide general guidelines for use by facilitators whose role is to support professionals as practitioner researchers in using the systematic problem-based methodology to develop – specifically to improve – their professional practice. For the purposes of these guidelines, I assume that the facilitators (two is the ideal for any one workshop) are independent of the practitioner researchers; they might be researchers (funded or unfunded), area teachers with a formal responsibility for supporting professional development or facilitators brought in by the institution. It is presumed here that the facilitators have no supporting role outside of the development workshops. I assume also that the practitioners are participating on a voluntary basis, and that they will be working in groups or teams with between two and five members (though any team of only two should be combined with another team for the purposes of workshop group discussions). For the most part, I assume there is a shared overarching problem, common to all the groups, and that there are few, if any, opportunities for in-depth discussion among practitioner participants between workshops. Although my focus is on the development workshops, I first make some comments about preparatory activities.

For anyone initiating a professional development process that makes use of these guidelines, I would suggest that efforts be made to obtain funding to cover teachers for the time they spend at the workshops. In England, where teachers in all sectors often feel beleaguered and undervalued, it has been crucially important for recruitment and retention to acknowledge and value the teachers' time and expertise – at a cost no greater than that of supply or relief cover during the normal working week. I would also suggest that refreshments and, where appropriate, lunch be provided free of charge at each workshop.

Negotiating participation can be time consuming, and a brief preliminary meeting with practitioners may be the easiest way to communicate key basic information and secure a commitment to participate. If there is already an agreed upon, shared, overarching problem, reading material about this can be distributed prior to the first workshop. At a minimum, the ethical guidelines for collaborative action research (ibid.) and other relevant ethical guidelines, as mentioned earlier, should also be distributed at this stage.

It is particularly important that facilitators using the problem-based methodology stress from the outset that they will not report back to institutional managers. Only managers who are directly involved in a project – that is, as workshop participants – should have access to teacher plans and reports. If the use of the problem-based methodology is to be part of a formal process of accountability (see section 9 below), then it should be the responsibility of the practitioner group or individual, not the facilitator, to submit a report of the development project. In general, the facilitator's role is to serve the practitioners, not to judge them.

Workshop 1

As stated earlier, the first problem-based methodology workshop requires a minimum of two and a half hours, including a break. Where there is an agreed upon overarching problem, a preliminary session in relation to this might be highly beneficial. This session might take place in the morning, with the methodology workshop following in the afternoon after lunch.

After introductions and any necessary discussion and clarification (e.g. in respect of ethical issues), the task of the facilitators is to take the practitioners, working in groups, through the first seven stages of the methodology (see section 7 above for the stages, including the amendment to stage (v)). For each of the stages apart from (vii), each group needs a sheet of A3 paper on which the task is written; for stage (vii) three sheets need to be provided for each group. At the end of each stage, the A3 sheets are displayed on the walls of the room, with each group having its own wall space. The groups then have the opportunity to reflect briefly on each others' responses during the break and before the end of the workshop. The morning ends with a plenary discussion.

In taking the practitioners through the first seven stages of the methodology, it is essential for the facilitators to maintain the pace and keep participants to the brief time available for each activity. Stages (i) through (iv) require about 10 minutes each, including administration. Stages (v) through (vii) require about 20 minutes each. Some groups may need support to remain focused on the specific tasks rather than getting sidetracked into other areas or a disempowering focus on constraints. The practitioners formulate their own responses to the tasks. All ideas need to be expressed in sentences so that complete thoughts are formed and are comprehensible to others. With regard to (v), the facilitators may need to stress that the practical problems formulated should be ones that the practitioners are able and keen to address within a specified timescale.

After the workshop, the practitioners begin stage (viii) of the methodology. The facilitators type the content of the A3 sheets to form a single document, with sections for each group of practitioners. This is then sent to all workshop participants, so that each practitioner group has a record of what its members had planned, and all groups have basic information about the others' plans.

Workshop 2

Workshop 2 is held about three months after the first workshop. This is a shorter workshop, the length of time required being dependent on the extent to which the substantive topic of the development process is to be explored independently of the problem-based methodology. For the methodology, the key idea is that the practitioners will benefit from time in which to talk to each other about their planned professional development.

There are four principal activities to encourage reflection on practice and to provide support for report writing. The first uses a 'triads' format, whereby participants sit in threes (not with other members of their own professional development group) and each takes a turn as an interviewer, interviewee and note taker. Interviewers are asked to use the following lead question and probes: 'What have you been doing since Workshop 1 to develop your [type of practice to be specified] practice, and why have you been doing it?', 'What has been going well with regard to the development of your [type of practice to be specified] practice?' and 'What has not been going well?' For the second activity, teachers are asked to handwrite individual interim progress reports in response to the same questions as those used during the interviews. To support this, each teacher can use the note taker's notes. Hard copies of the plans from Workshop 1 are also made available. For the third activity, the participants sit in their professional development groups and share the con- tent of their individual reports, comparing them with what they had planned at Workshop 1 and talking about what they might do next, that is, between Workshop 2 and Workshop 3 (usually three to four months hence). The facilitators may also specify other questions relating to the focus of the over-arching problem. The fourth activity is a plenary, during which all groups report on progress, difficulties and current plans.

Within a few weeks of the workshop, the facilitators send the participants electronic versions of their interim reports. (Electronic versions rather than hard copy are preferable because they are time-saving, allowing participants to cut and paste material for their final reports.)

Workshop 3

The key to the success of Workshop 3 lies in the preparation. Three weeks prior to the workshop, facilitators need to send a detailed communication to the practitioners, outlining their expectations for the workshop, includ-ing expectations with regard to practitioner workshop presentations and the structure and content of the final reports of their professional development (stages (ix) and (x) of the methodology). The suggested structure and content of the final reports is shown in Figure 10.1. Practitioners short of time are asked to focus on items 3, 5 and 6. A minimum of one report is sought for each group.

The discussions at the final workshop are largely led by the practitioners. Each practitioner group has 10 minutes in which to present the report of its development during the specified period. Each presentation is followed by a minimum of 10 minutes discussion. After a break, there is a plenary during which possible future plans are discussed.

9 Problem-based accountability

A common view of accountability is that it means 'doing what you are told and showing that you've done it' (Pratt, 2009, p. 6, citing Tyrrell Burgess's critique). This conception of accountability is now endemic in state-funded schools in England, following the centralization of education decision mak-ing consequent on the Education Reform Act 1988 (see my Chapter 6, section 3). Such a state of affairs is an almost inevitable outcome of two mistaken ideas: that objectives-based planning and evaluation is the only rational approach (an idea that has been called into question by the argument in this chapter) and that a democracy is enhanced when elected politicians make decisions that prescribe in considerable detail the behaviour of state-funded employees.

1. Our practical professional development problem(s) and its (their) rationale

Here we're asking for a restatement of the 'How can . . . ?' questions from Workshop 1 and an outline of why the problem(s) you formulated was (were) then seen to be important.

2. Our planned solutions and how we intended to test them

Here we're asking for a restatement of what you planned to do and how you thought you would evaluate the outcomes.

3. What we actually did and why

Here we're asking for a summary statement of, as the heading says, what you did and why you did it. This can include an explanation of how and why your plans were changed. Your problem focus may also have shifted; if so, please explain why.

4. [A heading and guidelines can be inserted here in relation to the focus of the overarching professional development problem.]

5. An evaluation of what we did

Please address the following three questions: (a) To what extent, if at all, has (have) your initial problem(s) been solved? (b) What unintended consequences (desirable and undesirable) have arisen from your adopted solution(s)? (c) With the benefit of hindsight, might another solution (other solutions) have been preferable?

6. What we've learnt about [focus of the overarching problem] from being involved in this research

7. What we plan to do next with regard to developing our [specified] practice

For this, we'd like you to formulate new problems that have developed out of your practice during the past [specify] months.

Figure 10.1 Suggested headings and content for final reports.

I stress that adopting a problem-based approach to the pursuit of improvement is not at odds with accountability; but the conception of accountability associated with it contrasts sharply with that described above. Problem-based accountability means taking seriously the idea that professionals, such as teachers in education institutions, are capable of acting independently and responsibly, and that although a community or society will wish to *proscribe* certain behaviours, it is unproductive and potentially dangerous to attempt to *prescribe* the detail of what professional practitioners will do. Excessively detailed prescription constrains creativity and coerces people to practise in accordance with the fallible ideas of others – it prevents them from learning from their own mistakes. Of course, those in favour of do-what-you're-told-and-show-that-you've-done-it accountability may wish to argue that professionals and other practitioners should not be allowed to make mistakes, and that it is the responsibility of elected policy makers and their appointees to decide what is to be done for the best in the name of all. But, inevitably, everyone makes mistakes, even those in positions of power. One consequence of centralized control is that mistakes are often writ large and practitioners are constrained to adhere to mistaken policies even when they become aware of negative consequences. Eventually, a clearly mistaken policy may be rescinded, but often not before damage has been done to, in the case of education, one or more generations of students. In a hierarchical society, those towards the top of the hierarchy, who make policy to be followed by others lower down, usually have a vested interest in concealing their mistakes. Their position of power is to a significant degree 'justified' by the claim that they are right in their thinking.

Problem-based accountability, as conceived here, is not, however, just a matter of checking that practitioners have not done what has been proscribed. Rather, it involves both an expanded idea of professional practice and systems for checking that practitioners are practising responsibly. A responsible practitioner is one who strives to make appropriate judgements in specific circumstances, who acts on judgement and who takes care to consider the consequences of her action – including unintended consequences, desirable and undesirable. A responsible practitioner is prepared to subject her policies and practices to the critical scrutiny of others. Successive governments in England have not, by this criterion, shown themselves to be responsible, because the unintended consequences of education policy as enacted or otherwise promoted by government have not been (and, as I write, are still not being) given appropriate consideration.

Two social mechanisms for problem-based accountability in respect of schools and teachers were noted in Chapter 6, section 2, quoted from Burgess (1975, p. 7): 'the whole educational organisation of the school can be reported to the governors or managers, and can be approved by them. . . . It would secure the public interest in the plans of individual schools' and, with regard to the development of student-initiated curricula, 'If the inspectors were to inspect – the work of the pupils in formulating problems, the progress of the proposed solutions . . . they would not only be earning their money but would be making a serious educational contribution' (ibid.). With regard to the latter (edited) quotation (and in accordance with Burgess's extended argument),

I emphasize that the problem-based accountability proposed in this chapter does not require a national or other kind of common curriculum.

What kind of evidence of responsible policy and action might schools and/or teachers be asked to provide? I propose that they be asked to provide an account of the following:

(a) the most significant professional and/or educational problems they are addressing
(b) the solutions they are adopting or have recently adopted
(c) the process by which the outcomes of these solutions are being or have been evaluated
(d) the consequences, including not only those that were/are intended but also consequences that were/are unintended (desirable and undesirable)
(e) what they have learnt, or are learning, from this process of problem solving and what new problems have been developed from it.

In producing such an account, schools and/or teachers might find it useful to adopt the problem-based methodology set out in section 7 above. Such an account of process could not, of course, be evaluated according to a set of tick boxes; rather, it would invite more complex judgements on the part of those whose responsibility it is to check that the school and/or teacher is behaving responsibly. In the case of school inspectors, one of their overarching roles – given their unique access to a range of professional and educational development strategies – would be that of disseminating accounts of interesting and good innovative practice. They would, of course, be expected to eschew fostering a culture of blame and shame.

My proposals for problem-based planning and evaluation, and problem-based professional development and accountability in particular, may seem somewhat unrealistic because I can offer no panacea for the social and political difficulties encountered by anyone who wishes to challenge the practice of objectives-based planning and evaluation in the workplace. But if we wish to improve the conduct and organization of teaching in formal institutions of education, we must contest the orthodoxy of the objectives model and adopt and test problem-based approaches such as the one offered in this chapter. This will be difficult for many of us; the public procedures we are permitted to adopt are limited. When the requirement to present plans using the objectives model is inescapable, we may decide to use a problem-based approach in private and then present our plans and any subsequent evaluations as though objectives had been used. But apart from the time-consuming nature (and bad faith) of this approach, it fails to address the problem of how to challenge the current orthodoxy, and it provides inadequate scope for testing ideas.

In many contexts, the wholesale abandonment of the objectives model will require a considerable ideological shift, but, as an immediate strategy, teachers and others can at least keep the debate alive by not colluding with the idea that no rational alternative exists. We can remind ourselves and each other that learning and the pursuit of improvement are open-ended processes in which new ideas are created in response to the discovery of error and inadequacy. If we really want to promote learning and pursue improvement, we must accept and work with uncertainty, and value systems and procedures that embrace open-endedness rather than deny it.

Teaching for a Better World

A certain amount of state control in education . . . is necessary, if the young are to be protected from a neglect which would make them unable to defend their freedom, and the state should see that all educational facilities are available to everybody. But too much state control in educational matters is a fatal danger to freedom, since it must lead to indoctrination.

—*Karl Popper,* The Open Society and Its Enemies,
Volume 1: The Spell of Plato

The future is open. It is not predetermined and thus cannot be predicted – except by accident. The possibilities that lie in the future are infinite. When I say 'It is our duty to remain optimists', this includes not only the openness of the future but also that which all of us contribute to it by everything we do: we are all responsible for what the future holds in store.

—*Karl Popper,* The Myth of the Framework:
In Defence of Science and Rationality

Introduction

This chapter revisits the book's principal themes to present a speculative account of how teaching can be directed towards the pursuit of a better world. Regarding the pursuit of a better world, I do not offer objectives or specific aims. For the reasons discussed at length in Chapter 10, I caution against anyone pursuing a better world in light of aims and objectives (or goals and targets); a problem-based approach will be significantly more conducive to progress. Such an approach is adopted in this chapter, in which I propose the following overarching problem: '*How can we improve the way we function in the world, specifically with regard to how we treat each other and ourselves, and the way we use the world's resources?*' In using a problem-based methodology, there is scope for the development of many varied responses to this problem, some of which will be better than others. Many will be similarly worthwhile and necessary. This chapter presents one set of ideas: a set that follows directly from the content of the book. To formulate the argument, some material used earlier in the book is, of necessity, repeated here.

At the heart of my argument is the idea of *teaching for transcendent learning*. I have been inspired for many years by Karl Popper's succinct depiction (requoted below) of what learning is and what it can achieve, namely transcendence:

> The process of learning, of the growth of subjective knowledge, is always fundamentally the same. It is *imaginative criticism*. This is how we transcend our local and temporal environment by trying to think of circumstances *beyond* our experience: by criticizing the universality, or the structural necessity, of what may, to us, appear (or what philosophers may describe) as the 'given' or as 'habit'; by trying to find, construct, invent, new situations – that is, *test* situations, *critical* situations; and by trying to locate, detect, and challenge our prejudices and habitual assumptions.
>
> (1979 [1972], p. 148)

Transcendent learning, as construed in this book and following Popper, is the kind of learning that enables us, collectively and individually, to progress well beyond what has hitherto been habitual and/or commonplace in respect of our thinking, practices, strategies and institutional systems.

1 Keeping faith with mass schooling

I assert here that children and adolescents have a right to avail themselves of appropriate educational facilities and that this right is one which the state should protect (see the first quotation at the head of this chapter from Popper, 2002a [1945], pp. 117–18). But, as I argued in Chapters 5 and 6, formal education is generally disappointing because it does little to facilitate the transcendence (individual and collective) of which humans are capable. I further argued that, in practice, schooling is often manipulative and coercive – a view shared with and put even more strongly by some authors (e.g. Harber, 2004), including many of those whose analysis of schooling has focused on the hidden curriculum (e.g. Gatto, 2005 [1992]). But notwithstanding my criticisms of schooling and my awareness of the variety of alternatives to conventional formal education (such as those proposed by supporters of Personalised Education Now – www.personalisededucationnow.org.uk), I have not lost faith in the potential to redeem our current education institutions, in particular our schools, so that they become both significantly more educative and less authoritarian – two improvements which are inextricably linked, the former being dependent on the latter.

Authoritarianism is manifested in dependence relationships which, to draw on the words of Roland Meighan, generally 'persist unless the dominant person [or group] decides otherwise, though reactions from the submissive persons [or groups] can occur' (Meighan and Siraj-Blatchford, 2003 [1981], p. 209 – the words in brackets are my own). By using Meighan's analysis of different forms of authoritarianism in education (ibid. and my Chapter 1, section 6), we can see that formal education, particularly schooling, is largely authoritarian in nature not only because it is often manipulative and coercive, but also because it serves to encourage at least some degree of dependence on the part of students. Children and adolescents experience authoritarianism in school and are in a sense prepared for its continuation in adult life – rather than being prepared for the independence and interdependence that are necessary for the realization of human learning potential and for social systems and structures that are open and democratic.

I have not blamed the disappointing outcomes of formal education on teachers, students or parents. Nor have I attributed educational weaknesses to scant resources (though I do not deny that economic matters are important and are the most important factor in some contexts). Nor have I focused on authoritarianism as the central issue. Instead I have argued that, in many societies, significant difficulties lie in the assumptions about learning that are embedded in present structures, strategies and practices, and in the way that schools are expected to serve many purposes, some of which conflict with the promotion of learning. We can see that schools are instrumental in the process of social selection that influences post-school opportunities, wealth and status. This process conflicts with the provision of a learning service in that it results in a tendency to penalize the discovery of error and specific limitation. In so doing it inhibits learning, because it discourages activity and damages confidence. Some learning is encouraged, but learning that leads to greater learning in the longer term is, overall, curtailed.

I have no panacea for these systemic ills, but my substantial experience of working with teachers and students fuels my optimism. Teachers and students have the power to bring about improvements, and when they sense their power, they are often inclined to seize opportunities to act and learn in light of their preferences, rather than in accordance with what they have previously been constrained to think possible. What I have offered in this book is an argument about the nature of the improvement that is needed – in the way that teaching and formal learning are conceived – and I have provided some specific ideas as to how teachers can organize their teaching and conduct themselves with students, and how professional development for teachers can be effectively facilitated.

2 The importance of optimism

Popper asserted that optimism is a duty (see the second quotation at the head of this chapter from Popper, 1994a, p. xiii). He perhaps overstated the case, but clearly optimism is crucial to progress. In order energetically and steadfastly to pursue improvements in how we function as a species, we need to believe that such improvements are possible. We also need to recognize that the future is open. What will happen has not been determined, and it is not true that there is nothing new under the sun. There are constraints, of course, but we can still find ways to challenge the status quo and set out optimistically, if somewhat cautiously, to create a new and better state of affairs. As individuals, we need to believe that we can be instrumental in bringing about progress. What each of us does can count. We are responsible for what we do, and also for what we can do but choose not to do.

Optimism is not always easy to maintain in the face of significant flaws in what appears to be human nature. But we can remind ourselves that, as a species, we are capable of individual and collective acts of compassion and altruism. We are often willing and able to act independently rather than merely follow the herd. We can be immensely resourceful and creative, trying our utmost to make situations better rather than worse. Collectively, spurred on by the efforts and successes of individuals and groups, we have made huge strides regarding developments in, for example, linguistic communication and related technologies, the arts, engineering and science. We are capable of learning on a scale that vastly outstrips that of any other animal, to the extent that we take for granted many of the capabilities we use daily in order to function in society and mostly overlook our potential for collective transcendence. Despite our capacity for negative behaviour, there is cause for optimism.

3 Some impediments to human transcendence

The first stage of my systematic problem-based methodology (Chapter 10, section 7) has been loosely addressed in the preceding paragraph. The positive human characteristics listed are my response to 'What is going well in the present situation and what do I/we anticipate will go well in the future?' To address the second stage of the methodology, what is not going well is the extent to which our negative characteristics find expression in, for example, egocentricity, complacency and wastefulness. Also, despite our positive traits, often we manipulate and are manipulated by others, and we are inclined to act with scant regard for the long-term consequences of our actions. At the risk of saying something trite, as a species we need to exploit our positive qualities more effectively and reduce the influence of the negative. The difficulties in achieving such a shift are enormous. For example, the inclination towards negative behaviours can be self-reinforcing, and for those who aspire to what might be called higher values, the negative behaviours of oneself and others can lead to despair. What often then develop are social systems and structures designed to curtail negative tendencies but which also limit the exercise and development of the positive.

So what might impede the advancement of our positive qualities? There are many potential answers to this question, but outlined below are three sets of impediments to progress all relevant to, or focused on, the conduct and organization of teaching in institutions of education. These impediments act as significant constraints on learning. They are all in existence now and, without decisive action, it seems likely they will continue.

Teaching in accordance with a fallacious assumption about learning

An evolutionary analysis shows that learning takes place *only* as the result of the learner's activity. There is no passive stage or aspect to learning, and there is no transfer of informational elements from the environment to the learner. Learning takes place only and entirely as the result of a process characterized by Popper, as quoted earlier, as 'imaginative criticism' (1979 [1972], p. 148). Leaving haphazard organic changes aside, every human disposition that develops afresh in our lifetime – that is, each preference and expectation that is not instinctual – has to be imagined in response to experience. Our preferences and expectations are challenged – in effect, criticized – by experience, and we, being discontented with the state of affairs this brings about, are stimulated to create new preferences and expectations. Learning takes place through a process of trial and error-elimination; it is what happens when, and only when, the learner has a problem, attempts to solve it and survives, leading to changes in her (or his) disposition(s) – and, as a corollary, changes in the world – that are not entirely the outcome of maturational or haphazard factors (see Part 1).

It follows that if we wish to promote the growth of learning – particularly learning that goes beyond the mundane – we need to find ways to encourage and support imaginative criticism by encouraging and supporting self-directed exploratory activity, that is, activity in which the learner can engage in extended and open-ended trial and error-elimination. And if we want to maximize our potential for learning, we need to encourage exploratory activity that is not only self-directed (and by implication, self-monitored, self-evaluated and self-regulated) but also self-initiated, rather than encouraging individuals to be dependent on others for decisions about the focus and substance of their learning (see Part 2).

*Inter*dependent action is, of course, important, but we can expect that the most effective expressions of interdependence will involve individuals who have the ability and inclination to make independent and critically informed decisions, and who have freely chosen to develop their ability to work *with* others. Collaborative activity is not enhanced by the involvement of people who are manipulative or submissive.

The above account of learning contrasts with the common, but mistaken, assumption that learning takes place, at least sometimes and to some degree, *by* instruction from without – not to be confused with the idea of learning *in response to* instruction from without (as discussed in Chapter 2, section 1). Many teachers, educationists and education policy makers act on the assumption that learning can involve the transfer of informational elements from the physical and/or social environment to the individual. It is assumed that, to some degree, learning happens to us, rather than being wholly the result of activity on our part. Learning is then viewed as a process or event that can potentially be controlled by a teacher, rather than merely being a process that can be encouraged or inhibited. When educationists act on the assumption that there is some transference of information from the environment to the learner, and that this transference can be at least partially controlled by the teacher, the natural inclination of children to engage in self-initiated and self-directed exploratory activity – trial and error-elimination – tends to be curtailed. That which cannot be controlled tends to be viewed with suspicion rather than treated as the primary resource.

In short, a major impediment to human progress is this: the activities and institutional structures that have come to characterize schooling vastly underestimate our potential for imaginative criticism, because they do not acknowledge the extent to which it lies at the heart of what we, including the youngest children, do in order to succeed at even the most basic tasks.

Teaching for dependence

In keeping with the fallacious view of learning described above, the kinds of relationships that professional teachers are encouraged to develop with learners are more often than not those in which the learner is dependent. There is much rhetoric about educating children and adolescents for independence. But in practice, teachers are encouraged by institutional systems and structures to value student compliance and conformity. Of particular significance is the fact that, worldwide, students in formal education institutions are mostly taught according to a curriculum that has been prescribed by their teachers, the school board, or local or central government. Teachers are expected to initiate most of the planned learning activities, and students are expected to rely on teachers for fundamental decisions about what to do and when to do it. So what most students learn most strongly is to do the bidding of others; that their initiative is not welcomed; that they can make choices (if they are fortunate) but not exercise preference; and that they will be undervalued and disadvantaged if they fail to meet the narrowly conceived expectations of both teacher and school. Without the opportunity to initiate curricula, students learn dependence (though, in some cases, they become rebellious). For many students, schooling is not only disappointing, it is also disempowering. Mostly, too, prior to entering higher education, students are not encouraged to question or criticize the material with which they are presented. The task of the student is to learn the syllabus, not question it. When school students are expected to ask questions, they are usually invited to do so within a framework set by the teacher.

Teaching for dependence severely limits opportunities for self-initiated exploratory activity and generally constrains self-directed exploratory activity; it inhibits the development of criticality and creativity, and, for many students, it saps confidence. Contrary to what may be claimed, it works against the development of full learner autonomy, that is, *the ability and inclination to make independent and critically informed decisions regarding the timing, location, method, purpose and content of planned learning* (see Chapter 5, section 3).

A damaging approach to planning and evaluation

A fêted and widely adopted approach to planning and evaluation is falsely touted as *the* rational alternative to a laissez-faire attitude to the pursuit of improvement (see the introduction to Chapter 10, and sections 2 and 3). The adoption of this approach, which involves the formulation of objectives (or 'targets'), is particularly problematic in complex situations in which significant learning is required. Among other weaknesses, the objectives-based (or target-based) approach to planning and evaluation does not encourage breadth of vision and assumes a closed view of human endeavour. It has two particularly serious weaknesses with potentially devastating consequences when adopted. First, it does not encourage the defence and maintenance of what is going well or is expected to go well. Second, it fails to acknowledge that any planned action will inevitably have unintended consequences, some of which may be undesirable.

Fortunately, and contrary to what is widely assumed, there are problem-based rational alternatives to objectives-based planning, one of which has been discussed in Chapter 10 and is partially illustrated in the present chapter. This problem-based approach avoids the flaws identified in the objectives-based model. It is also consistent with an evolutionary analysis of learning, as summarized above.

4 Addressing impediments to transcendent learning

The extent to which the above impediments to the promotion of human learning and, therefore, to human progress fall within our sphere of influence, acting individually or as members of groups, will depend on our circumstances. On the face of it, those who live in open and democratic societies seem likely to be able to do more than those who do not. But although the ideas discussed relate primarily to people with formal teaching roles, some can be extended to all those who have an aspiration, conscious or unconscious, to help another individual or group of individuals to learn. We may not be able to have a profound effect on the ubiquity of authoritarian systems, structures and practices in the short term, but we can personally pursue in our specific circumstances the move from harder to softer authoritarian forms, and we can try to find ways of bridging from softer forms to democratic approaches (Meighan and Siraj-Blatchford, 2003 [1981], pp. 212–13).

Most importantly, as teachers, we can construe the learner's role in light of an evolutionary analysis of learning and strive to find ways to encourage students to engage in critical and creative activity – imaginative criticism – and we can seek to encourage the development of full learner autonomy. Despite constraints, there will still often be scope for developing educational relationships in which teacher and student are partners in the educational process. We can encourage students to value and learn from each other. We can strive to find ways of discouraging biddability and dependence. Quite simply, teachers can take action in their relationships with students (whether individual students, small groups of students or whole classes).

Also, although we may not be able to do much to effect the overthrow of the limited and naïve view of planning and evaluation that dominates education policy making in many contexts, we can at least not collude with the myth that it is the only rational approach. And we can, whenever possible, use an alternative problem-based methodology for the pursuit of improvement, such as the one described and discussed in Chapter 10.

5 Teaching for transcendence

So, to continue with the use of the systematic problem-based methodology, in light of what I have written in sections 2, 3 and 4 above and given the broad overarching practical problem *'How can we improve the way we function in the world, specifically with regard to how we treat each other and ourselves, and the way we interact with the world's resources?'*, I propose the following more specific practical problem – referred to hereafter as *the problem of teaching for transcendence* – for immediate and sustained attention from teachers:

> How can we (a) facilitate the creation and maintenance of an environment (or environments) in which students can safely engage in exploratory activity that is self-initiated and self-directed, (b) encourage students to exercise and develop their facility for creativity and criticality and (c) support students to become fully autonomous lifelong learners?

With regard to (c), I acknowledge that this is what many teachers already strive to do, although I have questioned the extent to which school teachers are able to do it within conventional formal education. With regard to (a) and (b), more often than not the aspirations here expressed are not even on the education agenda. A safe environment, as conceived here, is one in which students are not penalized for the discovery of error and specific limitation, and where unnecessary risks – specifically, the risks of occurrences that would ultimately curtail learning, *including risks to the individual's confidence as a learner* – are avoided, as far as possible.

The next stage in the systematic problem-based methodology invites the practitioner (or group of practitioners) to make a list of strategies that might be adopted to solve the problem, and the selection of a strategy to adopt and test in practice.

In the context of my own philosophical and empirical research, I have proposed a set of principles and practices which follow from, and are defensible in light of, an evolutionary analysis of learning (Part 2). I have, in particular, criticized the intensive use of prescribed curricula (in Chapter 6) and have proposed what I see as a key teaching strategy, that of introducing, supporting and managing student-initiated curricula, whereby students take responsibility for decisions about the content of their planned programmes of study. Building on the work of Tyrrell Burgess (1975, 1977, 1979), Chapter 7 sets out generic principles for such curricula, for use by teachers working with students of any age, but with illustrations drawn from my work with primary school children.

What I have proposed could be adopted when planning an entire formal curriculum (as was the case in higher education at the School for Independent Study, 1974–91) or substantial parts thereof (as in the case of my primary classroom, 1981–87). Even in England, despite the demands of the national curriculum, student-initiated curricula could be developed in almost any school, at least on a limited basis – such as one day a week, every afternoon, or two weeks a term. So my proposed solution to the problem of teaching for transcendence does not require the immediate abandonment of prescribed curricula; indeed, I have not even suggested this as a long-term aim. I am merely suggesting a move towards the reduction in the intensive use of such curricula. What I have proposed is doable in many contexts.

An understanding of the case for student-initiated curricula requires that a distinction be made between a practice which I accept as necessary, namely curbing or curtailing certain learning aspirations on the grounds that they are morally unacceptable or have overly demanding resource implications, and trying to prescribe what is to be learnt on the assumption that what students are inclined to plan for themselves with regard to learning will invariably be inappropriate or inferior – a practice I reject. It is also important to understand that what I am proposing is neither subject-centred nor child-centred; rather, it focuses on the *student's learning problems* (not to be confused with the idea of learning difficulties). The approach is structured and involves significant interventions on the part of the teacher. I have not proposed a laissez-faire system of schooling in which students are encouraged to do as they please without reference to thoughts about standards and without critical evaluation and accountability (for a proposal in respect of problem-based teacher and school accountability, see Chapter 10, section 9).

6 Anticipating consequences

Some teachers and educationists, upon hearing about student-initiated curricula, have responded by suggesting that the intensive use of such curricula would constitute a disservice to young children, because the experience will not prepare them for later teaching in school; that is, it will not socialize them for an environment in which expressions of individuality are often not welcome and in which conformity and biddability are dominant values. It has also been put to me that most children will grow up to become adults whose employment opportunities will be restricted to fairly routine jobs that require little initiative. It is better, so the argument goes, that education institutions prepare children and adolescents for the future as it seems likely to be, rather than a future as they or we might wish it to be. To accept this argument is to abandon the prospect of creating a better world. It also implies that a major function of the teacher's role is to prepare students to expect and accept oppression. But teaching for full learner autonomy can also be viewed as preparation for oppression, in that individuals who are more confident, resourceful and resilient in the face of difficulties, and who are experienced in collaborative activity, are more likely to be able to work to eliminate oppression, rather than accept it. The latter view carries with it a more optimistic expectation of what we can achieve, both individually and collectively.

Pessimistic expectations about the effects of student-initiated curricula have been, in my experience and that of Burgess and many others who were involved in the School for Independent Study, unrealized (see Chapter 6, section 5). I repeat here that the use of such curricula did not result in a narrowing of the curriculum or a general failure on the part of students to develop social and other basic skills. Indeed, the opposite was true. For most students, the development of student-initiated curricula discouraged complacency and inertia, fostered sustained effort, and led to increased confidence, understanding and capability with regard to a range of socially relevant endeavours, including, in the case of the primary school students, literacy. The formal programmes of learning that students created, though different from those that teachers and external curriculum developers might have conceived, were not foolish or inappropriate. These curriculum initiatives did not fail in educational terms; their demise was brought about by changes in the political ideology of the country in which they were developed.

Present systems of mass schooling may be construed as largely efficient and effective, requiring only tweaking at the margins, but only by those who have low expectations of what most children and adolescents can achieve and who assume, wrongly, that learning can take place by instruction from without and can be controlled by a teacher. Student-initiated curricula take some time to set up (a week or more with school students, even longer with students in higher education), but that does not mean that it would be more efficient and effective to use some kind of prescribed curriculum, not even one designed as a means of short-circuiting the time spent working with students to ascertain their learning aspirations and helping them to plan their formal programmes of learning.

7 Testing practices and testing the theory

How, in general, are solutions to the practical problem of how to teach for transcendence to be evaluated? Given the broad overarching problem, it would be appropriate to consider evidence of success by reference to any apparent increase in the influence of positive human characteristics, such as those noted in section 2 above, and evidence of failure in respect of negative characteristics, such as those noted at the beginning of section 3. In relation to the problem of teaching for transcendence, plans could be developed to evaluate solutions according to whether, or to what extent, it has been possible to (a) create and maintain a safe place in which students have been encouraged to engage in exploratory activity that is self-initiated and self-directed, (b) encourage students to exercise and develop their facility for creativity and criticality and (c) support students to become fully autonomous lifelong learners. Of these evaluative criteria, the use of the first would seem to be relatively straightforward, the second slightly less so. Using the third criterion would be rather more problematic and would require that the solution be sustained for a substantial period, such as two years or more, before a full evaluation would be feasible. As with the proposal for testing my teaching hypothesis, the outcomes of practice in respect of the third criterion might be evaluated in part by the use of standardized tests to 'measure' changes in self-confidence, social skills, attitudes to learning, literacy and the use of oral language (but see Chapter 9, section 7, in respect of qualms regarding this proposal).

Concerns about the potential unintended consequences of a chosen solution will vary according to the specific situation. Were I to return to school teaching and again have an opportunity to use student-initiated curricula with children, I would look in greater detail at the implications of any intensive adoption of such curricula for the development of numeracy. But I would certainly not limit my critical reflection in respect of unintended consequences to this one area.

I hope that readers of this book will be encouraged to adopt the problem of teaching for transcendence and to develop and test solutions. In accordance with my problem-based methodology, what I mean by testing, with regard to practical solutions to practical problems, involves carrying out a review by addressing the questions 'To what extent, if at all, has the initial problem been solved?', 'What unintended and unexpected consequences (desirable or undesirable) have arisen?', 'With the benefit of hindsight, might another solution have been preferable?' and 'What new problems might now be formulated, and are they such as to require attention?' I hope that, for at least some teachers, the process of testing will be part of an action research project and that formal accounts of what has taken place and what has been learnt will be written up and disseminated.

In addition, as proposed in Chapter 9, scientific research could be carried out to test the theory of teaching set out in Part 2 of this book when accompanied by the systematic problem-based methodology presented in Chapter 10. In the meantime, we should not assume that the present conventions for deciding curriculum content have withstood the test of time and are likely to be better than any radically new initiative. That a particular way of doing things has seemed to work for a long time, even centuries, does not mean that it, or any of the assumptions embedded in it, have been rigorously tested.

8 What teachers are for – their role and purpose in promoting learning

Early in this book I made the case for construing teaching as any activity undertaken on the part of one individual with the intention, conscious or unconscious, of helping another individual or group of individuals to learn. Although the activities of teaching are many and varied, I have identified two endeavours which together characterize teaching and are, essentially, what teachers are for: teachers may be intent on helping another or others to learn something in particular, something conceived by them (the teachers) prior to and/or independent of their engagement with the learner, and something other than the general attributes associated with learning how to learn and the development of full learner autonomy; and they may have a more general intention to promote learning, without privileging any particular set of ideas or capabilities other than those that relate to learning in general. Although both endeavours are central to teaching, the value of the second tends to be underplayed in formal education – to the detriment of students' learning. In this book I have argued for a more profound conception of what teachers are for, one that does not reject either of the two more basic teaching endeavours, but which attaches greater importance to the second endeavour and is an extension of it.

In light of my interpretation of Popper's analysis of learning, in Part 1 of this book, and the argument, principles and practical proposals set out in subsequent chapters, I assert that the promotion of human transcendence should be construed as what teachers are for – that is, their role and purpose – and that this undertaking can be pursued by addressing the tripartite problem of teaching for transcendence set out in section 5 above. Although the overarching problem of improving how humans function in the world can be addressed in many different and important ways, the problem of teaching for transcendence must be effectively solved as part of a collective solution to the overarching problem. Any effective solution to the problem of teaching for transcendence will require teachers to encourage and support students in the initiation and development of their own formal programmes of learning – student-initiated curricula.

References

Adams, E. and Burgess, T. (1980), 'Conclusions and proposals', in T. Burgess and E. Adams (eds), *Outcomes of Education*. Basingstoke, UK: Macmillan Education, pp. 163–81.

— (1989), *Teachers' Own Records: A System Promoting Professional Quality*. Windsor, UK: NFER-NELSON.

— (1992), 'Recognizing achievement', in H. Berlak, F. M. Newmann, E. Adams, D. A. Archbald, T. Burgess, J. Raven and T. A. Romberg, *Toward a New Science of Educational Testing and Assessment*. New York, NY: State University of New York Press, pp. 117–37.

Agassi, J. (2008), *A Philosopher's Apprentice: In Karl Popper's Workshop*. Amsterdam, The Netherlands: Rodopi. First edition in 1993.

Andrews, I., Swann, J. and Ecclestone, K. (2007), 'Rolling out and scaling up: the effects of a problem-based approach to developing teachers' assessment practice'. Paper presented at the annual conference of the British Educational Research Association, University of London, 5–8 September.

Atkinson, E. and Swann, J. (2003), 'Decision-making in the real world: postmodernism versus fallibilist realism', in J. Swann and J. Pratt (eds), *Educational Research in Practice: Making Sense of Methodology*. London: Continuum, pp. 127–40.

Auld, R. (1976), *The William Tyndale Junior and Infants Schools: Report of the Public Inquiry Conducted by Mr Robin Auld, QC, into the Teaching, Organization and Management of the William Tyndale Junior and Infants Schools, Islington, London, N1*. London: Inner London Education Authority.

Bach-y-Rita, P., Tyler, M. E. and Kaczmarek, K. A. (2003), 'Seeing with the brain'. *International Journal of Human-Computer Interaction*, 15 (2), pp. 285–95.

Bailey, R. (1995), 'Karl Popper as educator'. *Interchange*, 26 (2), pp. 185–91.

— (2000), *Education in the Open Society – Karl Popper and Schooling*. Aldershot, UK: Ashgate.

— (2001), ' "Never answer an unasked question": interviews with Karl Popper on education'. *Research Intelligence*, 75, pp. 24–7.

Barnes, A. (2008), 'Towards practitioner empowerment: the impact of a problem-based approach to professional development on the leadership of gifted and talented mathematics education in the primary school'. Brighton, UK: University of Brighton (unpublished MA dissertation).

— (2009), 'A professional-academic synthesis: empowering gifted and talented co-ordinators to create bespoke professional development in gifted and talented mathematics education in English primary schools'. Paper presented at the 18th World Conference on Gifted and Talented Children, Vancouver, Canada, 3–7 August.

— (2010), 'Professional development: creating a bespoke programme'. *CPD Update e-bulletin*, October. Available at http://www.teachingexpertise.com/articles/professional-development-creating-bespoke-programme-10523 [accessed 19 February 2011].

Baxter, B. (1982), *Alienation and Authenticity: Some Consequences for Organized Work*. London: Tavistock Publications.

Berkson, W. and Wettersten, J. (1984), *Learning from Error: Karl Popper's Psychology of Learning*. La Salle, IL: Open Court Publishing.

Black, P., Harrison, C., Lee, C., Marshall, B. and Wiliam, D. (2003), *Assessment for Learning: Putting it into Practice*. Maidenhead, UK: Open University Press.

Blenkin, G. M. and Kelly, A. V. (1987), *The Primary Curriculum: A Process Approach to Curriculum Planning*. London: Paul Chapman Publishing.

Bloom, B. S. (ed.) (1956), *Taxonomy of Educational Objectives, The Classification of Educational Goals, Handbook 1: Cognitive Domain*. New York, NY: David McKay.

Blunkett, D. (2000), 'Influence or irrelevance: can social science improve government?' Speech made to a meeting convened by the [UK's] Economic and Social Research Council on 2 February 2000. Reprinted with permission in *Research Intelligence*, 71, March, pp. 12–21.

Brandes, D. and Phillips, H. (1977), *Gamesters' Handbook: 140 Games for Teachers and Group Leaders*. London: Hutchinson.

Briskman, L. (2009), 'Creative product and creative process in science and art', in M. Krausz, D. Dutton and K. Bardsley (eds), *The Idea of Creativity*. Leiden, The Netherlands: Koninklijke Brill NV, pp. 17–41. Essay first published in 1980 in *Inquiry*, 23 (1), pp. 83–106.

British Educational Research Association (2004), *Revised Ethical Guidelines for Educational Research*. Southwell, UK: British Educational Research Association. Available at http://www.bera.ac.uk/files/guidelines/ethica1.pdf [accessed 19 February 2011].

Brown, A. (1987), 'Metacognition, executive control, self-regulation, and other more mysterious mechanisms', in F. E. Weinert and R. H. Kluwe (eds), *Metacognition, Motivation, and Understanding*. Hillsdale, NJ: Lawrence Erlbaum Associates, pp. 65–116.

Brown, S. and McIntyre, D. (1993), *Making Sense of Teaching*. Buckingham, UK: Open University Press.

Bühler, K. (1934), *Sprachtheorie: Die Darstellungsfunktion der Sprache*. Jena, Germany: Gustav Fischer.

Burgess, T. (1975), 'Choice is not enough – go for responsibility'. *Where, the Education Magazine for Parents*, 100, pp. 5–7.

— (1977), *Education After School*. London: Victor Gollancz.

— (1979), 'New ways to learn'. *The Royal Society of Arts Journal*, CXXVII (5271), pp. 143–57.

— (1981), 'Bias is of the essence', in D. W. Piper (ed.), *Is Higher Education Fair?* Guildford, UK: Society for Research into Higher Education, pp. 1–16.

— (1985a), 'New laws for post school education'. *Higher Education Review*, 18 (1), pp. 25–42.

— (1985b), 'Applying Popper to social realities: practical solutions to practical problems'. *ETC: A Review of General Semantics*, 42 (3), pp. 299–309.

— (ed.) (1986), *Education for Capability*. Windsor, UK: NFER-NELSON.

— (1989), 'The great pretenders'. *The Times Educational Supplement*, 17 March, p. A17.

— (1992), 'Accountability with confidence', in T. Burgess (ed.), *Accountability in Schools*. Harlow, UK: Longman, pp. 3–14.

— (1999), 'Inquiry for "taught" masters', in J. Swann and J. Pratt (eds), *Improving Education: Realist Approaches to Method and Research*. London: Cassell Education, pp. 156–63.

— (2000), 'The logic of learning and its implications for higher education'. *Higher Education Review*, 32 (2), pp. 53–65.

— (2002), 'Towards a social science: a comment on Karl Popper's twenty seven theses'. Paper presented at the Karl Popper 2002 Centenary Congress, University of Vienna, 3–7 July.

Burgess, T. and Adams, E. (1980), 'The present inadequacy', in T. Burgess and E. Adams (eds), *Outcomes of Education*. Basingstoke, UK: Macmillan Education, pp. 3–14.

— (1985), *Records of Achievement at 16*. Windsor, UK: NFER-NELSON.

Burgess, T., and Swann, J. (2003), 'The rejectability of Karl Popper: why Popper's ideas have had so little influence on social practice'. *Higher Education Review*, 35 (2), pp. 57–65.

Butcher, C. (2009), 'Bloom's taxonomy'. Leeds, UK: Staff and Departmental Development Unit, University of Leeds. Available online at http://www.leeds.ac.uk/sddu/online/bloom.html [accessed 4 January 2010].

Campbell, D. T. (1974), 'Evolutionary epistemology', in P. A. Schilpp (ed.), *The Philosophy of Karl Popper, Book 1*. La Salle, IL: Open Court Publishing, pp. 413–63.

Carr, W., and Kemmis, S. (1986), *Becoming Critical: Education, Knowledge and Action Research*. London: The Falmer Press.

Codd, J. A. (2005), 'Academic freedom and the commodification of knowledge in the modern university'. *Learning for Democracy*, 1 (1), pp. 69–87.

Cohen, L., Manion, L. and Morrison, K. (1996), *A Guide to Teaching Practice*, 4th edn. London: Routledge.

— (2007), *Research Methods in Education*, 6th edn. London: Routledge. First edition in 1980.

Cottingham, J. (1984), *Rationalism*. London: Paladin Books.

Cross, H. (1988), 'Innovation in higher education: the School for Independent Study'. *New Era in Education*, 69 (3), pp. 80–4.

Dearden, R. F. (1976), *Problems in Primary Education*. London: Routledge & Kegan Paul.

Department of Education and Science/Welsh Office (1987), *The National Curriculum 5–16: A Consultation Document*. London: Department of Education and Science/Welsh Office. Published in July.

Dewey, J. (1916), *Democracy and Education: An Introduction to the Philosophy of Education*. New York, NY: Macmillan.

— (1963), *Experience and Education*. New York, NY: Macmillan. First published in 1938.

— (1990), *The School and Society and The Child and the Curriculum*. Chicago, IL: University of Chicago Press. *The School and Society*, first published in 1900; *The Child and the Curriculum*, first published in 1902.

Driver, R. and Bell, B. (1986), 'Students' thinking and the learning of science: a constructivist view'. *The School Science Review*, 67 (240), March, pp. 443–56.

Driver, R. and Oldham, V. (1986), 'A constructivist approach to curriculum development in science'. *Studies in Science Education*, 13, pp. 105–22.

Ecclestone, K. (2002), *Learning Autonomy in Post-16 Education: The Politics and Practice of Formative Assessment*. London: Routledge.

Edelman, G. M. (1992), *Bright Air, Brilliant Fire: On the Matter of the Mind*. New York, NY: Basic Books.

Elliott, J (1976), *Developing Hypotheses about Classrooms from Teachers' Practical Constructs: An Account of the Work of the Ford Teaching Project*. Grand Forks, ND: University of North Dakota.

Elliott, J. and Adelman, C. (1975), 'Teacher education for curriculum reform: an interim report of the work of the Ford Teaching Project'. *British Journal of Teacher Education*, 1 (1), pp. 105–14.

Finch, J. (1986), *Research and Policy: The Uses of Qualitative Methods in Social and Educational Research*. Basingstoke, UK: Falmer Press.

Floreano, D., Husbands, P., and Nolfi, S. (2008), 'Evolutionary robotics', in B. Siciliano and O. Khatib (eds), *Springer Handbook of Robotics*. Berlin: Springer, pp. 1422–51.

Freire, P. (1972), *Pedagogy of the Oppressed*. Harmondsworth, UK: Penguin Books (trans. M. B. Ramos).

Gatto, J. T. (2005), *Dumbing Us Down: The Hidden Curriculum of Compulsory Schooling*. Gabriola Island, Canada: New Society Publishers. First edition in 1992.

Glasersfeld, E. von (1985), 'Reconstructing the concept of knowledge'. *Archives de Psychologie*, 53, pp. 91–101.

— (1989), 'Constructivism in education', in T. Husen and T. N. Postlethwaite (eds), *The International Encyclopedia of Education*, Supplementary Volume 1. Oxford: Pergamon Press, pp. 162–3.

Goodman, P. (1971), *Compulsory Miseducation*. Harmondsworth, UK: Penguin Books. First edition in 1962.

Gray, J. (2004), *Consciousness: Creeping Up on the Hard Problem*. Oxford, UK: Oxford University Press.

Guardian, The (1989), 'First-class degrees: 1989', *The Guardian*, 19 September, pp. 27–31.

Hacohen, M. H. (2000), *Karl Popper – the Formative Years, 1902–1945: Politics and Philosophy in Interwar Vienna*. Cambridge, UK: Cambridge University Press.

Hammersley, M. (1998), 'Get real! a defence of realism', in P. Hodkinson (ed.), *The Nature of Educational Research: Realism, Relativism or Post-Modernism?* Manchester, UK: Manchester Metropolitan University, pp. 7–23.

Harber, C. (2004), *Schooling as Violence: How Schools Harm Pupils and Societies*. London: RoutledgeFalmer.

Hark, M. R. M. ter (2004), *Popper, Otto Selz and the Rise of Evolutionary Epistemology*. Cambridge, UK: Cambridge University Press.

— (2006), 'The historical roots of Popper's theory of the searchlight: a tribute to Otto Selz', in I. C. Jarvie, K. Milford and D. Miller (eds), *Karl Popper: A Centenary Assessment, Volume 1 – Life and Times, and Values in a World of Facts*. Aldershot, UK: Ashgate, pp. 37–56.

— (2009), 'Popper's theory of the searchlight: a historical assessment of its significance', in Z. Parusniková and R. S. Cohen (eds), *Rethinking Popper*. Dordrecht, The Netherlands: Springer, pp. 175–84.

Hein, A. (1980), 'The development of visually guided behavior', in C. S. Harris (ed.), *Visual Coding and Adaptability*. Hillsdale, NJ: Lawrence Erlbaum Associates, pp. 51–67.

Hein, A., Held, R. and Gower, E. C. (1970), 'Development and segmentation of visually controlled movement by selective exposure during rearing'. *Journal of Comparative and Physiological Psychology*, 73 (2), pp. 181–7.

Held, R. and Hein, A. (1963), 'Movement-produced stimulation in the development of visually guided behavior'. *Journal of Comparative and Physiological Psychology*, 56 (5), pp. 872–6.

Holt, J. (1969), *How Children Fail*. Harmondsworth, UK: Penguin Books. First edition in 1964.

Howson, C. (1984), 'Popper's solution to the problem of induction'. *The Philosophical Quarterly*, 34 (135), pp. 143–7.

Hume, D. (1999), 'An enquiry concerning human understanding', in S. M. Cahn (ed.), *Classics of Western Philosophy*, 5th edn. New York, NY: Hackett, pp. 628–96. Hume's text first published in 1748.

— (2010), *A Treatise of Human Nature*. Lawrence, KS: Neeland Media LLC (Digireads.com). First edition in 1739–1740.

Illich, I. (1973), *Deschooling Society*. Harmondsworth, UK: Penguin Books. First edition in 1970.

James, R. (1980), *Return to Reason: Popper's Thought in Public Life*. Shepton Mallet, UK: Open Books Publishing.

Jarvie, I. C. (2009), 'The rationality of creativity', in M. Krausz, D. Dutton and K. Bardsley (eds), *The Idea of Creativity*. Leiden, The Netherlands: Koninklijke Brill NV, pp. 43–62. First published in 1981 in D. Dutton and M. Krausz (eds), *The Concept of Creativity in Science and Art*. The Hague: Martinus Nijhoff Publishers, pp. 109–28.

Katz, D. (1937) *Animals and Men: Studies in Comparative Psychology*. London: Longmans, Green & Co.

Kemmis, S. and McTaggart, R. (eds) (1988), *The Action Research Planner*. Victoria, Australia: Deakin University Press.

Kerr, J. F. (1968), 'The problem of curriculum reform', in J. F. Kerr (ed.), *Changing the Curriculum*. London: University of London Press, pp. 13–38.

Klappholz, K. and Agassi, J. (1959), 'Methodological prescriptions in economics'. *Economica*, XXVI (101–104), February, pp. 60–74.

Krick, E. V. (1969), *An Introduction to Engineering and Engineering Design*, 2nd edn. New York, NY: John Wiley and Sons. First edition in 1965.

Lewin, K. (1946), 'Action research and minority problems'. *Journal of Social Issues*, 2, pp. 34–6.

Little, G. R. (1981), 'Social models: blueprints or processes?' *Impact of Science on Society*, 31 (4), pp. 439–47.

Meighan, R. (1981), *A Sociology of Educating*. London: Holt, Reinhart and Winston.

Meighan, R. and Siraj-Blatchford, I. (2003), *A Sociology of Educating*, 4th edn. London: Continuum. First edition in 1981.

Miller, D. (1982), 'Conjectural knowledge: Popper's solution of the problem of induction', in P. Levinson (ed.), *In Pursuit of Truth: Essays on the Philosophy of Karl Popper on the Occasion of His 80th Birthday*. Atlantic Highlands, NJ: Humanities Press, pp. 17–49.

— (1985), 'Editor's Introduction', in D. Miller (ed.), *Popper Selections*. Princeton, NJ: Princeton University Press, pp. 9–22.

— (1994), *Critical Rationalism: A Restatement and Defence*. Chicago, IL, Open Court Publishing.

— (2006a), *Out of Error: Further Essays on Critical Rationalism*. Aldershot, UK: Ashgate.

— (2006b), 'Darwinism is the application of situational logic to the state of ignorance', in I. C. Jarvie, K. Milford and D. Miller (eds), *Karl Popper: A Centenary Assessment, Volume 3 – Science*. Aldershot, UK: Ashgate, pp. 155–62.

Mossio, M. and Taraborelli, D. (2008), 'Action-dependent perceptual invariants: from ecological to sensorimotor approaches'. *Consciousness and Cognition*, 17 (4), pp. 1324–40 (doi:10.1016/j.concog.2008.08.002).

Munz, P. (2001), 'The progression of values or mankind's Siberian dilemma'. Te Tapuae o Rehua Lecture, New Zealand Historical Association Conference, Christchurch, 2 December.

Naish, M. and Hartnett, A. (1975), 'What theory cannot do for teachers'. *Education for Teaching*, 96, pp. 12–19.

Niiniluoto, I. (2006), 'World 3: a critical defence', in I. C. Jarvie, K. Milford and D. Miller (eds), *Karl Popper: A Centenary Assessment, Volume 2 – Metaphysics and Epistemology*. Aldershot, UK: Ashgate, pp. 59–69.

Norman, D. A. (1980), 'What goes on in the mind of the learner?', in W. J. McKeachie (ed.), *Learning, Cognition, and College Teaching*. San Francisco, CA: Jossey-Bass, pp. 37–49.

Nørretranders, T. (1998), *The User Illusion: Cutting Consciousness Down to Size*. London: Penguin Books (trans. J. Sydenham). First published in Danish in 1991.

Notturno, M. A. (2000), *Science and the Open Society: The Future of Karl Popper's Philosophy*. Budapest: Central European University Press.

Organisation for Economic Co-operation and Development (2003), *New Challenges for Educational Research*. Paris: OECD.

Perkinson, H. J. (1971), *The Possibilities of Error: An Approach to Education*. New York, NY: David McKay.

— (1984), *Learning From Our Mistakes: A Reinterpretation of Twentieth-Century Educational Theory*. Westport, CT: Greenwood Press.

Petersen, A. F. (1988), *Why Children and Young Animals Play: A New Theory of Play and Its Role in Problem Solving*. Monograph of The Royal Danish Academy of Sciences and Letters, Copenhagen, *Historisk-filosofiske Meddelelser*, 54, pp. 1–57.

— (1992), 'On emergent pre-language and language evolution and transcendent feedback from language production on cognition and emotion in early man', in J. Wind, B. Chiarelli and B. Bichakjian (eds), *Language Origin: A Multidisciplinary Approach*. Dordrecht, Netherlands: Kluwer Academic Publishers, pp. 449–64.

— (2000), 'Emergent consciousness considered as a solution to the problem of movement', in R. L. Amoroso, R. Antunes, C. Coelho, M. Farias, A. Leite and P. Soares (eds), *Science and the Primacy of Consciousness: Intimation of a 21st Century Revolution*. Orinda, CA: The Noetic Press, pp. 8–16.

Phillips, D. C. (1987), *Philosophy, Science, and Social Inquiry: Contemporary Methodological Controversies in Social Science and Related Applied Fields of Research*. Oxford, UK: Pergamon Press.

— (1992a), 'On castigating constructivists', in H. Alexander (ed.), *Philosophy of Education 1992: Proceedings of the Forty-Eighth Annual Meeting of the Philosophy of Education Society*. Urbana, IL: Philosophy of Education Society, University of Illinois, pp. 312–15.

— (1992b), *The Social Scientist's Bestiary: A Guide to Fabled Threats to, and Defenses of, Naturalistic Social Science*. Oxford, UK: Pergamon Press.

— (1995), 'The good, the bad, and the ugly: the many faces of constructivism'. *Educational Researcher*, 24 (7), pp. 5–12. Reprinted as chapter 1 of Phillips (2000).

— (1999), 'How to play the game: a Popperian approach to the conduct of educational research', in G. Zecha (ed.), *Critical Rationalism and Educational Discourse*. Amsterdam, The Netherlands: Rodopi, pp. 170–90.

— (2000), *The Expanded Social Scientist's Bestiary: A Guide to Fabled Threats to, and Defences of, Naturalistic Social Science*. Lanham, MD: Rowman & Littlefield.

Phillips, D. C., and Burbules, N. C. (2000), *Postpositivism and Educational Research*. Lanham, MD: Rowman & Littlefield.

Popham, W. J., Eisner, E. W., Sullivan, H. J., and Tyler, L. L. (1969), *Instructional Objectives*. Chicago, IL: Rand McNally & Company.

Popper, K. R. (1961), *The Poverty of Historicism*. London: Routledge & Kegan Paul. First edition in 1957.

— (1972a), *The Logic of Scientific Discovery*. London: Hutchinson. First published in German in 1934. First English edition in 1959.

— (1972b), *Conjectures and Refutations: The Growth of Scientific Knowledge*. London: Routledge. First edition in 1963.

— (1974), 'Replies to my critics', in P. A. Schilpp (ed.), *The Philosophy of Karl Popper, Book II*. La Salle, IL: Open Court Publishing, pp. 961–1197.

— (1979), *Objective Knowledge: An Evolutionary Approach*. Oxford, UK: Oxford University Press. First edition in 1972.

— (1982), *The Open Universe: An Argument for Indeterminism*. London: Hutchinson. From the Postscript to the Logic of Scientific Discovery, written mainly during the years 1951–56, ed. by W. W. Bartley, III.

— (1985a), *Realism and the Aim of Science*. London: Routledge. First edition in 1983. From the Postscript to the Logic of Scientific Discovery, written mainly during the years 1951–56, ed. by W. W. Bartley, III.

— (1985b), 'The problem of induction (1953, 1974)', in D. Miller (ed.), *Popper Selections*. Princeton, NJ: Princeton University Press, pp. 101–17.

— (1985c), 'The problem of demarcation (1974)', in D. Miller (ed.), *Popper Selections*. Princeton, NJ: Princeton University Press, pp. 118–30.

— (1985d), 'Piecemeal social engineering (1944)', in D. Miller (ed.), *Popper Selections*. Princeton, NJ: Princeton University Press, pp. 304–18.

— (1990), *A World of Propensities*. Bristol, UK: Thoemmes Antiquarian Books.

— (1992a), *Unended Quest: An Intellectual Autobiography*. London: Routledge. First published as 'Autobiography of Karl Popper', in P. A. Schilpp (ed.) (1974), *The Philosophy of Karl Popper, Book 1*. La Salle, IL: Open Court Publishing, pp. 3–181.

— (1992b), *In Search of a Better World: Lectures and Essays from Thirty Years*. London: Routledge.

— (1994a), *The Myth of the Framework: In Defence of Science and Rationality*. London: Routledge (ed. by M. A. Notturno).

— (1994b), *Knowledge and the Body-Mind Problem: In Defence of Interaction*. London: Routledge (ed. by M. A. Notturno).

— (1998), *The World of Parmenides: Essays on the Presocratic Enlightenment*. London: Routledge (ed. A. F. Petersen, with assistance from J. Mejer).

— (1999), *All Life is Problem Solving*. London: Routledge (some chapters trans. by P. Camiller).

— (2002a), *The Open Society and Its Enemies, Volume 1: The Spell of Plato*. London: Routledge. First edition in 1945.

— (2002b), *The Open Society and Its Enemies, Volume 2: Hegel and Marx*. London: Routledge. First edition in 1945.

— (2008), *The Two Fundamental Problems of the Theory of Knowledge*. London: Routledge (ed. T. E. Hansen; trans. by A. Pickel and J. Kinroy). First published in German in 1979, using drafts and preliminary work from 1930–33.

Popper, K. R. and Eccles, J. C. (1977), *The Self and Its Brain: An Argument for Interactionism*. London: Springer International.

Postman, N. and Weingartner, C. (1969), *Teaching as a Subversive Activity*. Harmondsworth, UK: Penguin Books.

Pratt, J. (1976), 'What's wrong with the study of public administration?' London: Centre for Institutional Studies, North East London Polytechnic (unpublished paper).

— (1999), 'Testing policy', in J. Swann and J. Pratt (eds), *Improving Education: Realist Approaches to Method and Research*. London, Cassell, pp. 39–52.

— (2003), 'A Popperian approach to policy research', in J. Swann and J. Pratt (eds), *Educational Research in Practice: Making Sense of Methodology*. London: Continuum, pp. 51–66.

— (2009), 'Editorial: the next four decades'. *Higher Education Review*, 42 (1), pp. 3–8.

Pratt, J. and Cocking, J. (1999), 'Making modularity work'. *Teaching in Higher Education*, 4 (1), pp. 107–19.

Pratt, J. and Swann, J. (2003), 'Doing good research', in J. Swann and J. Pratt (eds), *Educational Research in Practice: Making Sense of Methodology*. London: Continuum, pp. 175–93.

Pring, R. (2004), *Philosophy of Educational Research*, 2nd edn. London: Continuum. First edition in 2000.

Raven, J. (1977), *Education, Values and Society: The Objectives of Education and the Nature and Development of Competence*. London: H. K. Lewis & Co.

Reimer, E. (1971), *School is Dead: Alternatives in Education*. New York, NY: Doubleday. First edition in 1970.

Robbins, D. (1988), *The Rise of Independent Study: The Politics and the Philosophy of an Educational Innovation, 1970–87*. Milton Keynes, UK: Society for Research into Higher Education and Open University Press.

Russell, J. (2009), 'New Labour's great mistake is to think we are all automatons'. *Guardian*, 14 July. Available at http://www.guardian.co.uk/commentisfree/2009/jul/14/targets-nhs-care-crime-bureaucracy [accessed 9 February 2011].

Seth, A. K., McKinstry, J. L., Edelman, G. M. and Krichmar, J. L. (2004), 'Visual binding through reentrant connectivity and dynamic synchronization in a brain-based device'. *Cerebral Cortex*, 14 (11), pp. 1185–99 (doi:10.1093/cercor/bhh079).

Skinner, B. F. (1968), *The Technology of Teaching*. New York, NY: Meredith Corporation.

— (1974), *About Behaviourism*. London: Jonathan Cape.

Somekh, B. (1995), 'The contribution of action research to development in social endeavours: a position paper on action research methodology'. *British Educational Research Journal*, 21 (3), pp. 339–55.

Stenhouse, L. (1975), *An Introduction to Curriculum Research and Development*. London: Heinemann Educational Books.

Stephenson, J. (1980), 'Higher education: School for Independent Study', in T. Burgess and E. Adams (eds), *Outcomes of Education*. Basingstoke, UK: Macmillan Education, pp. 132–49.

— (1981), 'Student planned learning', in D. Boud (ed.), *Developing Student Autonomy in Learning*. London: Kogan Page, pp. 145–59.

Suzuki, M., Floreano, D., and Di Paolo, E. A. (2005), 'The contribution of active body movement to visual development in evolutionary robots'. *Neural Networks*, 18, pp. 656–65. Available at http://www.informatics.sussex.ac.uk/users/ezequiel/suzuki_floreano_dipaolo.pdf [accessed 4 January 2011].

Swann, J. (1976), 'Karl Popper: some implications for the curriculum'. London: London University Institute of Education (unpublished MA dissertation).

— (1983), 'Teaching and the logic of learning'. *Higher Education Review*, 15 (2), pp. 31–57.

— (1988), 'How can classroom practice be improved?: an investigation of the logic of learning in classroom practice'. London: Council for National Academic Awards (unpublished PhD thesis).

— (1995), 'Realism, constructivism, and the pursuit of truth'. *Higher Education Review*, 27 (3), pp. 37–55.

— (1997), 'How can we make better plans?' *Higher Education Review*, 30 (1), pp. 37–55.

— (1999a), 'What happens when learning takes place?' *Interchange*, 30 (3), pp. 257–82.

— (1999b), 'Making better plans: problem-based versus objectives-based planning', in J. Swann and J. Pratt (eds), *Improving Education: Realist Approaches to Method and Research*. London: Cassell, pp. 53–66.

— (1999c), 'The logic-of-learning approach to teaching: a testable theory', in J. Swann and J. Pratt (eds), *Improving Education: Realist Approaches to Method and Research*. London: Cassell, pp. 109–20.

— (2000a). 'Be prepared: a check list of arguments against a national curriculum'. *Education Now*, 27, p. 2.

— (2000b), 'How can research lead to improvement in education?' *Prospero*, 6 (3/4), pp. 130–8.

— (2003a), 'How science can contribute to the improvement of educational practice'. *Oxford Review of Education*, 29 (2), pp. 253–68.

— (2003b), 'A Popperian approach to research on learning and method', in J. Swann and J. Pratt (eds), *Educational Research in Practice: Making Sense of Methodology*. London: Continuum, pp. 11–34.

— (2005), 'Education research and the chimera of secure knowledge'. *Higher Education Review*, 38 (1), pp. 32–47.

— (2006), 'How to avoid giving unwanted answers to unasked questions: realizing Karl Popper's educational dream', in I. C. Jarvie, K. Milford and D. Miller (eds), *Karl Popper: A Centenary Assessment, Volume 3 – Science*. Aldershot, UK: Ashgate, pp. 261–70.

— (2008), 'Student-initiated curricula: a cornerstone of learning for democracy', in *Yearbook of the Institute of History 'G. Barit', Cluj-Napoca Series Humanistica*, Romanian Academy, Branch of Cluj-Napoca. Bucharest: Romanian Academy Publishing House, pp. 43–52.

Swann, J., Andrews, I., and Ecclestone, K. (2011), 'Rolling out and scaling up: the effects of a problem-based approach to developing teachers' assessment practice'. *Educational Action Research*, 19 (4), in press.

Swann, J., and Arthurs, J. (1999), 'Empowering lecturers: a problem-based approach to improve assessment practice'. *Higher Education Review*, 31 (2), pp. 50–74.

Swann, J., and Brown, S. (1997), 'The implementation of a national curriculum and teachers' classroom thinking'. *Research Papers in Education*, 12 (1), pp. 91–114.

Swann, J., and Ecclestone, K. (1999a), 'Empowering lecturers to improve assessment practice in higher education', in J. Swann and J. Pratt (eds), *Improving Education: Realist Approaches to Method and Research*. London: Cassell, pp. 89–100.

— (1999b), 'Improving lecturers' assessment practice in higher education: a problem-based approach'. *Educational Action Research*, 7 (1), pp. 63–84.

Swann, J., Wiliam, D. and Black, P. (2003), 'Assessing learning how to learn'. Paper presented at the annual conference of the British Educational Research Association, Heriot-Watt University, Edinburgh, 11–13 September.

Swartz, R. M., Perkinson, H. J., and Edgerton, S. G. (1980), *Knowledge and Fallibilism: Essays on Improving Education*. New York, NY: New York University Press.

Technician Education Council (1976), *TEC Guidance Notes No. 1: The Presentation of Educational Objectives in TEC Units*. London: Technician Education Council.

Tennant, M. (2006) *Psychology and Adult Learning*, 3rd edn. London: Routledge. First edition in 1988.

Thorne, B. (2001), 'What's worth fighting for?' A paper given to the Oxfordshire branch of the National Association of Head Teachers, 3 March, 2000. *Education Today*, 51 (1), pp. 20–4.

Tyler, R. W. (1949), *Basic Principles of Curriculum and Instruction*. Chicago, IL: University of Chicago Press.

Wächtershäuser, G. (1993), 'Light and life: on the nutritional origins of sensory perception', in G. Radnitzky and W. W. Bartley, III (eds), *Evolutionary Epistemology, Rationality, and the Sociology of Knowledge*. Peru, IL: Open Court, pp. 121–38.

Watson, J. B. (1913), 'Psychology as the behaviorist views it'. *Psychological Review*, 20 (2), pp. 158–77.

Wettersten, J. (1999), 'The critical rationalists' quest for an effective liberal pedagogy', in G. Zecha (ed.), *Critical Rationalism and Educational Discourse*. Amsterdam, The Netherlands: Rodopi, pp. 93–115.

Wiliam, D. (2006), 'The half-second delay: what follows?' *Pedagogy, Culture & Society*, 14 (1), pp. 71–81.

Wragg, T. (1988), *Education in the Market Place: The Ideology Behind the 1988 Education Bill*. London: National Union of Teachers. Later published as chapter 14 of T. Wragg (2003), *The Art and Science of Teaching and Learning: The Selected Works of Ted Wragg*. London: Routledge.

Publisher Acknowledgements

A small proportion of material in the book has been excerpted from previous publications, as follows:

Swann, J., Andrews, I., and Ecclestone, K. (2011), 'Rolling out and scaling up: the effects of a problem-based approach to developing teachers' assessment practice'. *Educational Action Research*, 19 (4), in press (by the permission of the publisher, Taylor & Francis Ltd, http://wwwtandf.co.uk/journals).

Swann, J. (2009), 'Popperian epistemology and the curriculum: the legacy of Tyrrell Burgess'. *Higher Education Review*, 42 (1), pp. 9–16 (by permission of Tyrrell Burgess Associates).

Swann, J. (2009), 'Learning: an evolutionary analysis'. *Educational Philosophy and Theory* (Journal of the Philosophy of Education Society of Australasia), 41 (3), pp. 256–69 (by permission of Blackwell Publishing).

Swann, J. (2009), 'Popperian selectionism and its implications for education, or "what to do about the myth of learning by instruction from without?"', in Z. Parusniková and R. S. Cohen (eds), *Rethinking Popper*. Dordrecht, The Netherlands: Springer, pp. 379–88 (copyright © 2009 Springer Science+Business Media B.V.) (with kind permission from Springer Science+Business Media B.V.).

Swann, J. (2008), 'Student-initiated curricula: a cornerstone of learning for democracy', in *Yearbook of the Institute of History 'G. Barit', Cluj-Napoca Series Humanistica*, Romanian Academy, Branch of Cluj-Napoca. Bucharest: Romanian Academy Publishing House, pp. 43–52 (by permission of Romanian Academy Publishing House).

Swann, J. (2007), 'The myth of learning by instruction from without'. *Higher Education Review*, 40 (1), pp. 37–51 (by permission of Tyrrell Burgess Associates).

Swann, J. (2007), 'Teaching for a better world: the why and how of student-initiated curricula', in D. Aspin and J. Chapman (eds), *Values Education and Lifelong Learning: Principles, Policies, Programmes*. Dordrecht, The Netherlands: Springer, pp. 279–94 (copyright © 2007 Springer) (with kind permission from Springer Science+Business Media B.V.).

Swann, J. (2006), 'How to avoid giving unwanted answers to unasked questions: realizing Karl Popper's educational dream', in I. C. Jarvie, K. Milford and D. Miller (eds), *Karl Popper: A Centenary Assessment, Volume 3 – Science*. Aldershot, UK: Ashgate, pp. 261–71 (copyright © the author) (by permission of the publisher).

Swann, J. (2005), 'Education research and the chimera of secure knowledge'. *Higher Education Review*, 38 (1), pp. 32–47 (by permission of Tyrrell Burgess Associates).

Swann, J. (2005), 'Editorial: learning for democracy'. *Learning for Democracy*, 1 (1), pp. 7–10 (by permission of Tyrrell Burgess Associates).

Swann, J., and Burgess, T. (2005), 'The usefulness of Karl Popper's selectionist theory of learning for educational practice'. *Learning for Democracy*, 1 (3), pp. 7–22 (by permission of Tyrrell Burgess Associates).

Swann, J. (2003), 'How science can contribute to the improvement of educational practice'. *Oxford Review of Education*, 29 (2), pp. 253–68 (by permission of the publisher, Taylor & Francis Ltd, http://www.tandf.co.uk/journals).

Swann, J. (2002), 'Reality: how to make it better'. *Higher Education Review*, 34 (3), pp. 21–33 (by permission of Tyrrell Burgess Associates).

Swann, J. (1999), 'What happens when learning takes place?' *Interchange*, 30 (3), pp. 257–82 (copyright © Kluwer Academic Publishers) (with kind permission from Springer Science+Business Media B.V.).

Swann, J. (1998), 'What doesn't happen in teaching and learning?' *Oxford Review of Education*, 24 (2), pp. 211–23 (by permission of the publisher, Taylor & Francis Ltd, http://www.tandf.co.uk/journals).

Swann, J. (1997), 'How can we make better plans?' *Higher Education Review*, 30 (1), pp. 37–55 (by permission of Tyrrell Burgess Associates).

Swann, J. (1995), 'Realism, constructivism, and the pursuit of truth'. *Higher Education Review*, 27 (3), pp. 37–55 (by permission of Tyrrell Burgess Associates).

Swann, J. (1983), 'Teaching and the logic of learning'. *Higher Education Review*, 15 (2), pp. 31–57 (by permission of Tyrrell Burgess Associates.

Index